THE DARKNESS

REBIRTH
VOLUME 3

THE DARKNESS CREATED BY:
MARC SILVESTRI, GARTH ENNIS
AND DAVID WOHL

published by
Top Cow Productions, Inc.
Los Angeles

THE DARKNESS®

REBIRTH
VOLUME 3

writer: **David Hine** • artist: **Jeremy Haun**

colorist: **John Rauch** • letterer: **Troy Peteri**

original editions edited by **Bryan Rountree** & **Betsy Gonia**

For this edition, cover art by: **Jeremy Haun** & **John Rauch**

For this edition, book design and layout by: **Addison Duke**

Want more info? Check out:

www.topcow.com

for news & exclusive
Top Cow merchandise!

For Top Cow Productions, Inc.:

Marc Silvestri - CEO

Matt Hawkins - President & COO

Betsy Gonia - Managing Editor

Elena Salcedo - Operations Manager

Ryan Cady - Production Assistant

COMIC SHOP LOCATOR SERVICE

888-COMIC-BOOK

888-266-4226

To find the comic shop nearest you, call:
1-888-COMICBOOK

IMAGE COMICS, INC.
Robert Kirkman - Chief Operating Officer
Erik Larsen - Chief Financial Officer
Todd McFarlane - President
Marc Silvestri - Chief Executive Officer
Jim Valentino - Vice-President

Eric Stephenson - Publisher
Ron Richards - Director of Business Development
Jennifer de Guzman - Director of Trade Book Sales
Kat Salazar - PR & Marketing Coordinator
Jeremy Sullivan - Digital Marketing Coordinator
Jamie Parreno - Online Marketing Coordinator
Emilio Bautista - Sales Assistant
Branwyn Bigglestone - Senior Accounts Manager
Emily Miller - Accounts Manager
Jessica Ambriz - Administrative Assistant
Tyler Shainline - Events Coordinator
David Brothers - Content Manager
Jonathan Chan - Production Manager
Drew Gill - Art Director
Meredith Wallace - Print Manager
Monica Garcia - Senior Production Artist
Jenna Savage - Production Artist
Addison Duke - Production Artist
IMAGECOMICS.COM

Darkness: Rebirth Volume 3 Trade Paperback.
JANUARY 2014. FIRST PRINTING. ISBN: 978-1-60706-806-8. $17.99 USD

TABLE OF CONTENTS

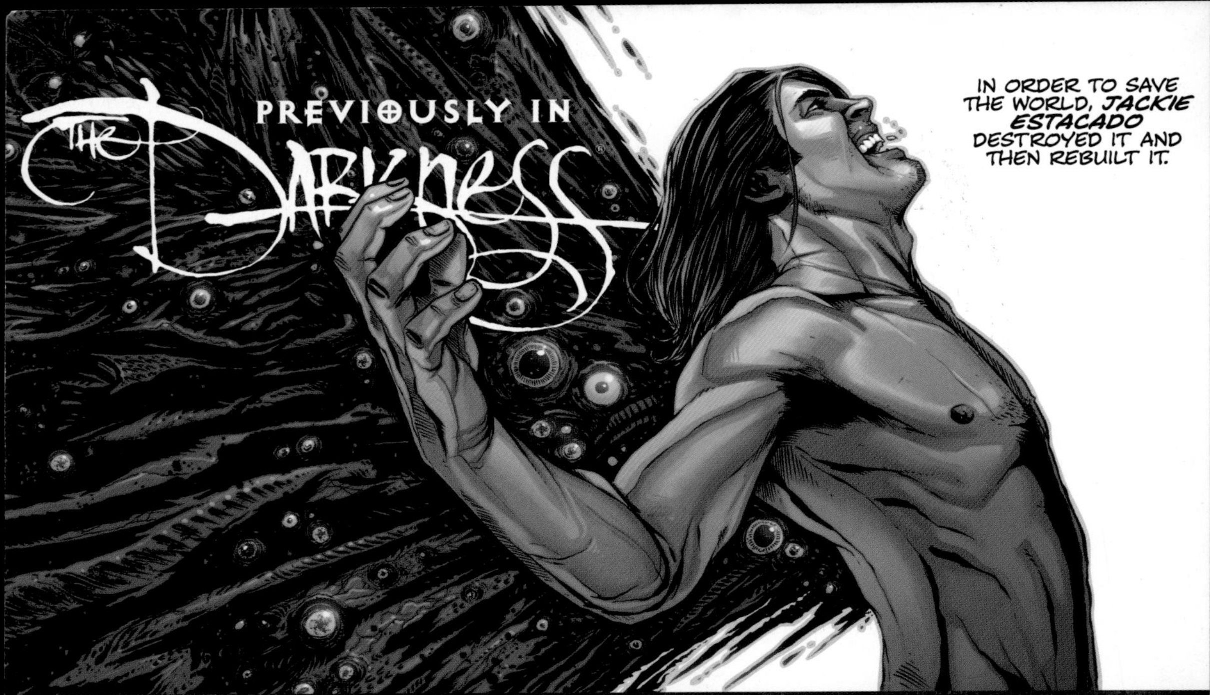
PREVIOUSLY IN
THE DARKNESS
IN ORDER TO SAVE THE WORLD, JACKIE ESTACADO DESTROYED IT AND THEN REBUILT IT.

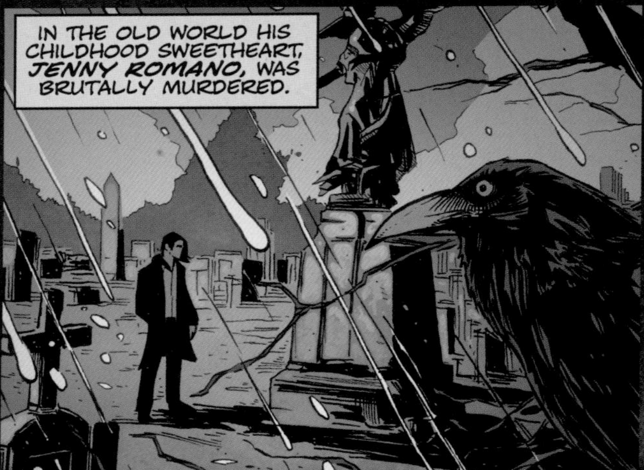
IN THE OLD WORLD HIS CHILDHOOD SWEETHEART, JENNY ROMANO, WAS BRUTALLY MURDERED.

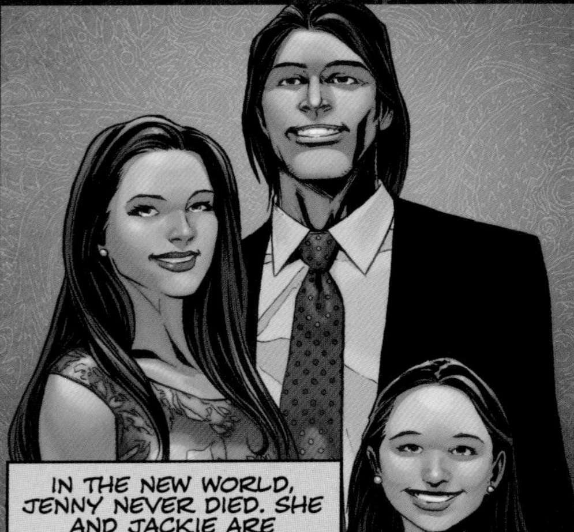
IN THE NEW WORLD, JENNY NEVER DIED. SHE AND JACKIE ARE MARRIED AND HAVE A CHILD NAMED HOPE.

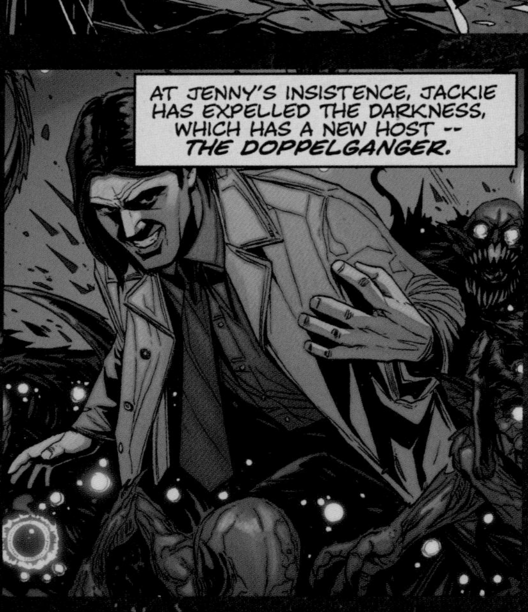
AT JENNY'S INSISTENCE, JACKIE HAS EXPELLED THE DARKNESS, WHICH HAS A NEW HOST -- THE DOPPELGANGER.

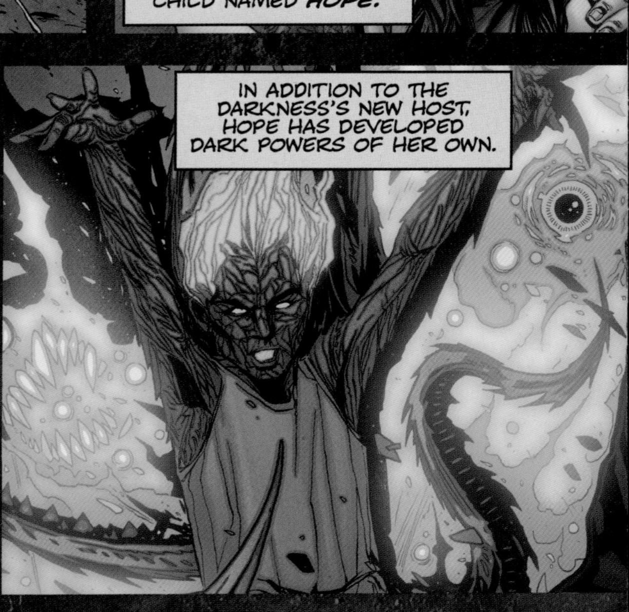
IN ADDITION TO THE DARKNESS'S NEW HOST, HOPE HAS DEVELOPED DARK POWERS OF HER OWN.

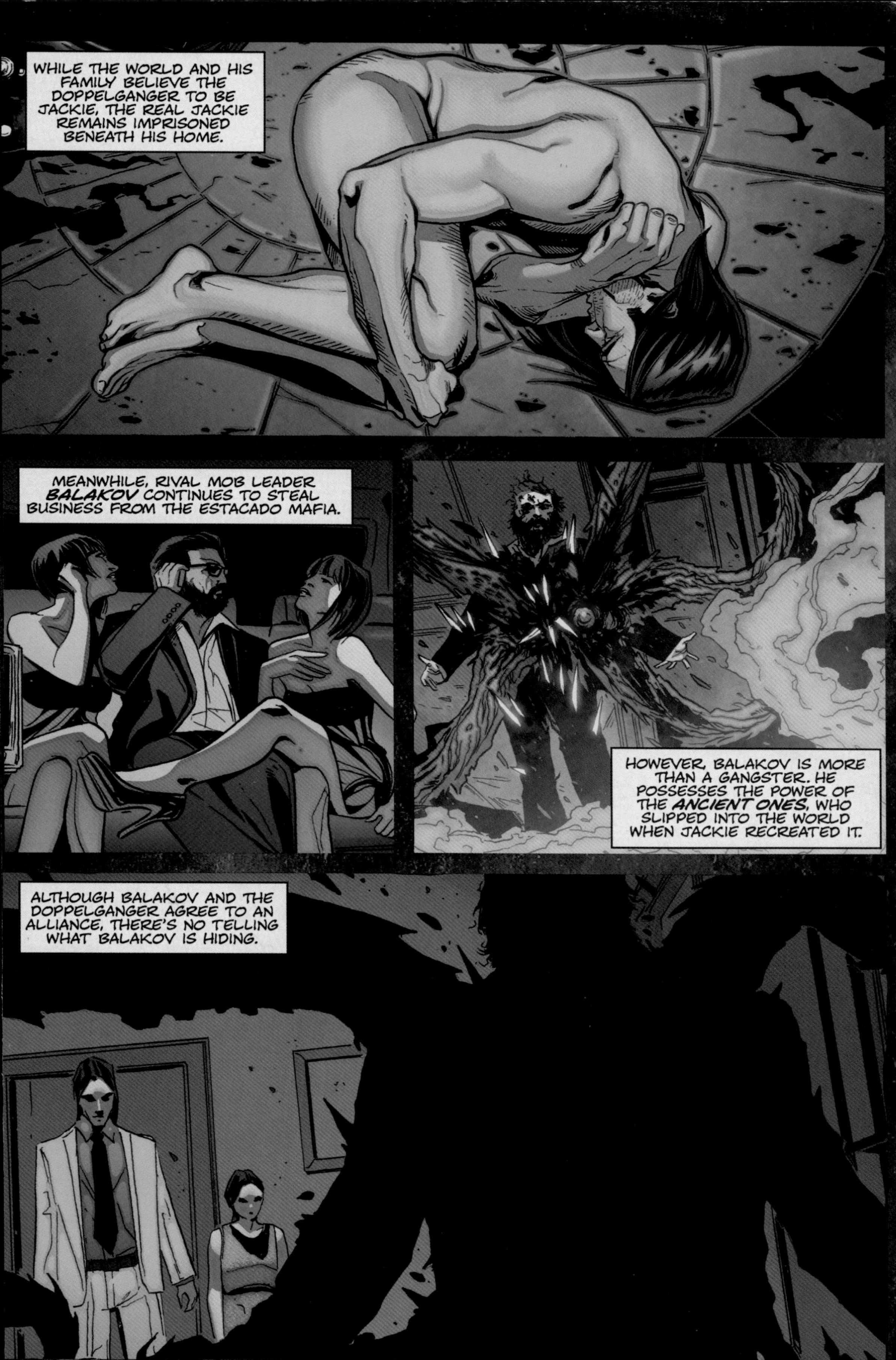
WHILE THE WORLD AND HIS FAMILY BELIEVE THE DOPPELGANGER TO BE JACKIE, THE REAL JACKIE REMAINS IMPRISONED BENEATH HIS HOME.
MEANWHILE, RIVAL MOB LEADER BALAKOV CONTINUES TO STEAL BUSINESS FROM THE ESTACADO MAFIA.
HOWEVER, BALAKOV IS MORE THAN A GANGSTER. HE POSSESSES THE POWER OF THE ANCIENT ONES, WHO SLIPPED INTO THE WORLD WHEN JACKIE RECREATED IT.
ALTHOUGH BALAKOV AND THE DOPPELGANGER AGREE TO AN ALLIANCE, THERE'S NO TELLING WHAT BALAKOV IS HIDING.

"HOPE'S ADVENTURES UNDERGROUND"
PART
I

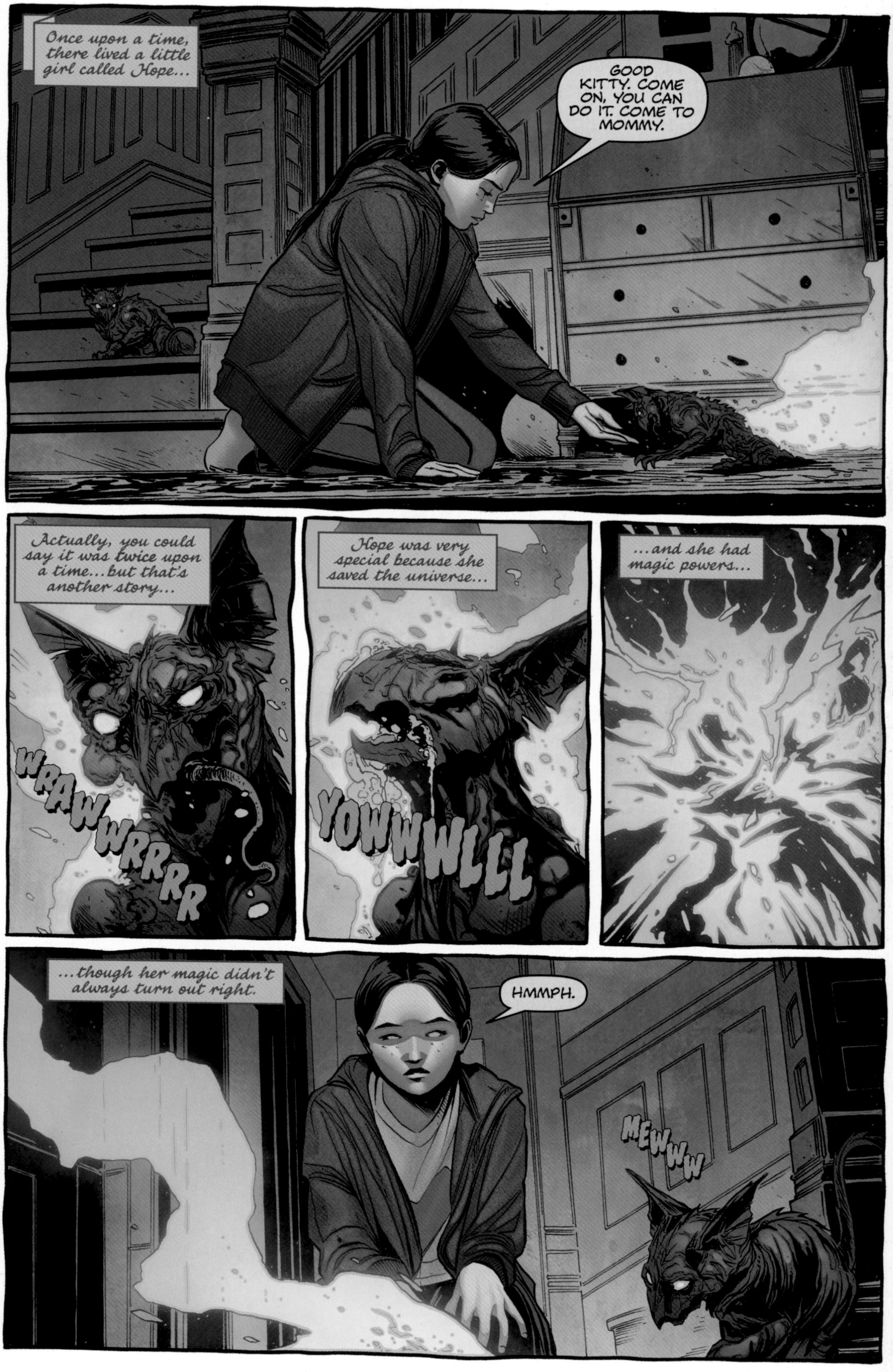
Once upon a time, there lived a little girl called Hope...
GOOD KITTY. COME ON, YOU CAN DO IT. COME TO MOMMY.
Actually, you could say it was twice upon a time...but that's another story...
WRAWWRRRRR
Hope was very special because she saved the universe...
YOWWWLLL
...and she had magic powers...
...though her magic didn't always turn out right.
HMMPH.
MEWWW

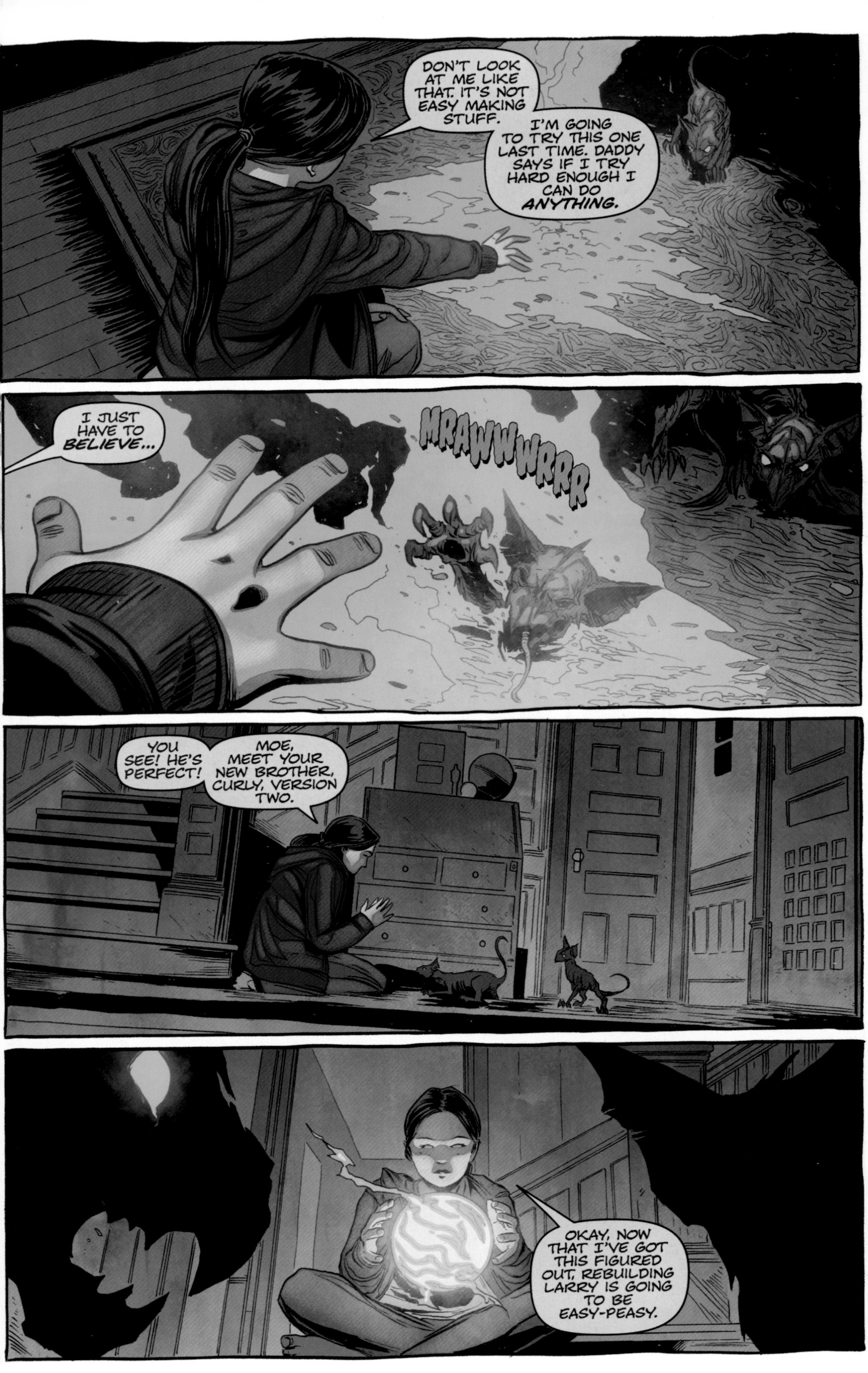

DON'T LOOK AT ME LIKE THAT. IT'S NOT EASY MAKING STUFF.
I'M GOING TO TRY THIS ONE LAST TIME. DADDY SAYS IF I TRY HARD ENOUGH I CAN DO *ANYTHING.*
I JUST HAVE TO *BELIEVE...*
MRAWWWRRR
YOU SEE! HE'S PERFECT!
MOE, MEET YOUR NEW BROTHER, CURLY, VERSION TWO.
OKAY, NOW THAT I'VE GOT THIS FIGURED OUT, REBUILDING LARRY IS GOING TO BE EASY-PEASY.

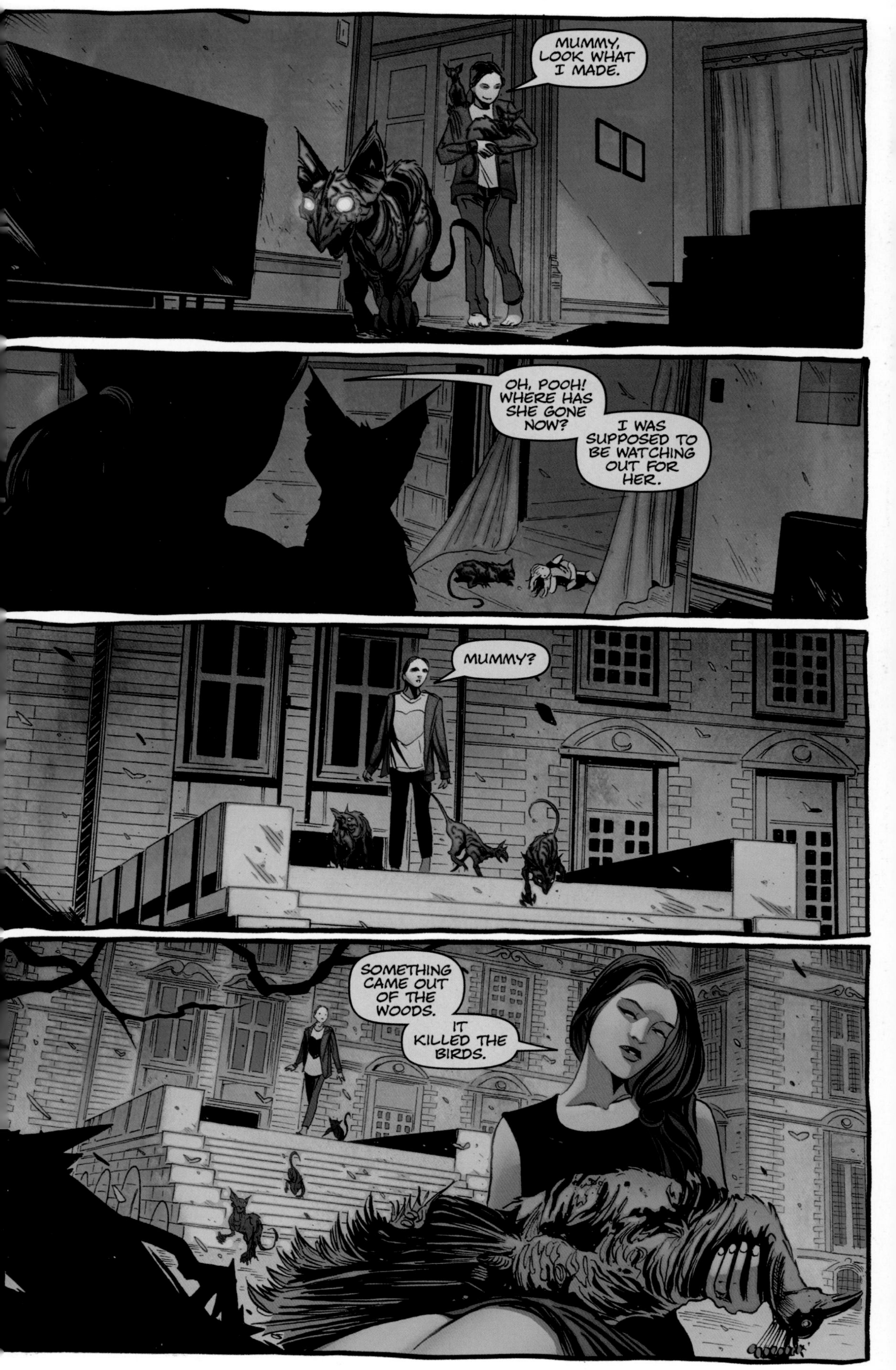
MUMMY, LOOK WHAT I MADE.
OH, POOH! WHERE HAS SHE GONE NOW?
I WAS SUPPOSED TO BE WATCHING OUT FOR HER.
MUMMY?
SOMETHING CAME OUT OF THE WOODS.
IT KILLED THE BIRDS.

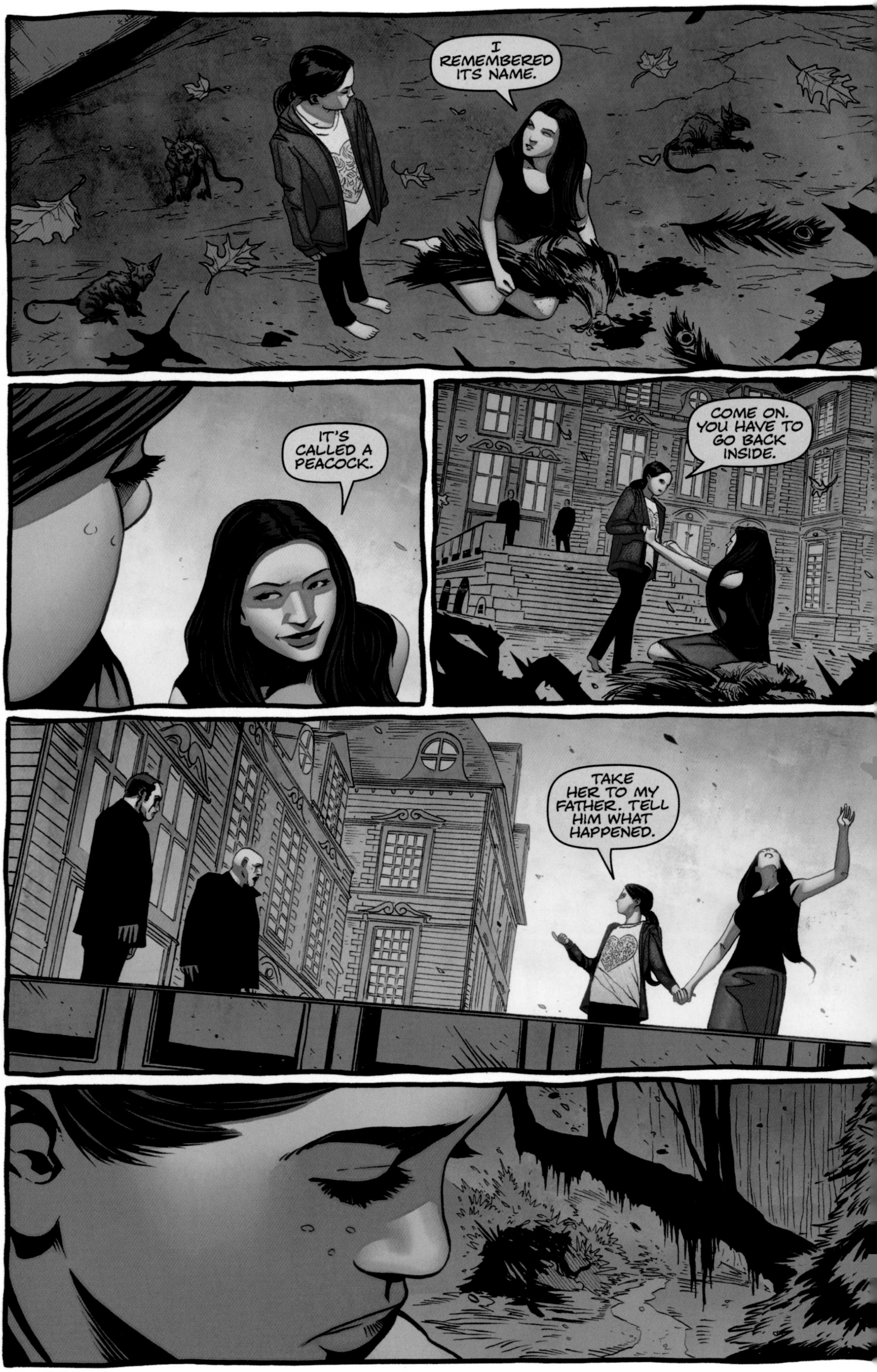
I REMEMBERED ITS NAME.
IT'S CALLED A PEACOCK.
COME ON. YOU HAVE TO GO BACK INSIDE.
TAKE HER TO MY FATHER. TELL HIM WHAT HAPPENED.

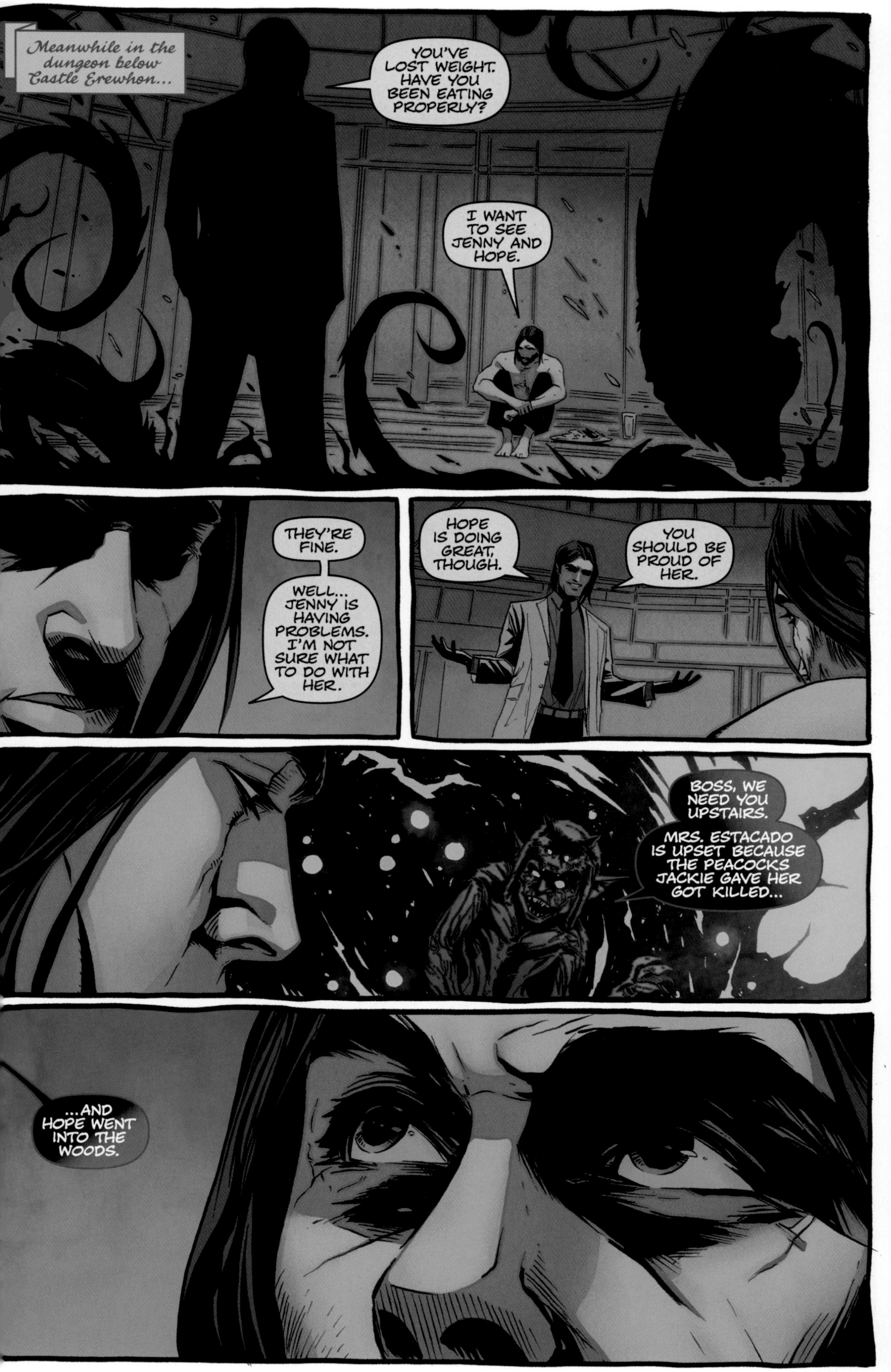
Meanwhile in the dungeon below Castle Erewhon...
YOU'VE LOST WEIGHT. HAVE YOU BEEN EATING PROPERLY?
I WANT TO SEE JENNY AND HOPE.
THEY'RE FINE.
WELL... JENNY IS HAVING PROBLEMS. I'M NOT SURE WHAT TO DO WITH HER.
HOPE IS DOING GREAT, THOUGH.
YOU SHOULD BE PROUD OF HER.
BOSS, WE NEED YOU UPSTAIRS.
MRS. ESTACADO IS UPSET BECAUSE THE PEACOCKS JACKIE GAVE HER GOT KILLED...
...AND HOPE WENT INTO THE WOODS.

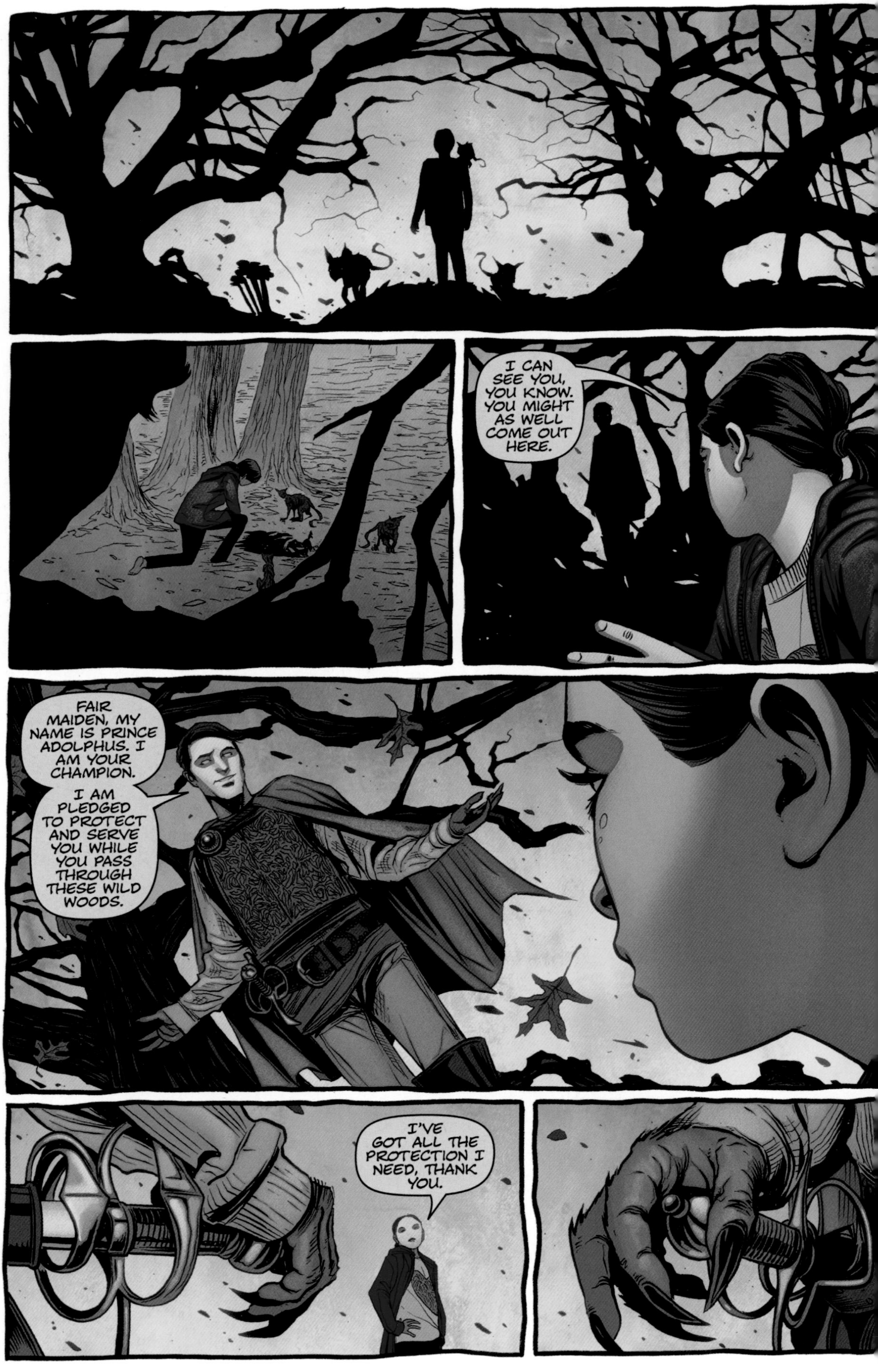
I CAN SEE YOU, YOU KNOW. YOU MIGHT AS WELL COME OUT HERE.
FAIR MAIDEN, MY NAME IS PRINCE ADOLPHUS. I AM YOUR CHAMPION.
I AM PLEDGED TO PROTECT AND SERVE YOU WHILE YOU PASS THROUGH THESE WILD WOODS.
I'VE GOT ALL THE PROTECTION I NEED, THANK YOU.

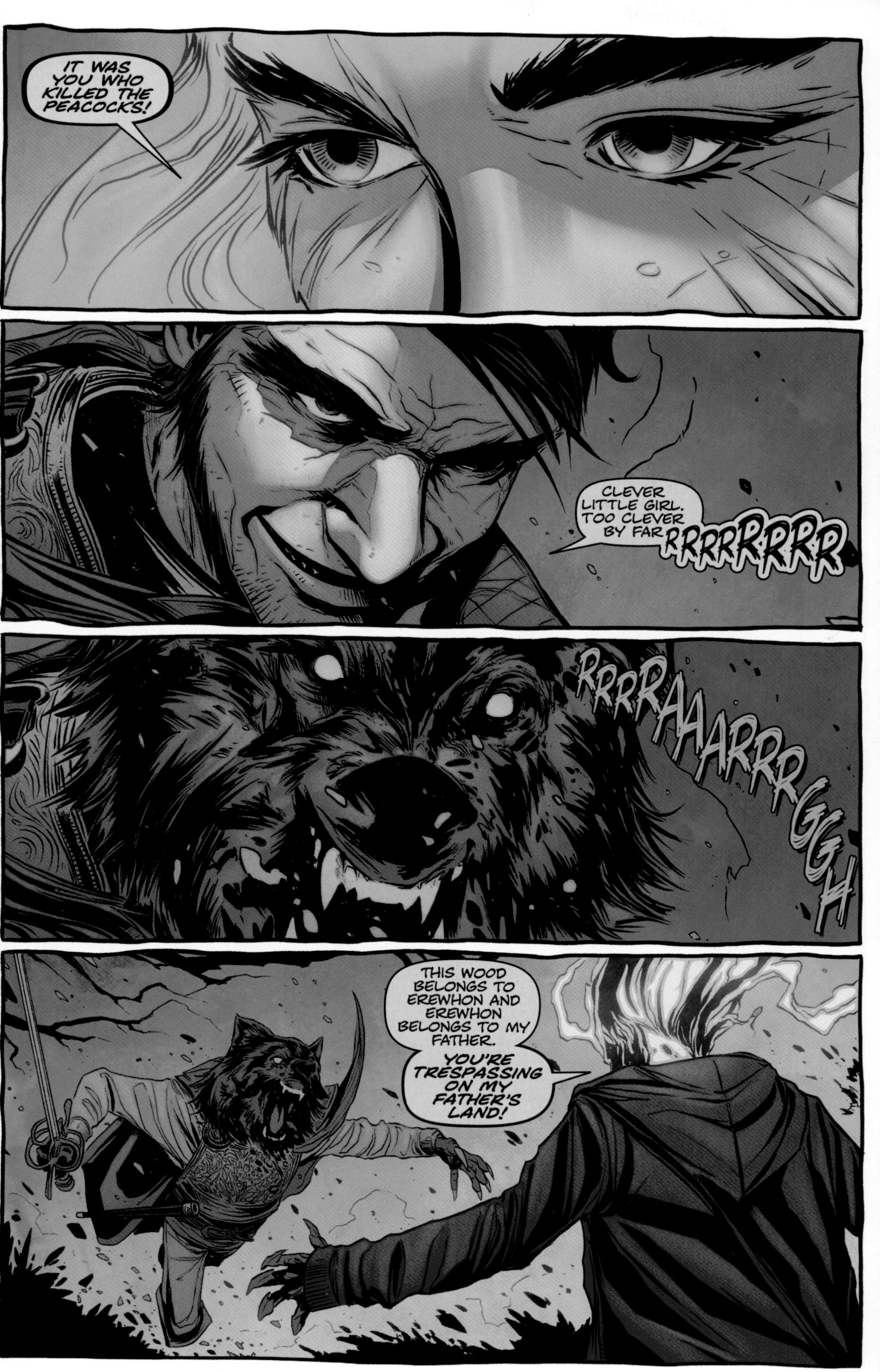
IT WAS YOU WHO KILLED THE PEACOCKS!
CLEVER LITTLE GIRL. TOO CLEVER BY FAR
RRRRRRRR
RRRRAAARRRGGGH
THIS WOOD BELONGS TO EREWHON AND EREWHON BELONGS TO MY FATHER.
YOU'RE TRESPASSING ON MY FATHER'S LAND!

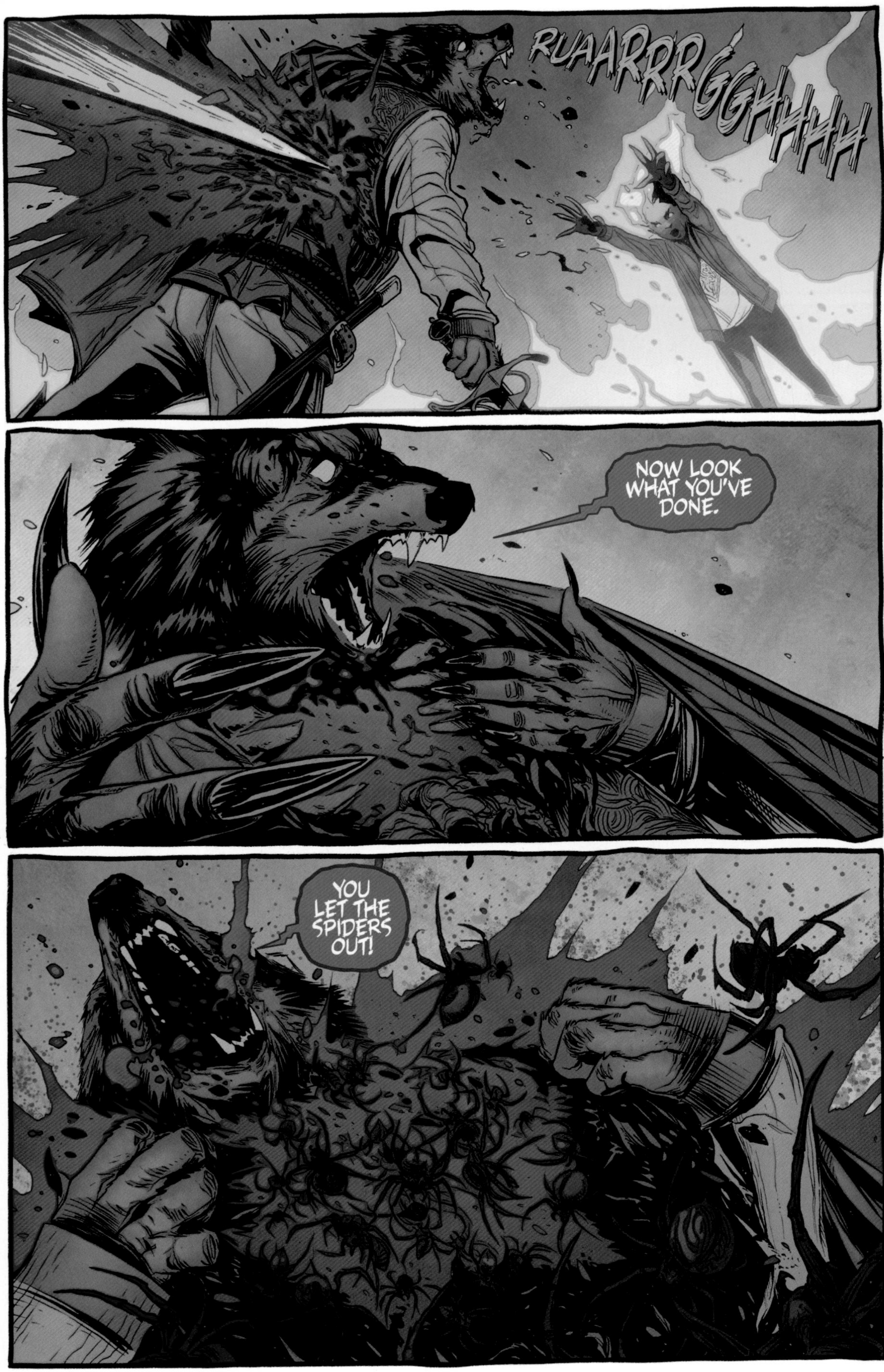
RUAARRRGGHHHH
NOW LOOK WHAT YOU'VE DONE.
YOU LET THE SPIDERS OUT!

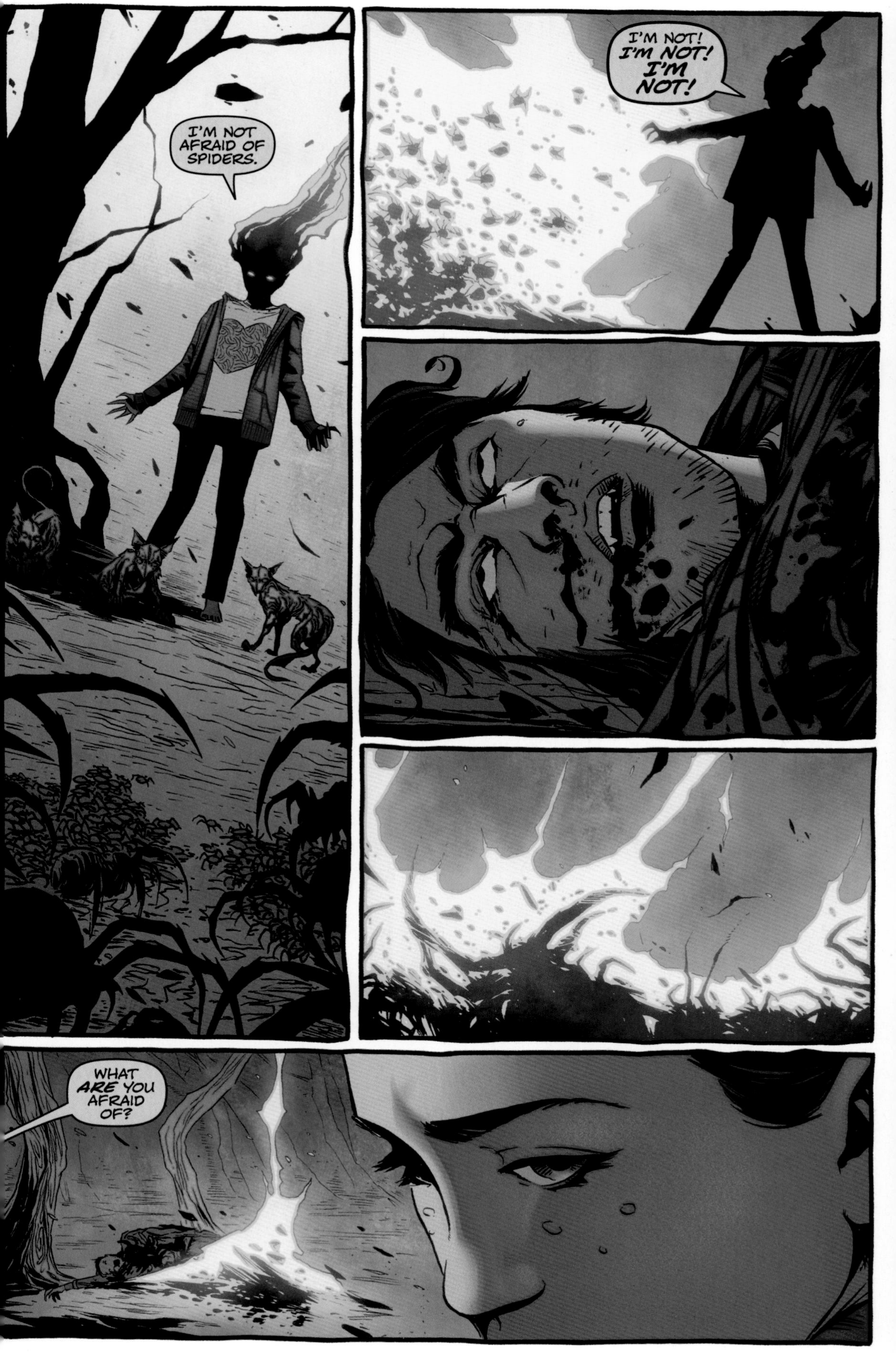
I'M NOT AFRAID OF SPIDERS.
I'M NOT! I'M NOT! I'M NOT!
WHAT ARE YOU AFRAID OF?

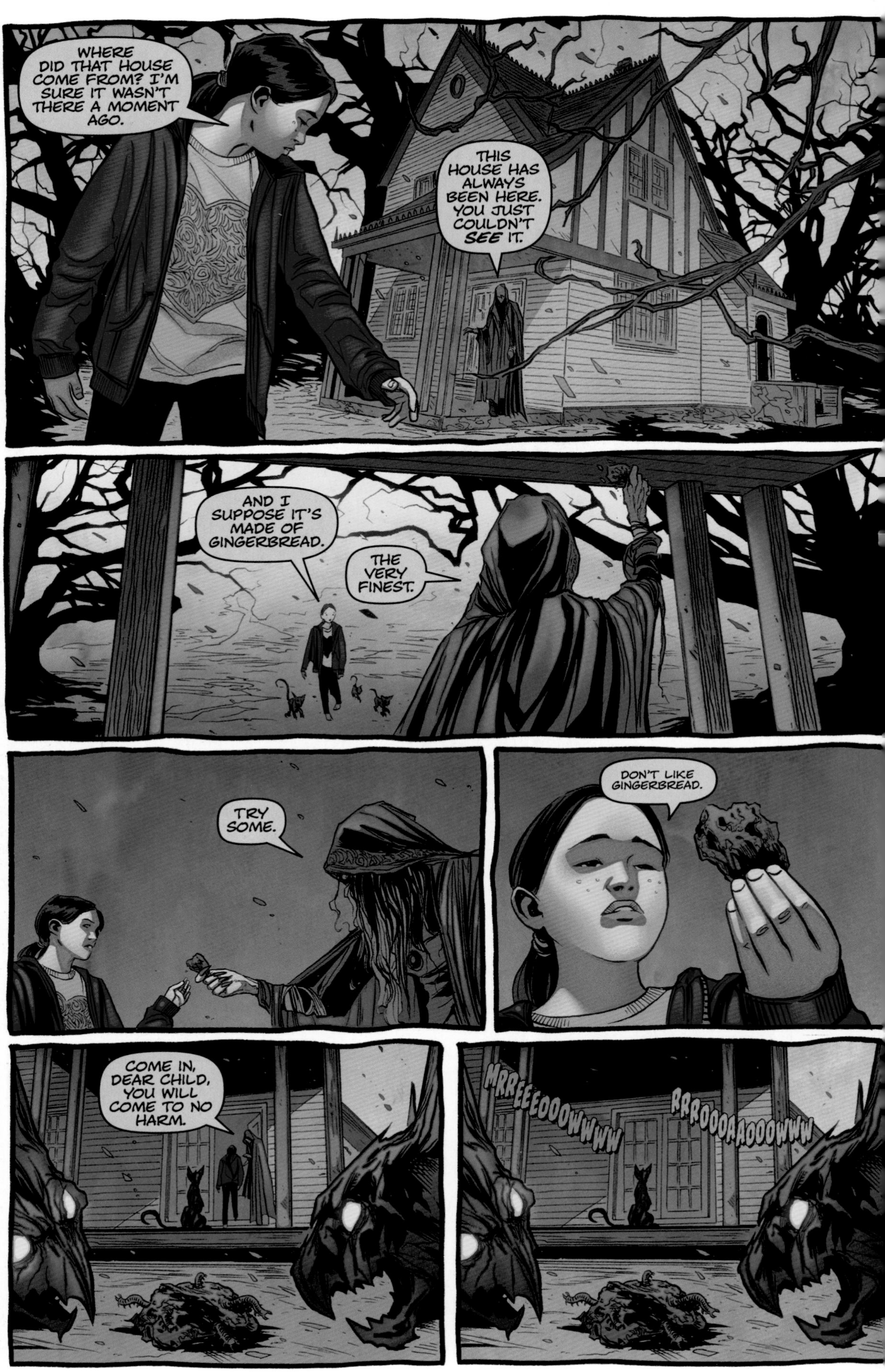
WHERE DID THAT HOUSE COME FROM? I'M SURE IT WASN'T THERE A MOMENT AGO.
THIS HOUSE HAS ALWAYS BEEN HERE. YOU JUST COULDN'T *SEE* IT.
AND I SUPPOSE IT'S MADE OF GINGERBREAD.
THE VERY FINEST.
TRY SOME.
DON'T LIKE GINGERBREAD.
COME IN, DEAR CHILD, YOU WILL COME TO NO HARM.
MRREEEOOOWWWW
RRROOOAAOOOWWW

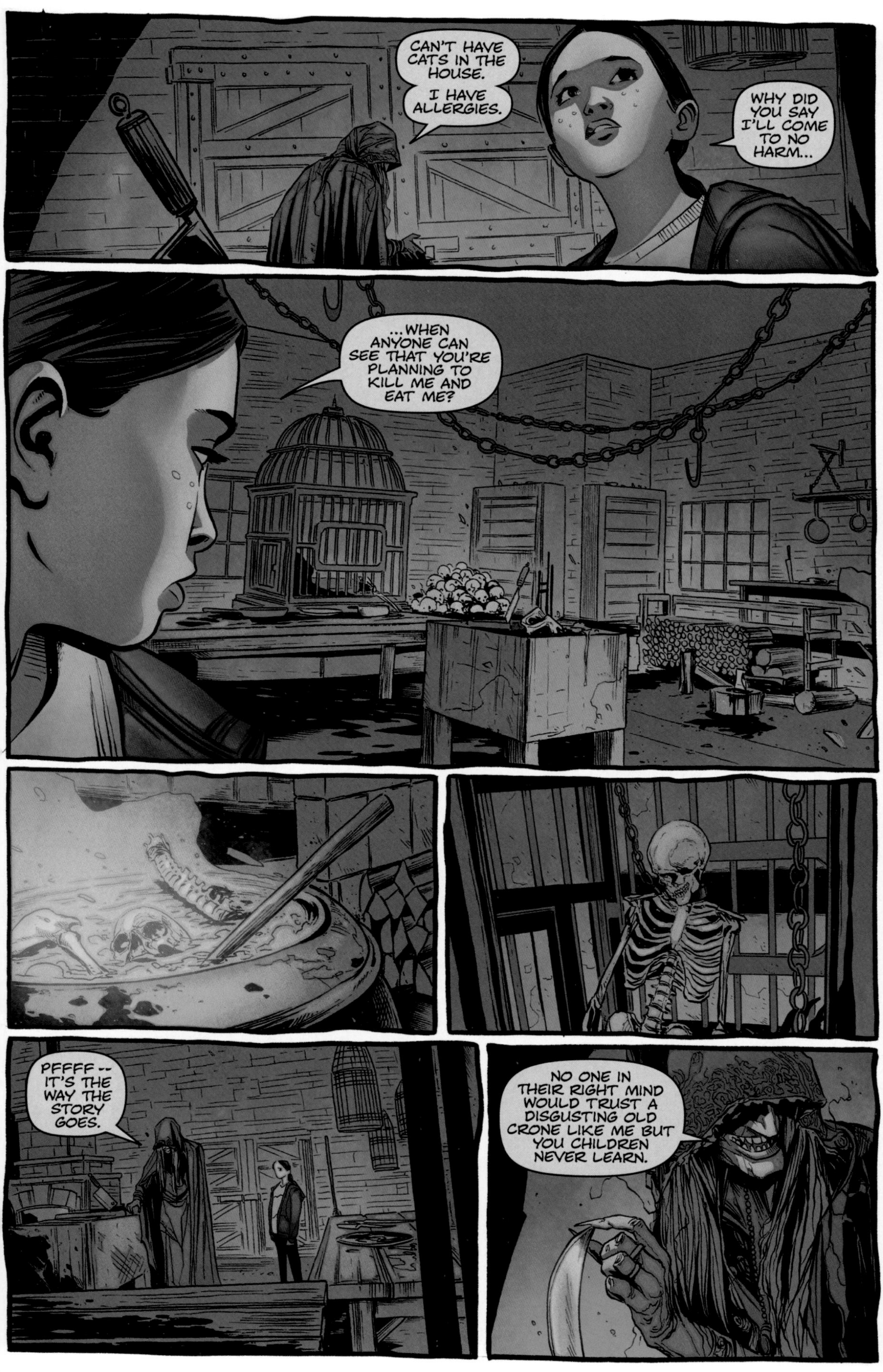
CAN'T HAVE CATS IN THE HOUSE.
I HAVE ALLERGIES.
WHY DID YOU SAY I'LL COME TO NO HARM...
...WHEN ANYONE CAN SEE THAT YOU'RE PLANNING TO KILL ME AND EAT ME?
PFFFF-- IT'S THE WAY THE STORY GOES.
NO ONE IN THEIR RIGHT MIND WOULD TRUST A DISGUSTING OLD CRONE LIKE ME BUT YOU CHILDREN NEVER LEARN.

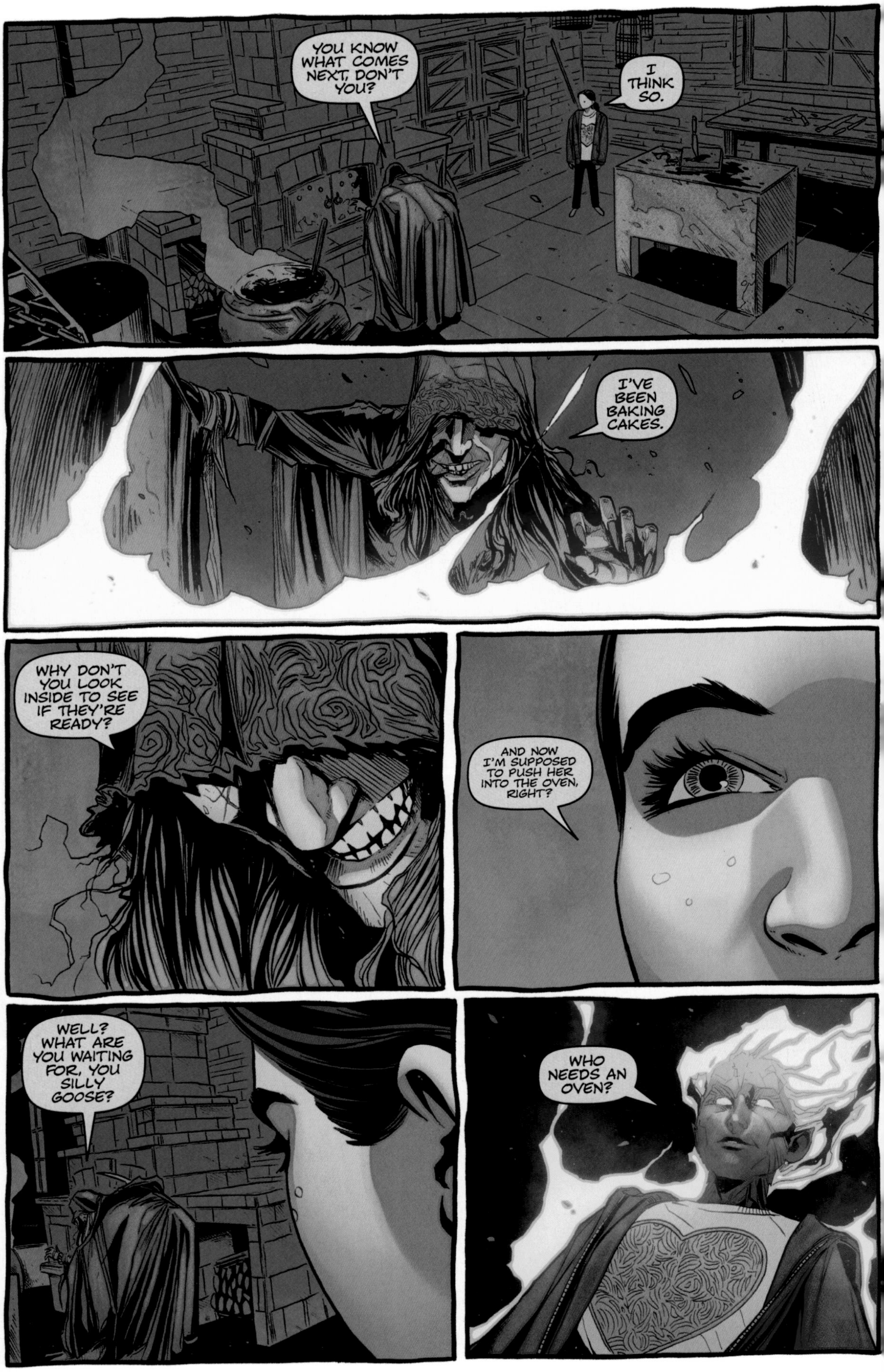
YOU KNOW WHAT COMES NEXT, DON'T YOU?
I THINK SO.
I'VE BEEN BAKING CAKES.
WHY DON'T YOU LOOK INSIDE TO SEE IF THEY'RE READY?
AND NOW I'M SUPPOSED TO PUSH HER INTO THE OVEN, RIGHT?
WELL? WHAT ARE YOU WAITING FOR, YOU SILLY GOOSE?
WHO NEEDS AN OVEN?

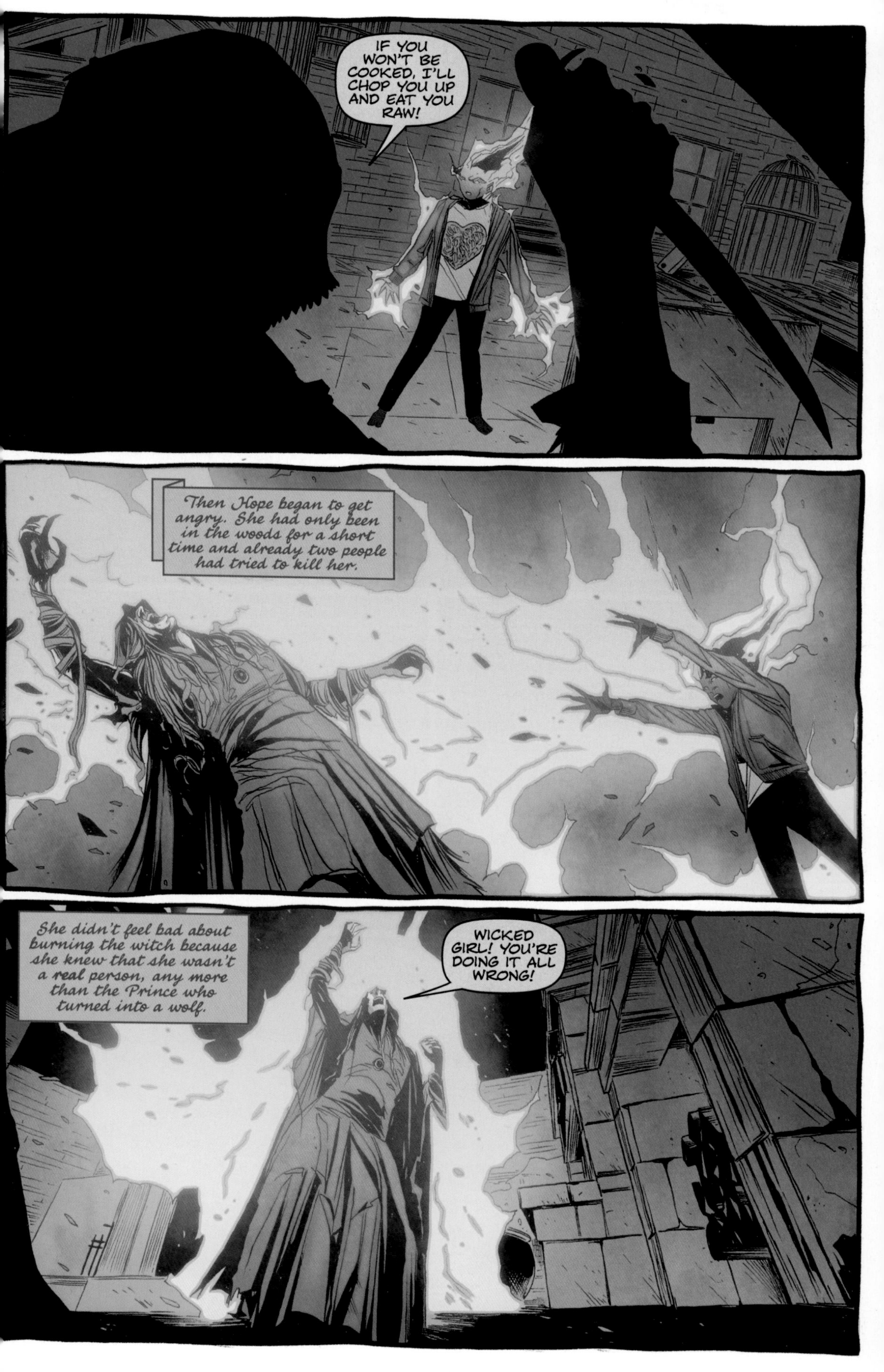
IF YOU WON'T BE COOKED, I'LL CHOP YOU UP AND EAT YOU RAW!
Then Hope began to get angry. She had only been in the woods for a short time and already two people had tried to kill her.
She didn't feel bad about burning the witch because she knew that she wasn't a real person, any more than the Prince who turned into a wolf.
WICKED GIRL! YOU'RE DOING IT ALL WRONG!

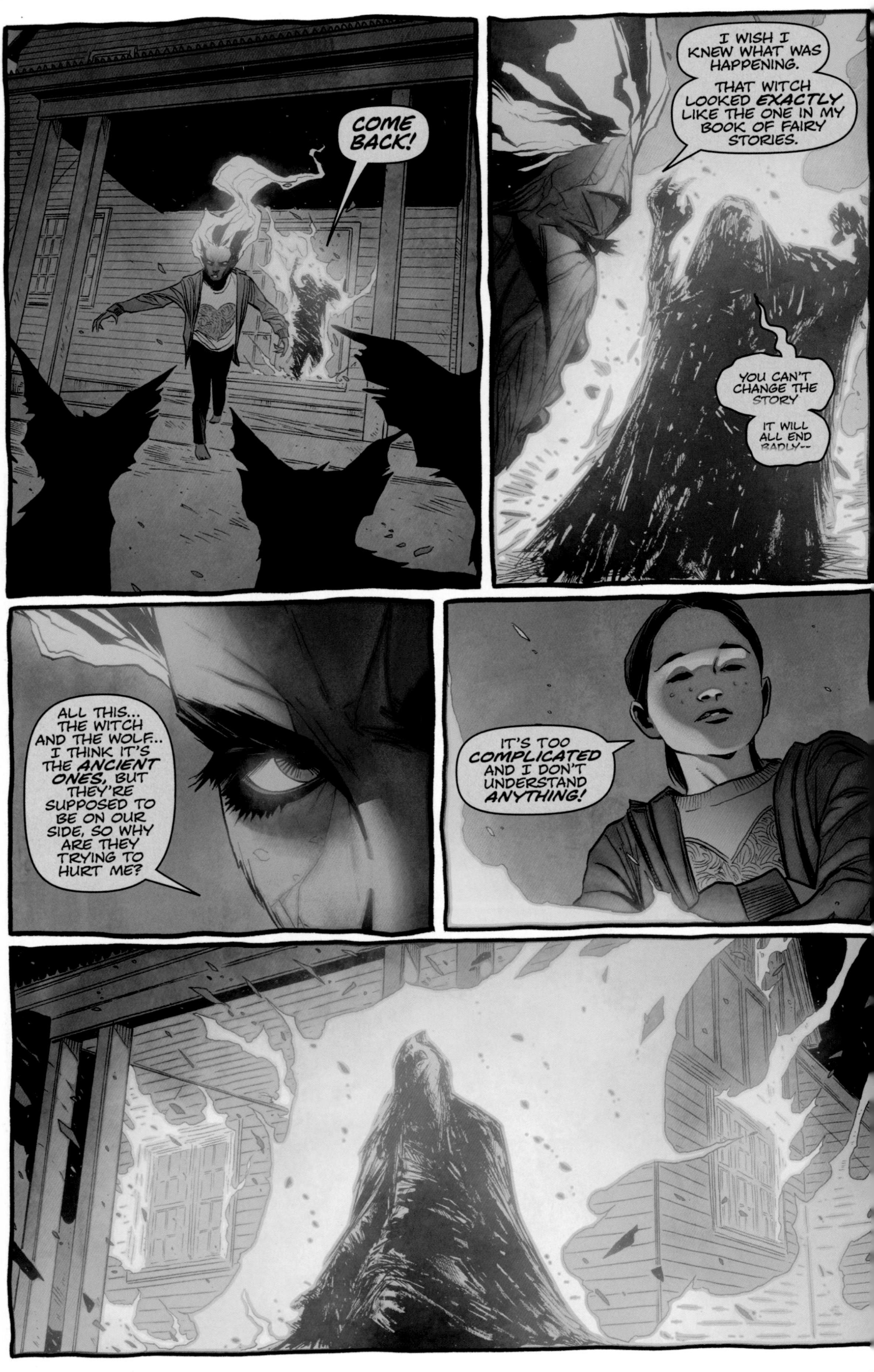
COME BACK!
I WISH I KNEW WHAT WAS HAPPENING.
THAT WITCH LOOKED EXACTLY LIKE THE ONE IN MY BOOK OF FAIRY STORIES.
YOU CAN'T CHANGE THE STORY
IT WILL ALL END BADLY--
ALL THIS... THE WITCH AND THE WOLF... I THINK IT'S THE ANCIENT ONES, BUT THEY'RE SUPPOSED TO BE ON OUR SIDE, SO WHY ARE THEY TRYING TO HURT ME?
IT'S TOO COMPLICATED AND I DON'T UNDERSTAND ANYTHING!

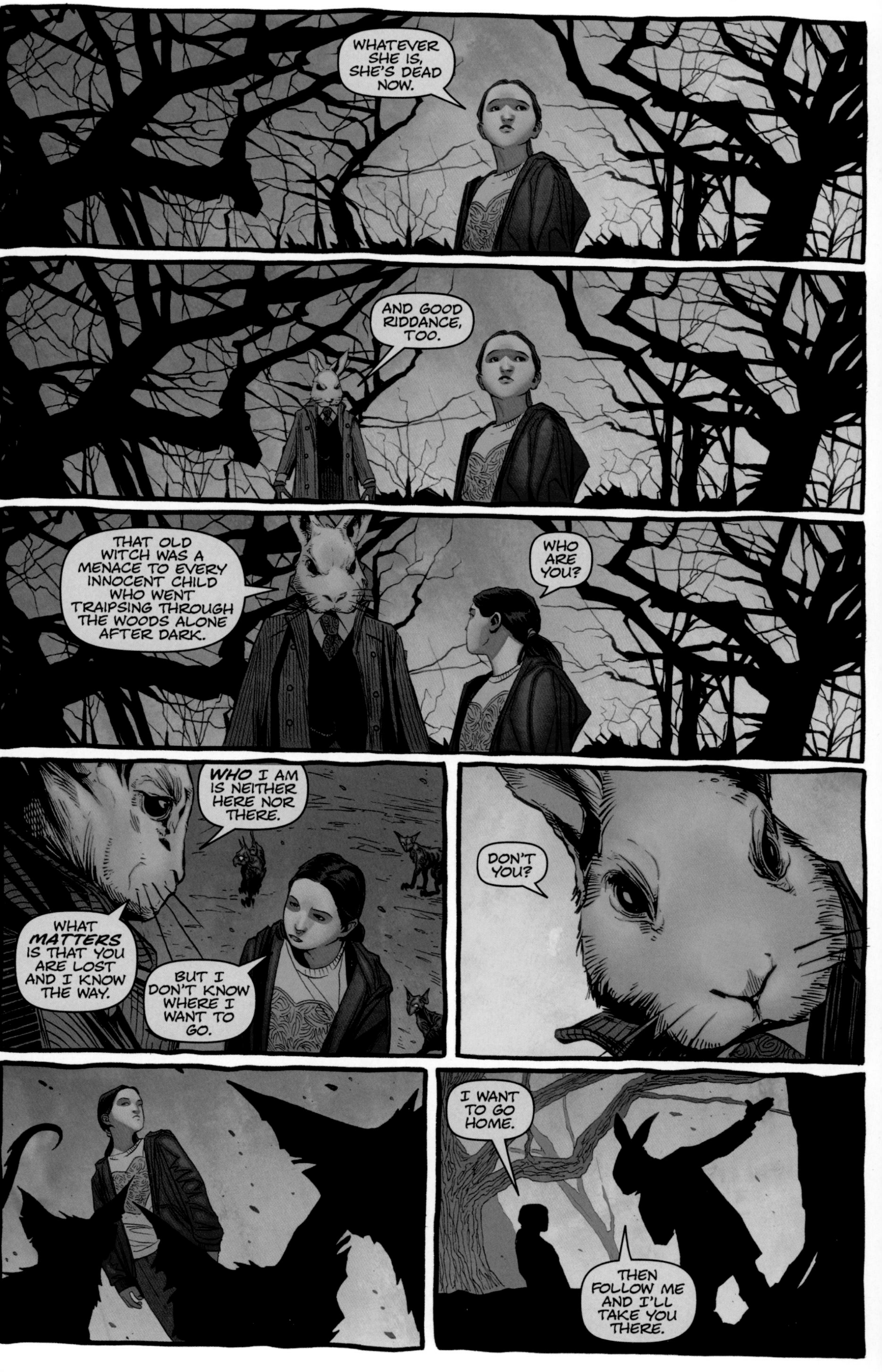
WHATEVER SHE IS, SHE'S DEAD NOW.
AND GOOD RIDDANCE, TOO.
THAT OLD WITCH WAS A MENACE TO EVERY INNOCENT CHILD WHO WENT TRAIPSING THROUGH THE WOODS ALONE AFTER DARK.
WHO ARE YOU?
WHO I AM IS NEITHER HERE NOR THERE.
WHAT MATTERS IS THAT YOU ARE LOST AND I KNOW THE WAY.
BUT I DON'T KNOW WHERE I WANT TO GO.
DON'T YOU?
I WANT TO GO HOME.
THEN FOLLOW ME AND I'LL TAKE YOU THERE.

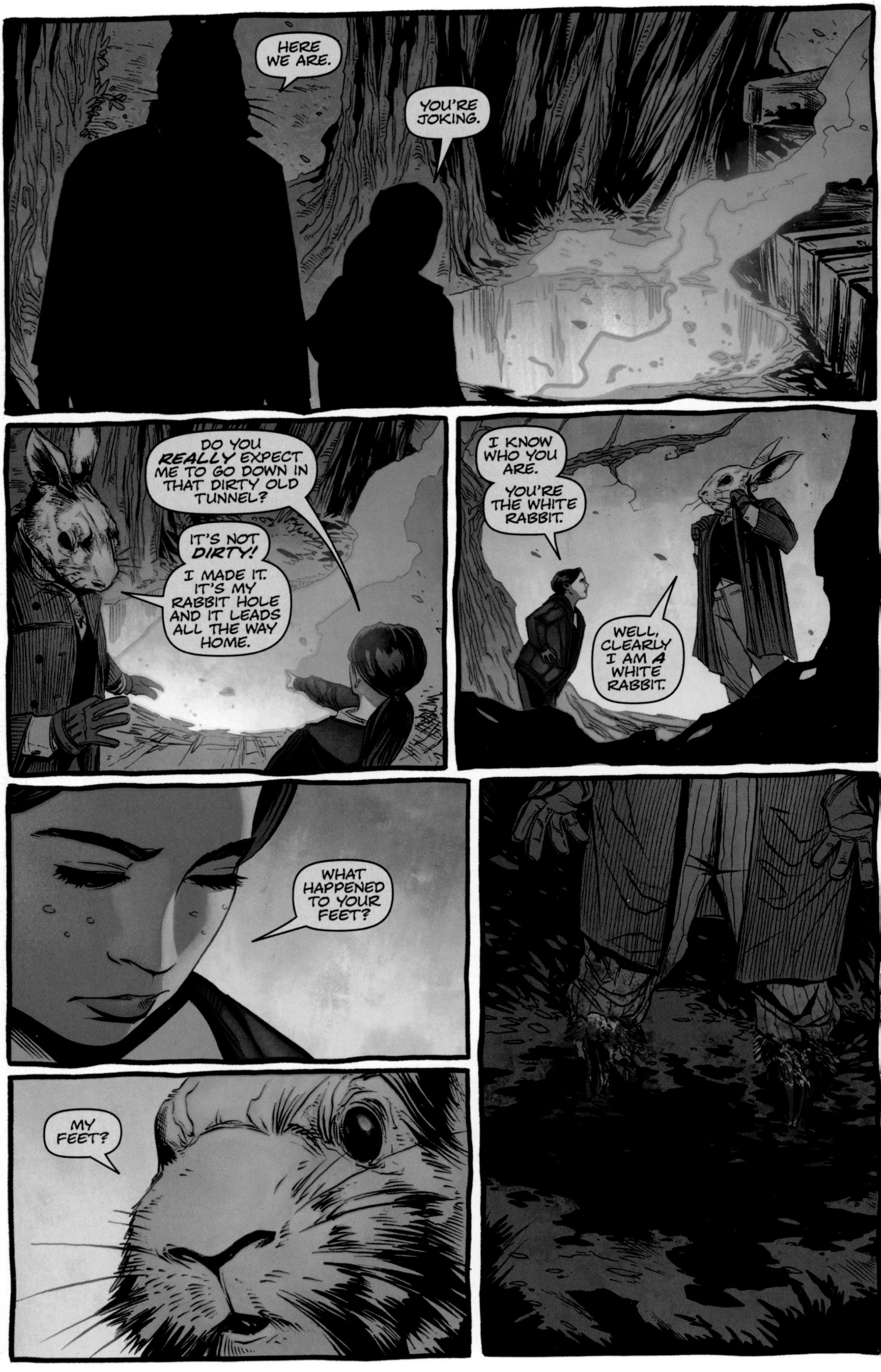
HERE WE ARE.
YOU'RE JOKING.
DO YOU *REALLY* EXPECT ME TO GO DOWN IN THAT DIRTY OLD TUNNEL?
IT'S NOT *DIRTY!*
I MADE IT. IT'S MY RABBIT HOLE AND IT LEADS ALL THE WAY HOME.
I KNOW WHO YOU ARE.
YOU'RE THE WHITE RABBIT.
WELL, CLEARLY I AM *A* WHITE RABBIT.
WHAT HAPPENED TO YOUR FEET?
MY FEET?

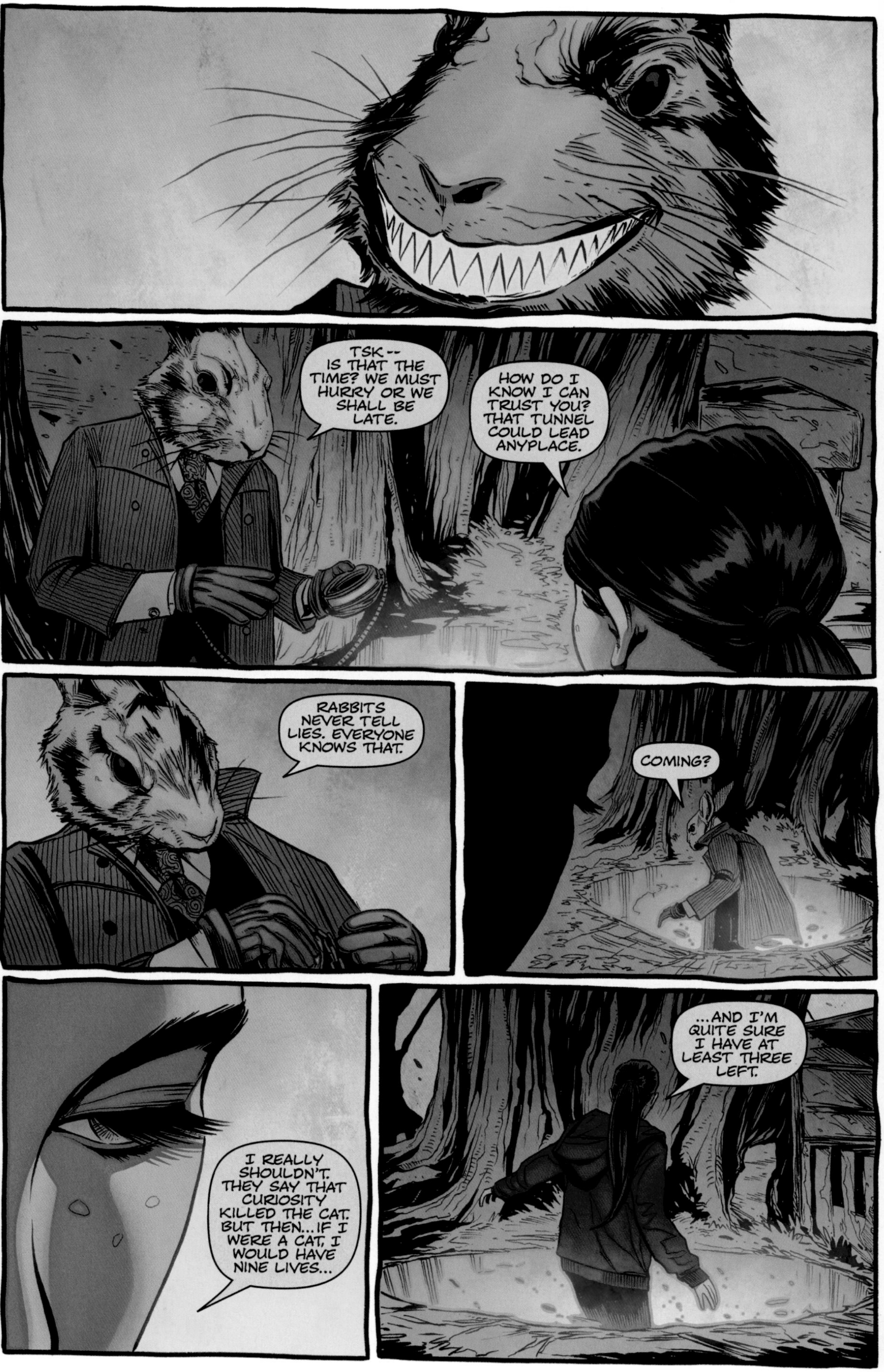
TSK-- IS THAT THE TIME? WE MUST HURRY OR WE SHALL BE LATE.
HOW DO I KNOW I CAN TRUST YOU? THAT TUNNEL COULD LEAD ANYPLACE.
RABBITS NEVER TELL LIES. EVERYONE KNOWS THAT.
COMING?
I REALLY SHOULDN'T. THEY SAY THAT CURIOSITY KILLED THE CAT. BUT THEN...IF I WERE A CAT, I WOULD HAVE NINE LIVES...
...AND I'M QUITE SURE I HAVE AT LEAST THREE LEFT.

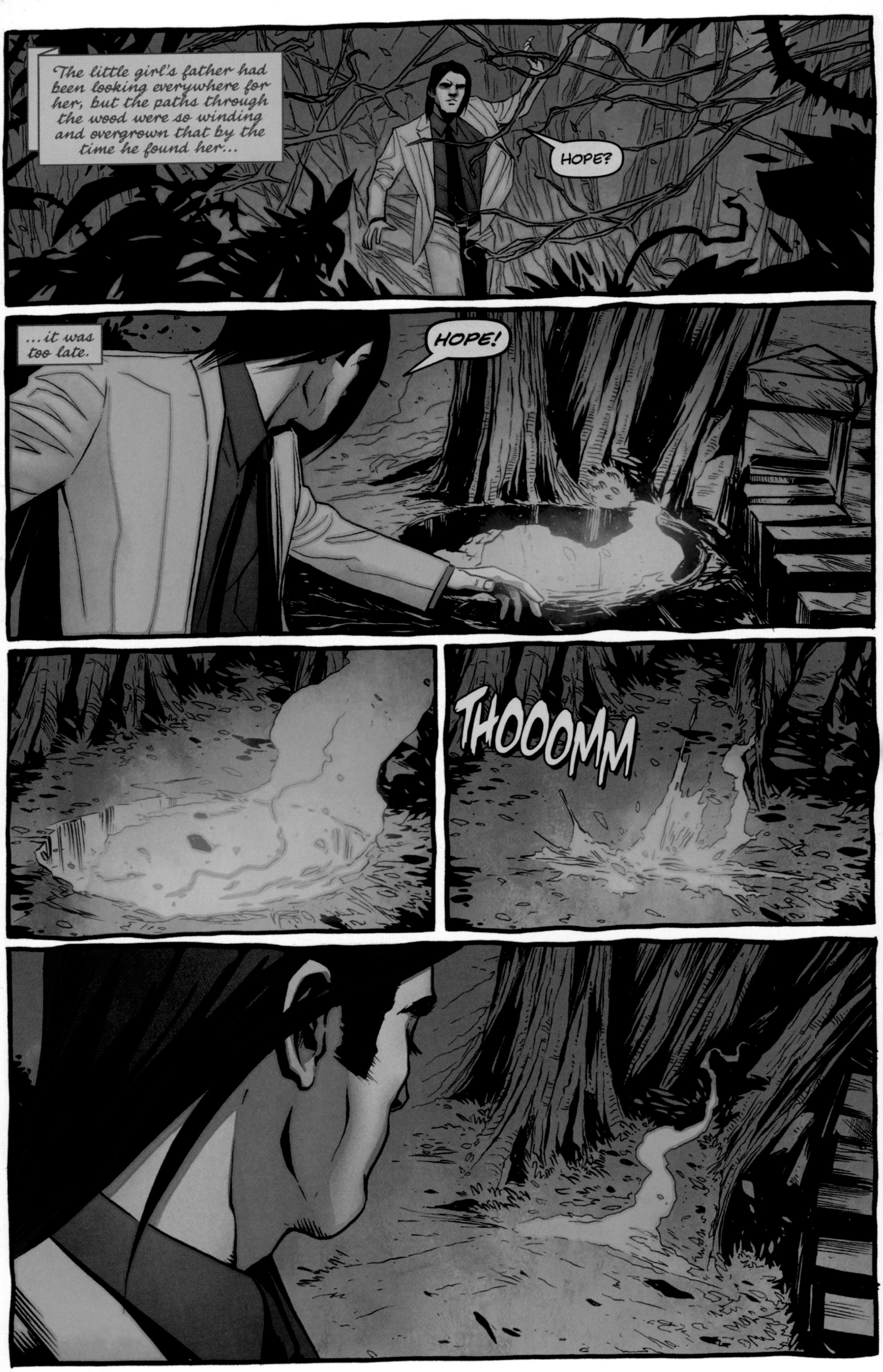
The little girl's father had been looking everywhere for her, but the paths through the wood were so winding and overgrown that by the time he found her...
HOPE?
...it was too late.
HOPE!
THOOOMM

by David Hine

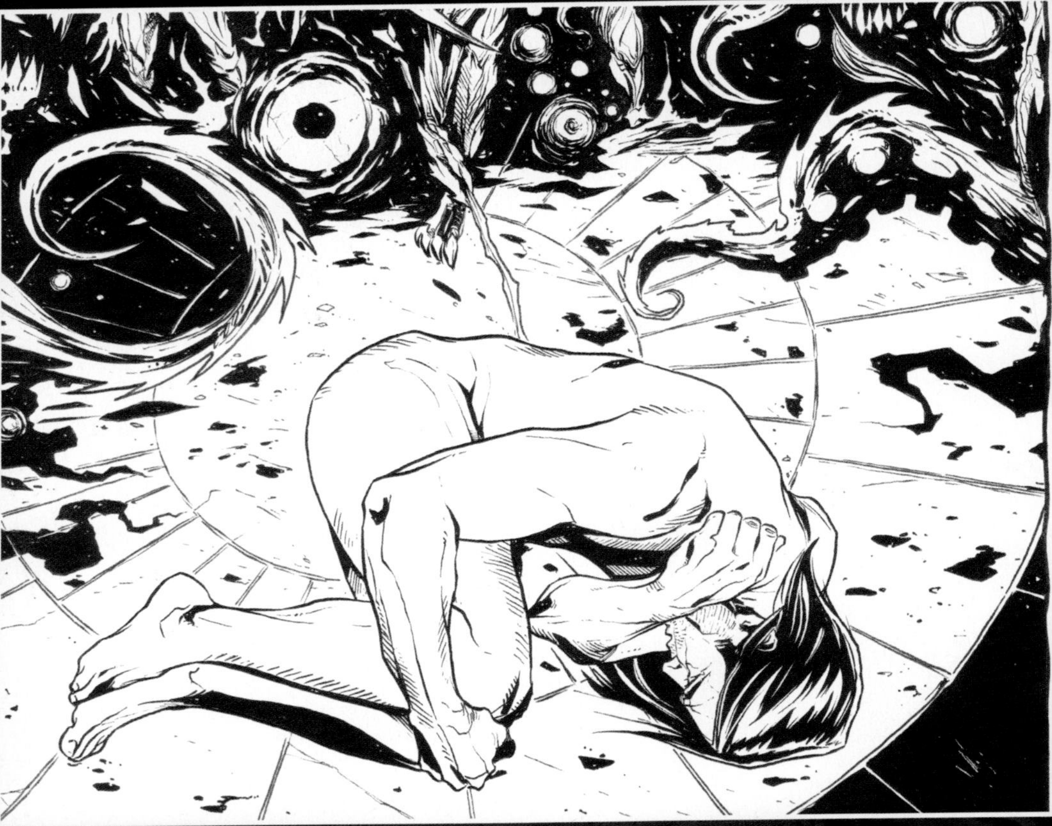

Jackie shivered, hugging his thin, bare chest. The damp, chill atmosphere had penetrated all the way to his bones but it wasn't just the cold that made his body shake. He knew he was becoming feverish. It was impossible to follow any single train of thought. He slipped in and out of sleep, dreaming of unspeakable horrors and waking to the reality of the Darkness. Slimy oil-black coils slithered across the stone floor and touched his foot with an obscene caress. He drew away with a shudder and saw that his feet were white as bone. He held his arms up in front of his face; hairless forearms and wrists stick thin. The Doppelganger was right. He was losing weight fast; faster than seemed possible, unless he had been down there longer than he thought. Time was impossible to measure. There was no day or night. The pale light from the overhead lamps was constant – just enough to see the Darkness undulating in the shadows.

Cathead and the other Darklings were gone. Carrying out their master's business, no doubt. He did his best to get news of Jenny and Hope from them, but they were unreliable messengers, given to inventing stories to torment him. At least the Doppelganger didn't lie to him, as far as he knew. Hope was lost in the woods. Jenny was lost in her own delusions.

He had to get out. He had never, in all his life, been so weak, so helpless. Even before the Darkness had come into his world, he had always been able to look after himself. No one messes with Jackie Estacado. He laughed and the sound of his own voice frightened him more than anything. It sounded like the high-pitched giggle of a madman.

He needed to eat. That was the thing. He had barely touched the food that the Doppelganger brought him. That was a mistake. He had to eat, get his strength back, get his mind sharp so he could work out how to get the hell out of there and take his life back. He reached for the tray of food, dragged it across the floor towards him. A steak, green beans, boiled potatoes. Long gone cold, but he was suddenly hungrier than he had been for as long as he could remember. He picked up the knife and fork in his numb fingers and cut the steak clumsily.

As the steel sliced through the grey meat, blind white maggots writhed onto the plate and he grunted with horror and disgust. He kicked the tray away from him, maggots spilling across the floor. How could the meat have putrefied so quickly? Perhaps it had been days, not hours, since the Doppelganger had been there. A Darkness tentacle slid out of the shadows and the maggots wriggled towards it, burrowing into the slick black flesh. Jackie shuddered, praying he would not be there to see what hatched from that unholy union.

He closed his eyes and sleep took him. He dreamed that he was Jackie Estacado, and in his dream he took back everything he had lost with bullets and blades and fists.

Later he woke to see a bulky figure bending to place a tray of fresh food onto the floor nearby. The man's back was towards him but as he stood he glimpsed his profile.

"Lorenzo? Thank Christ. You have to get me out of here. I don't know what he's been telling you. That person walking around up there…that's not…"

He stopped talking, trying desperately to gather his thoughts. If Lorenzo was down here, he must know about the Darkness and he must know there were two versions of Jackie. Why was the Doppelganger trusting him? Lorenzo stood with his back to Jackie, not moving, apparently waiting for orders.

"Lorenzo. For fuck's sake, turn around and tell me you know who I am."

He turned then and Jackie knew that there was no help here. Lorenzo's face had the pallid complexion of a corpse with a tracery of veins visible through the translucent skin – black veins. His eyes were pools of darkness. An oily black liquid oozed from them, trickling down his cheeks like the tears of the dead. When he spoke his voice was as hollow and empty of expression as his eyes.

"You're Jackie Estacado."
"What did he do to you?"
"He made me part of him. He made me whole."

From the shadows a tendril snaked through the air. Lorenzo reached out automatically, his fingers stroking it like a pet.

"HOPE'S ADVENTURES UNDERGROUND"
PART
2

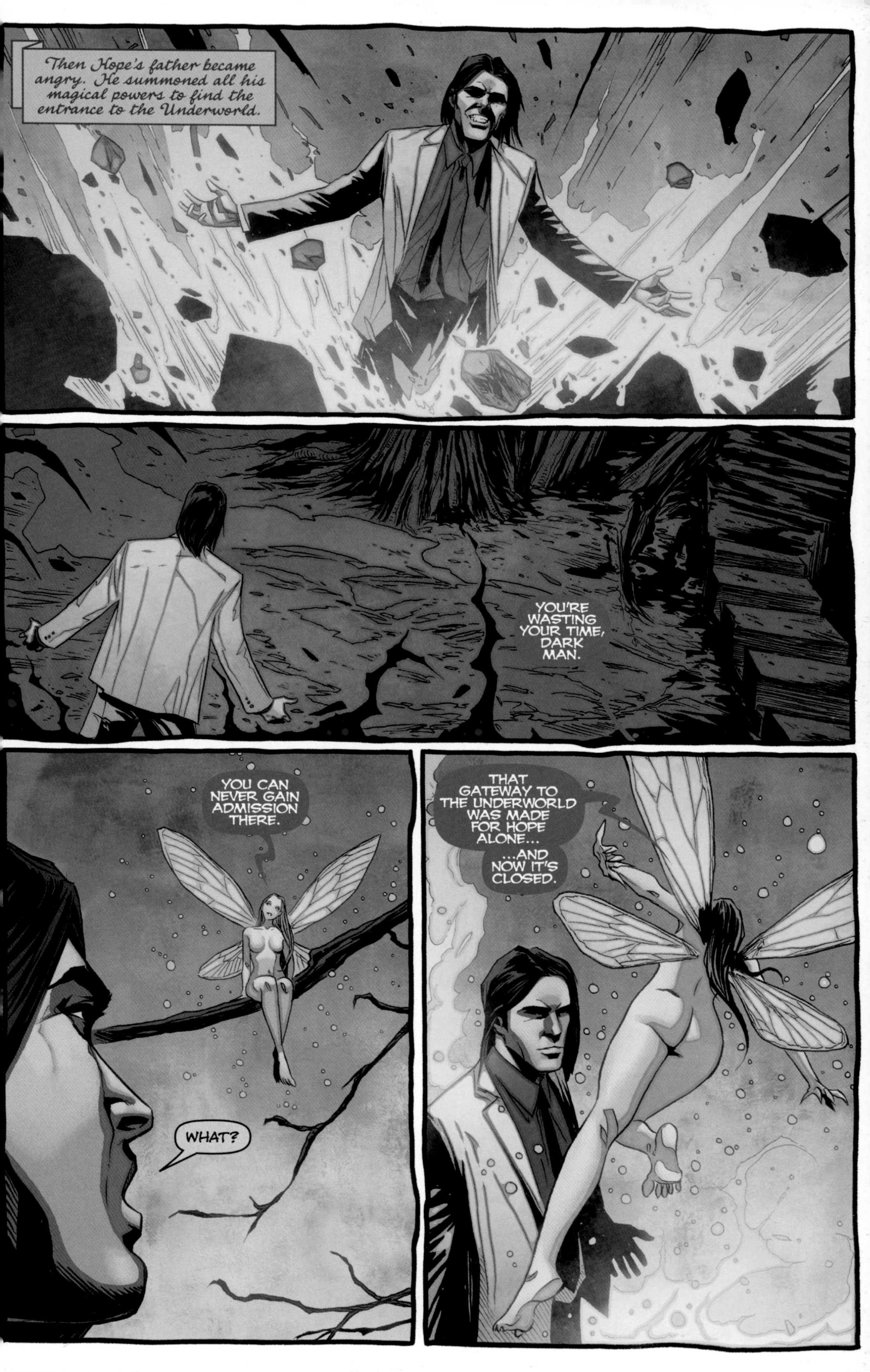
Then Hope's father became angry. He summoned all his magical powers to find the entrance to the Underworld.
YOU'RE WASTING YOUR TIME, DARK MAN.
YOU CAN NEVER GAIN ADMISSION THERE.
WHAT?
THAT GATEWAY TO THE UNDERWORLD WAS MADE FOR HOPE ALONE...
...AND NOW IT'S CLOSED.

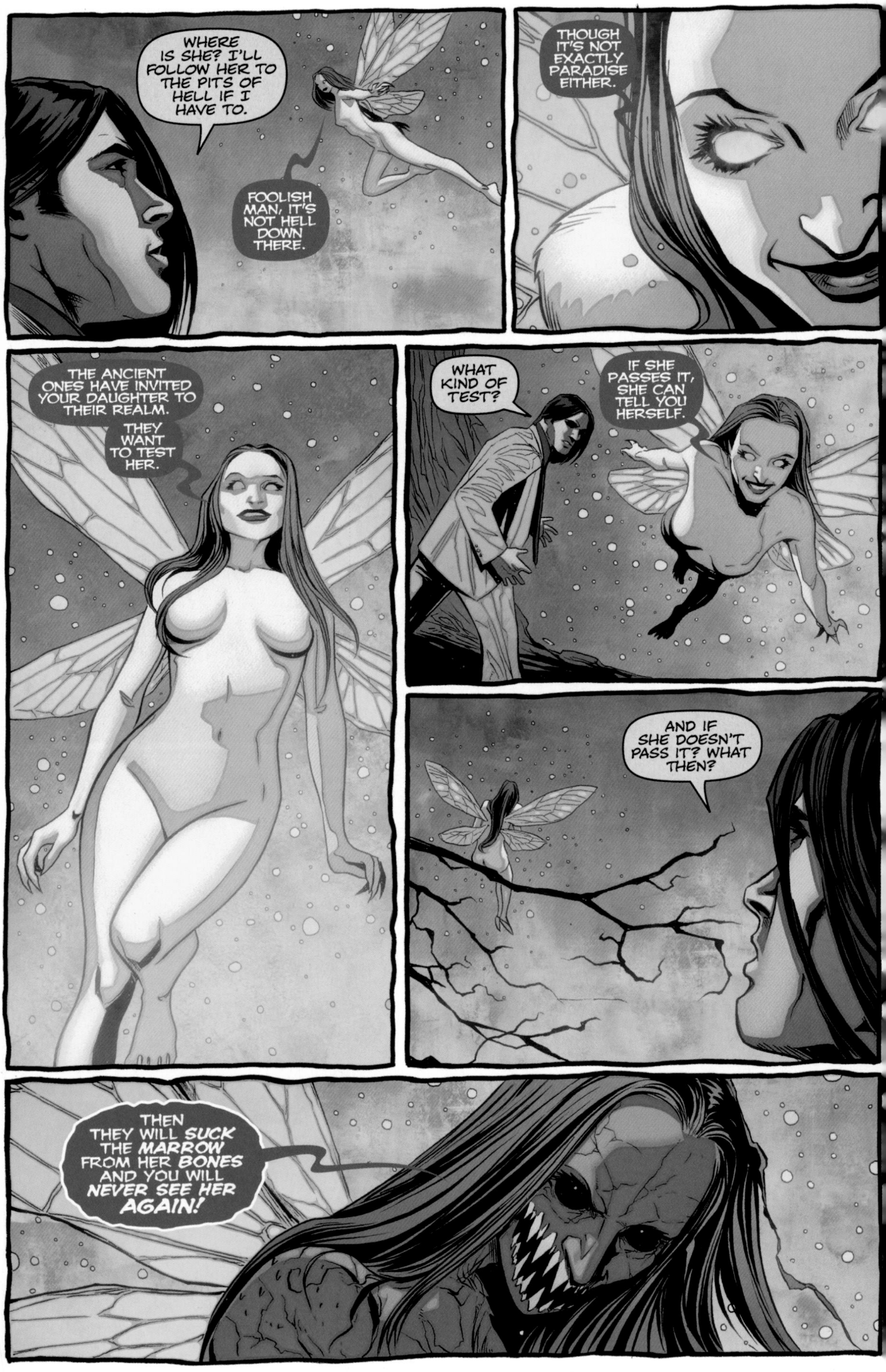
WHERE IS SHE? I'LL FOLLOW HER TO THE PITS OF HELL IF I HAVE TO.
FOOLISH MAN, IT'S NOT HELL DOWN THERE.
THOUGH IT'S NOT EXACTLY PARADISE EITHER.
THE ANCIENT ONES HAVE INVITED YOUR DAUGHTER TO THEIR REALM.
THEY WANT TO TEST HER.
WHAT KIND OF TEST?
IF SHE PASSES IT, SHE CAN TELL YOU HERSELF.
AND IF SHE DOESN'T PASS IT? WHAT THEN?
THEN THEY WILL SUCK THE MARROW FROM HER BONES AND YOU WILL NEVER SEE HER AGAIN!

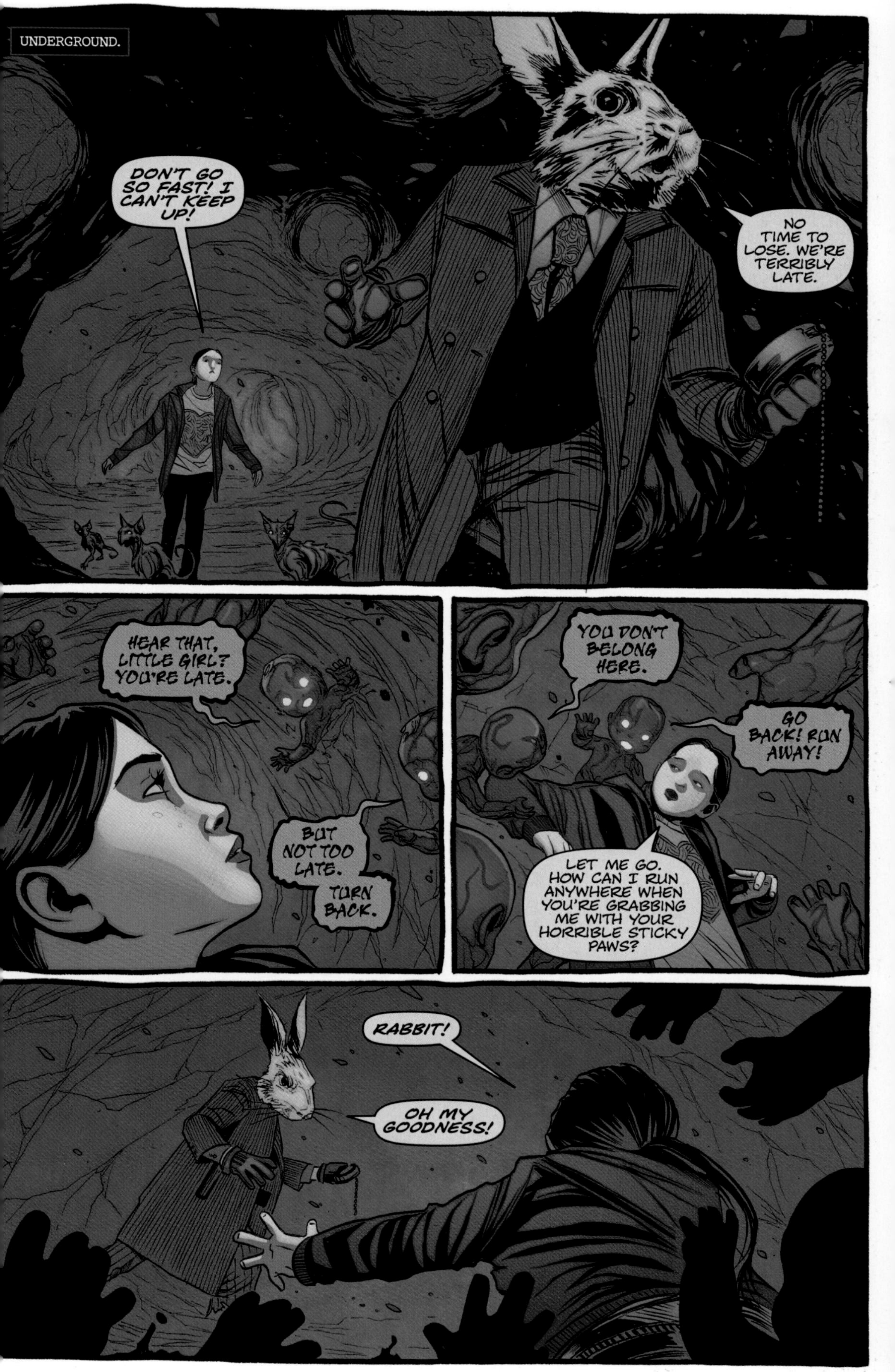
UNDERGROUND.
DON'T GO SO FAST! I CAN'T KEEP UP!
NO TIME TO LOSE. WE'RE TERRIBLY LATE.
HEAR THAT, LITTLE GIRL? YOU'RE LATE.
BUT NOT TOO LATE.
TURN BACK.
YOU DON'T BELONG HERE.
GO BACK! RUN AWAY!
LET ME GO. HOW CAN I RUN ANYWHERE WHEN YOU'RE GRABBING ME WITH YOUR HORRIBLE STICKY PAWS?
RABBIT!
OH MY GOODNESS!

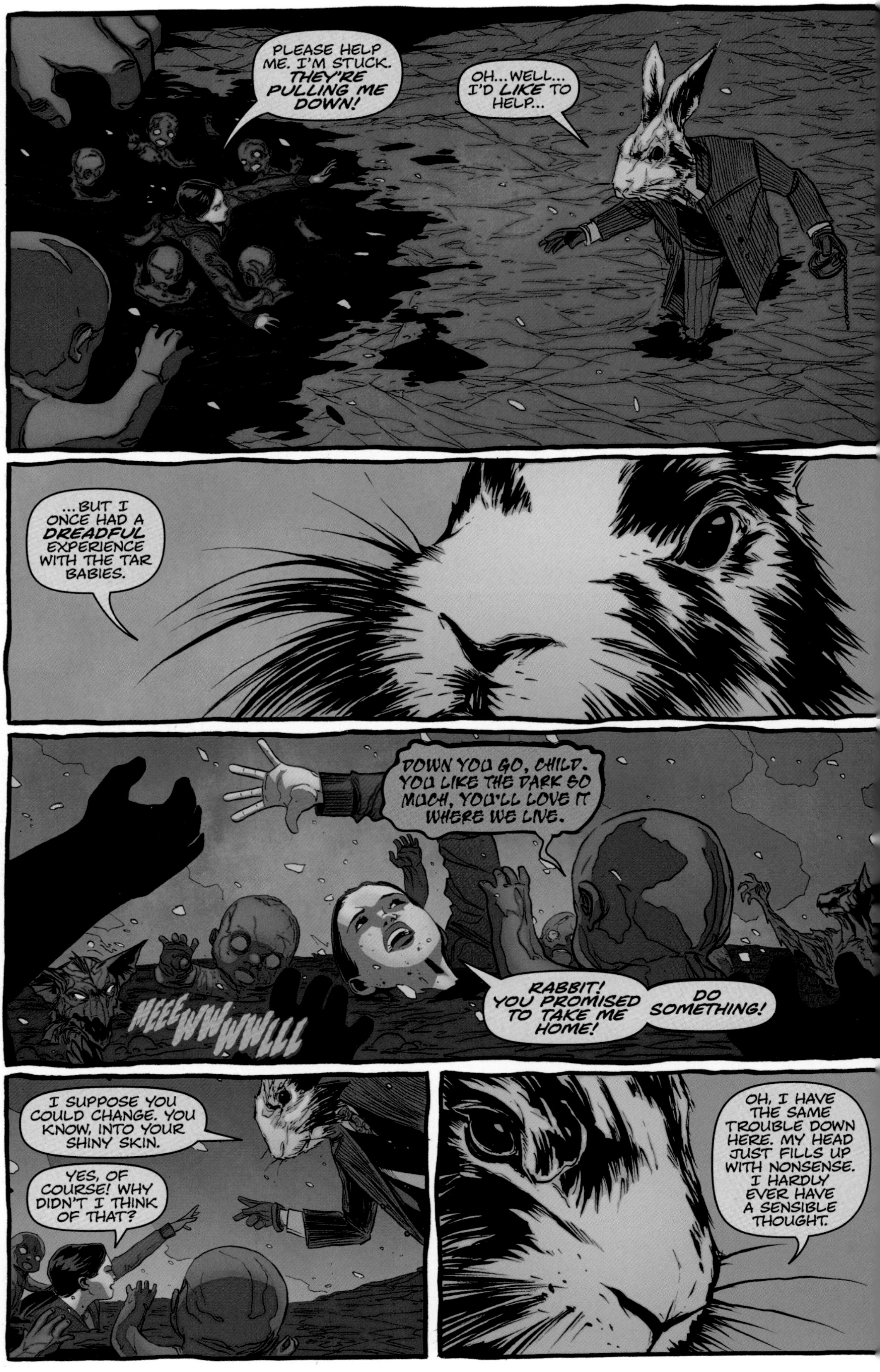
PLEASE HELP ME. I'M STUCK. THEY'RE PULLING ME DOWN!
OH...WELL... I'D LIKE TO HELP...
...BUT I ONCE HAD A DREADFUL EXPERIENCE WITH THE TAR BABIES.
DOWN YOU GO, CHILD. YOU LIKE THE DARK SO MUCH, YOU'LL LOVE IT WHERE WE LIVE.
MEEEWWWWWLLL
RABBIT! YOU PROMISED TO TAKE ME HOME!
DO SOMETHING!
I SUPPOSE YOU COULD CHANGE. YOU KNOW, INTO YOUR SHINY SKIN.
YES, OF COURSE! WHY DIDN'T I THINK OF THAT?
OH, I HAVE THE SAME TROUBLE DOWN HERE. MY HEAD JUST FILLS UP WITH NONSENSE. I HARDLY EVER HAVE A SENSIBLE THOUGHT.

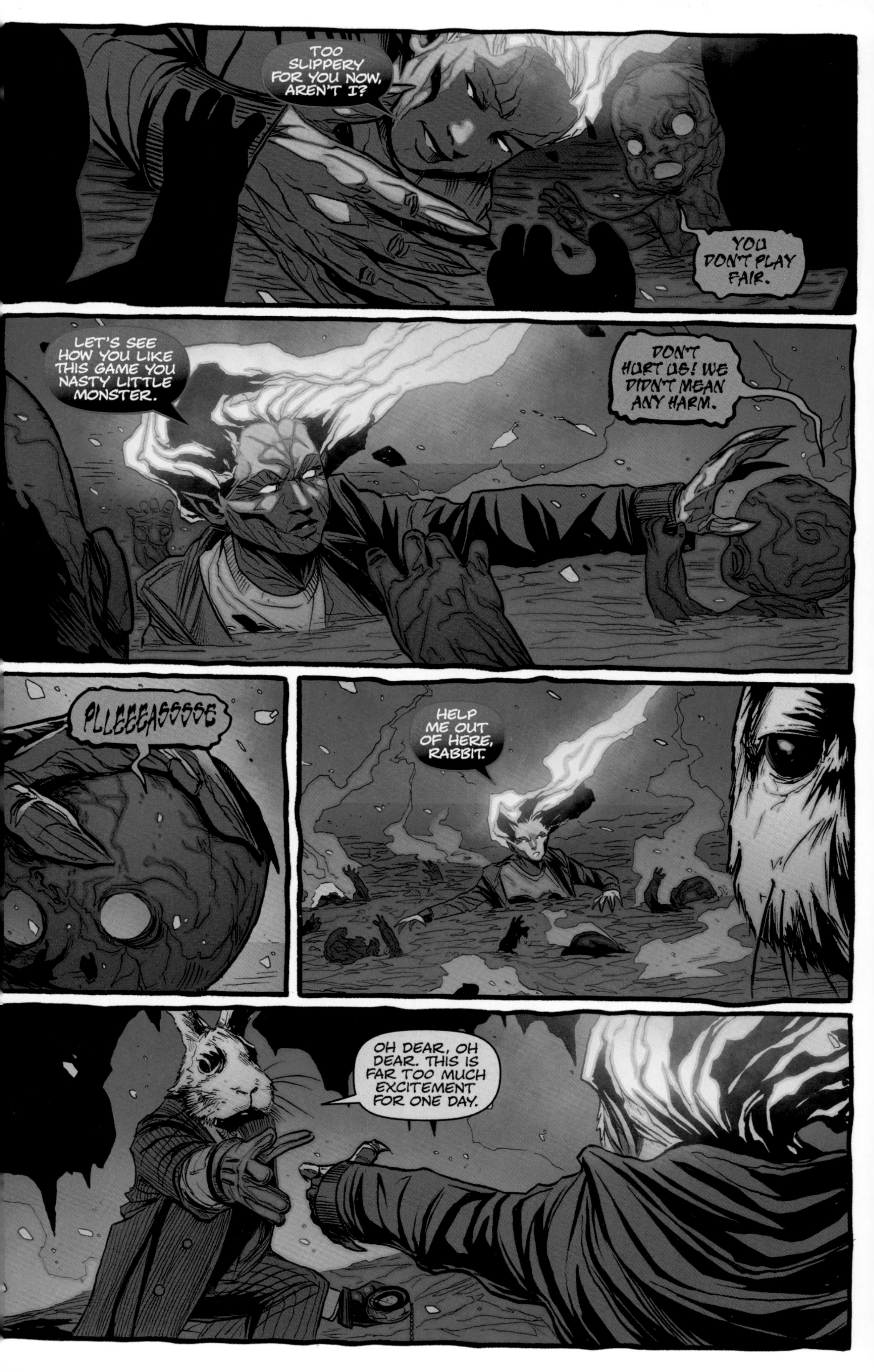
TOO SLIPPERY FOR YOU NOW, AREN'T I?
YOU DON'T PLAY FAIR.
LET'S SEE HOW YOU LIKE THIS GAME YOU NASTY LITTLE MONSTER.
DON'T HURT US! WE DIDN'T MEAN ANY HARM.
PLLEEEASSSSE
HELP ME OUT OF HERE, RABBIT.
OH DEAR, OH DEAR. THIS IS FAR TOO MUCH EXCITEMENT FOR ONE DAY.

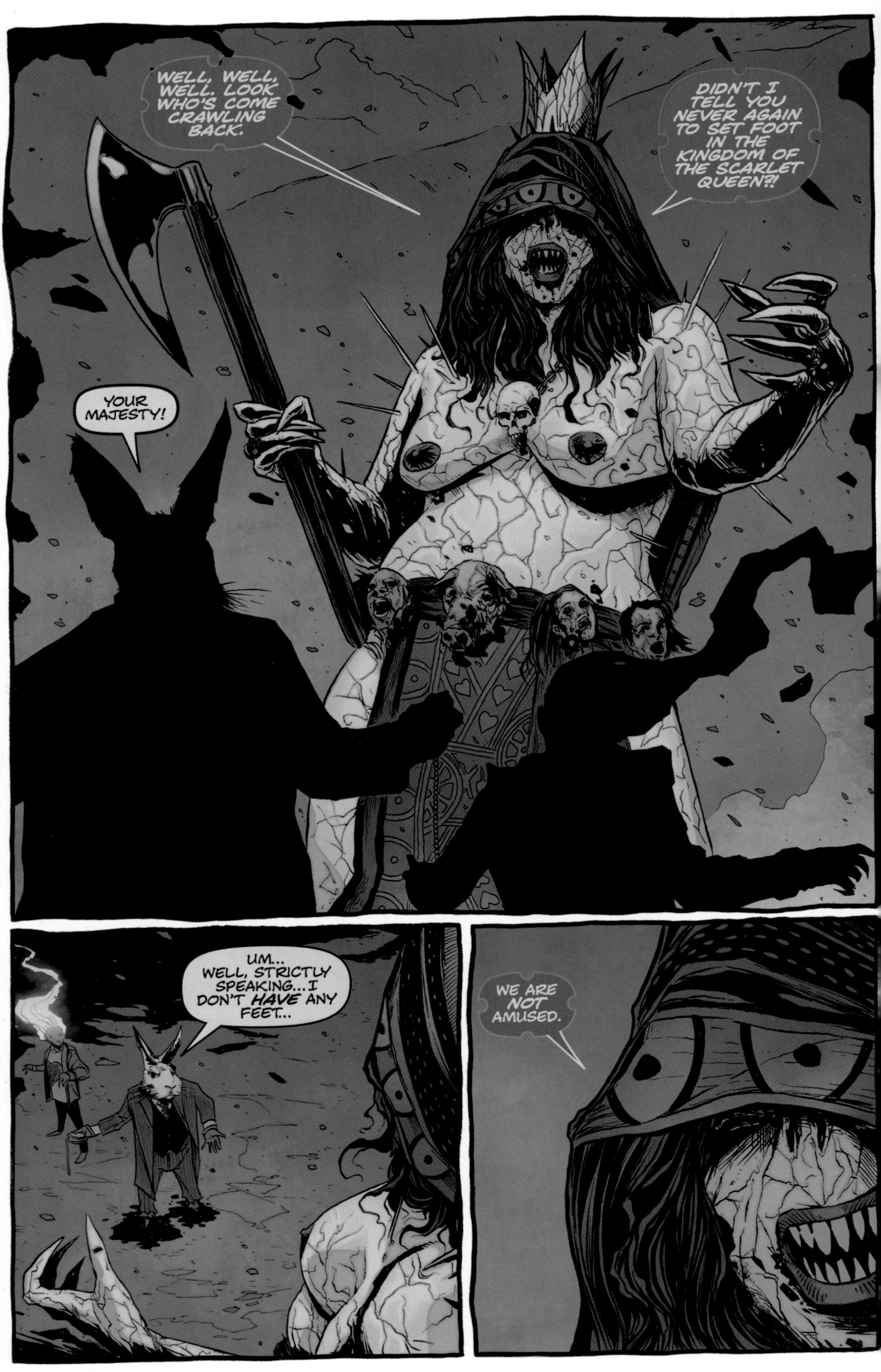
WELL, WELL, WELL. LOOK WHO'S COME CRAWLING BACK.
DIDN'T I TELL YOU NEVER AGAIN TO SET FOOT IN THE KINGDOM OF THE SCARLET QUEEN?!
YOUR MAJESTY!
UM... WELL, STRICTLY SPEAKING... I DON'T *HAVE* ANY FEET...
WE ARE *NOT* AMUSED.

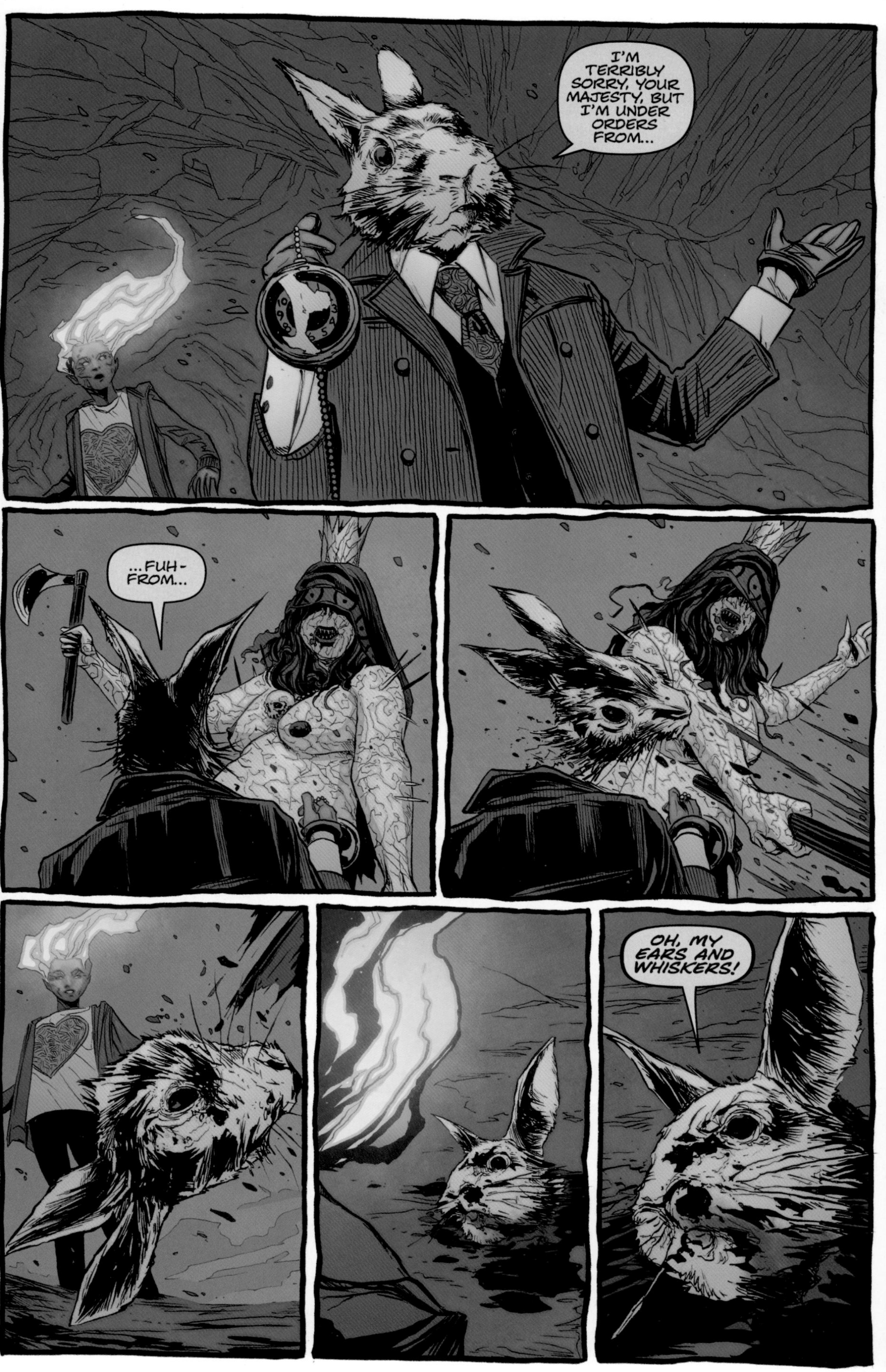
I'M TERRIBLY SORRY, YOUR MAJESTY, BUT I'M UNDER ORDERS FROM...
...FUH- FROM...
OH, MY EARS AND WHISKERS!

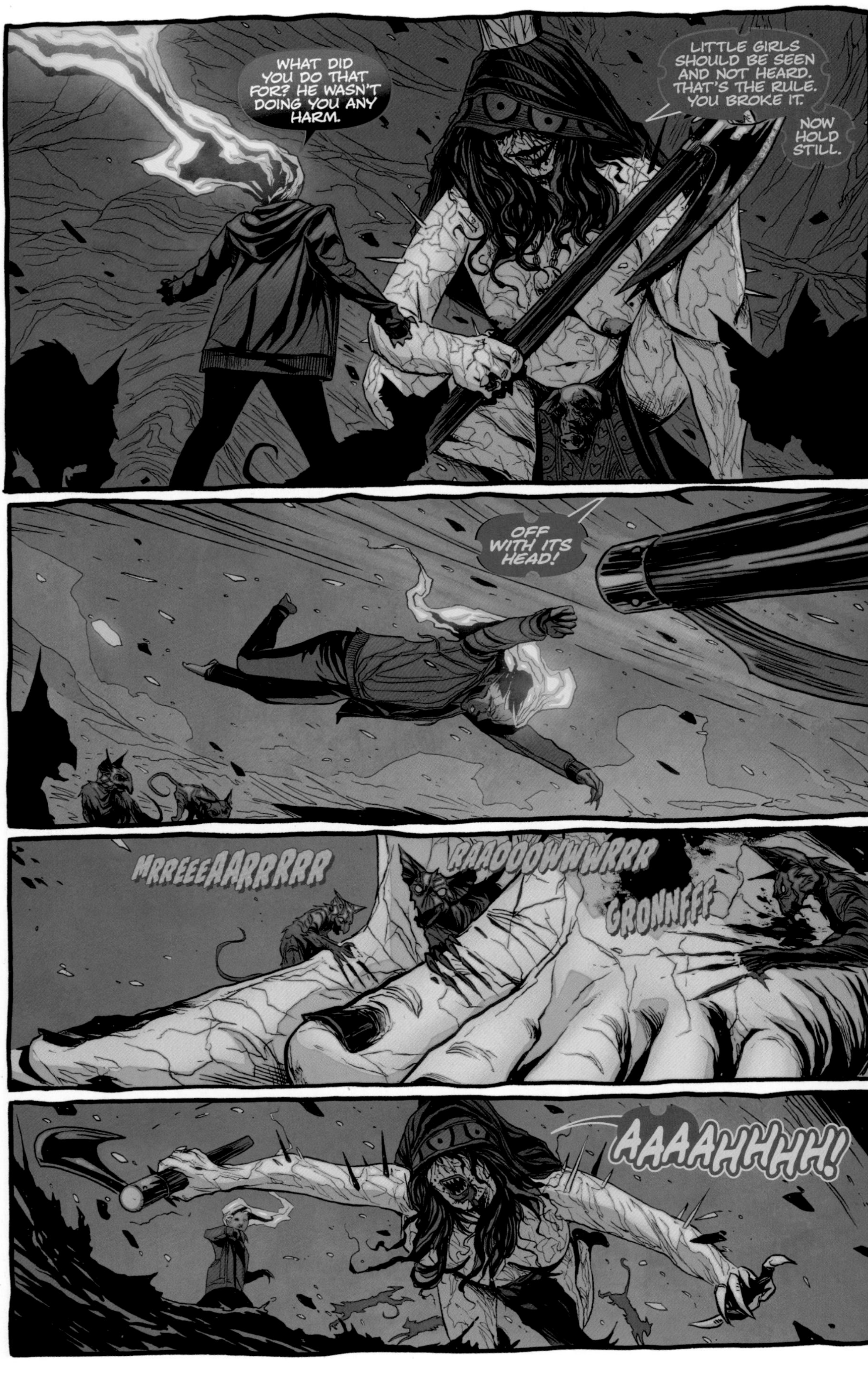
WHAT DID YOU DO THAT FOR? HE WASN'T DOING YOU ANY HARM.
LITTLE GIRLS SHOULD BE SEEN AND NOT HEARD. THAT'S THE RULE. YOU BROKE IT.
NOW HOLD STILL.
OFF WITH ITS HEAD!
MRREEEAARRRRR
RAADOOWWWRRR
GRONNFFF
AAAAHHHH!

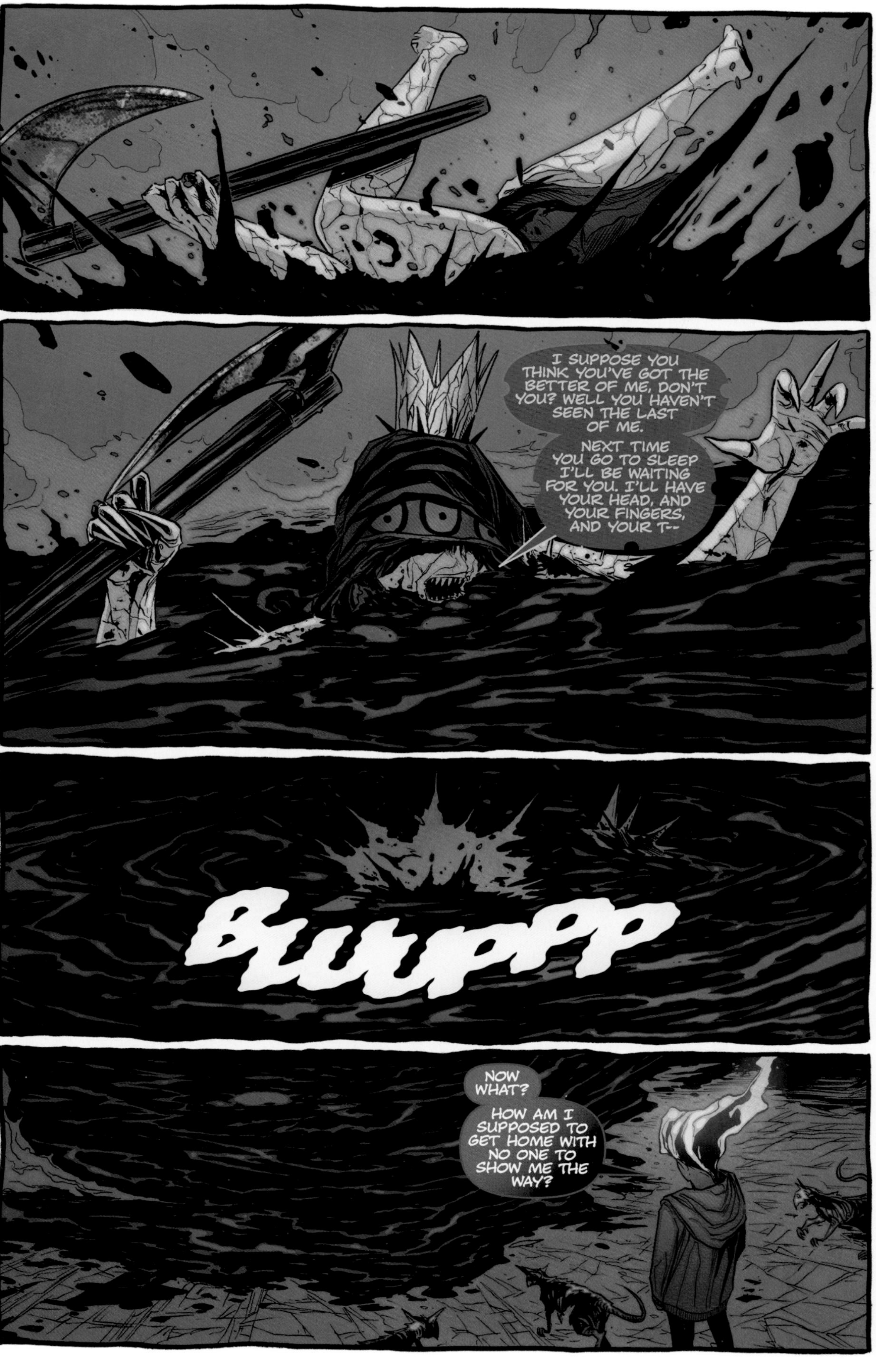
I SUPPOSE YOU THINK YOU'VE GOT THE BETTER OF ME, DON'T YOU? WELL YOU HAVEN'T SEEN THE LAST OF ME.
NEXT TIME YOU GO TO SLEEP I'LL BE WAITING FOR YOU. I'LL HAVE YOUR HEAD, AND YOUR FINGERS, AND YOUR T--
BLUPPP
NOW WHAT?
HOW AM I SUPPOSED TO GET HOME WITH NO ONE TO SHOW ME THE WAY?

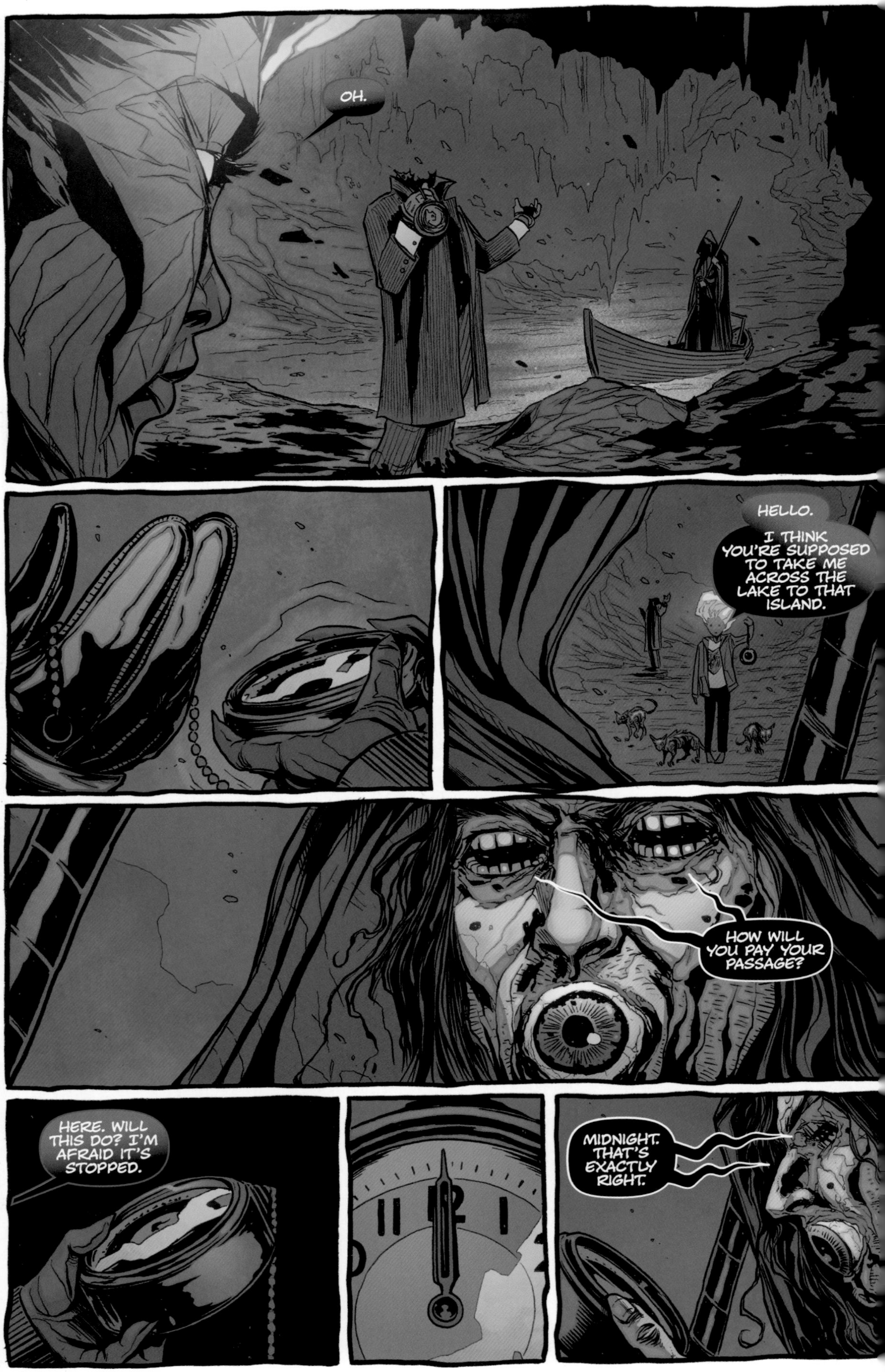

OH.
HELLO.
I THINK YOU'RE SUPPOSED TO TAKE ME ACROSS THE LAKE TO THAT ISLAND.
HOW WILL YOU PAY YOUR PASSAGE?
HERE. WILL THIS DO? I'M AFRAID IT'S STOPPED.
MIDNIGHT. THAT'S EXACTLY RIGHT.

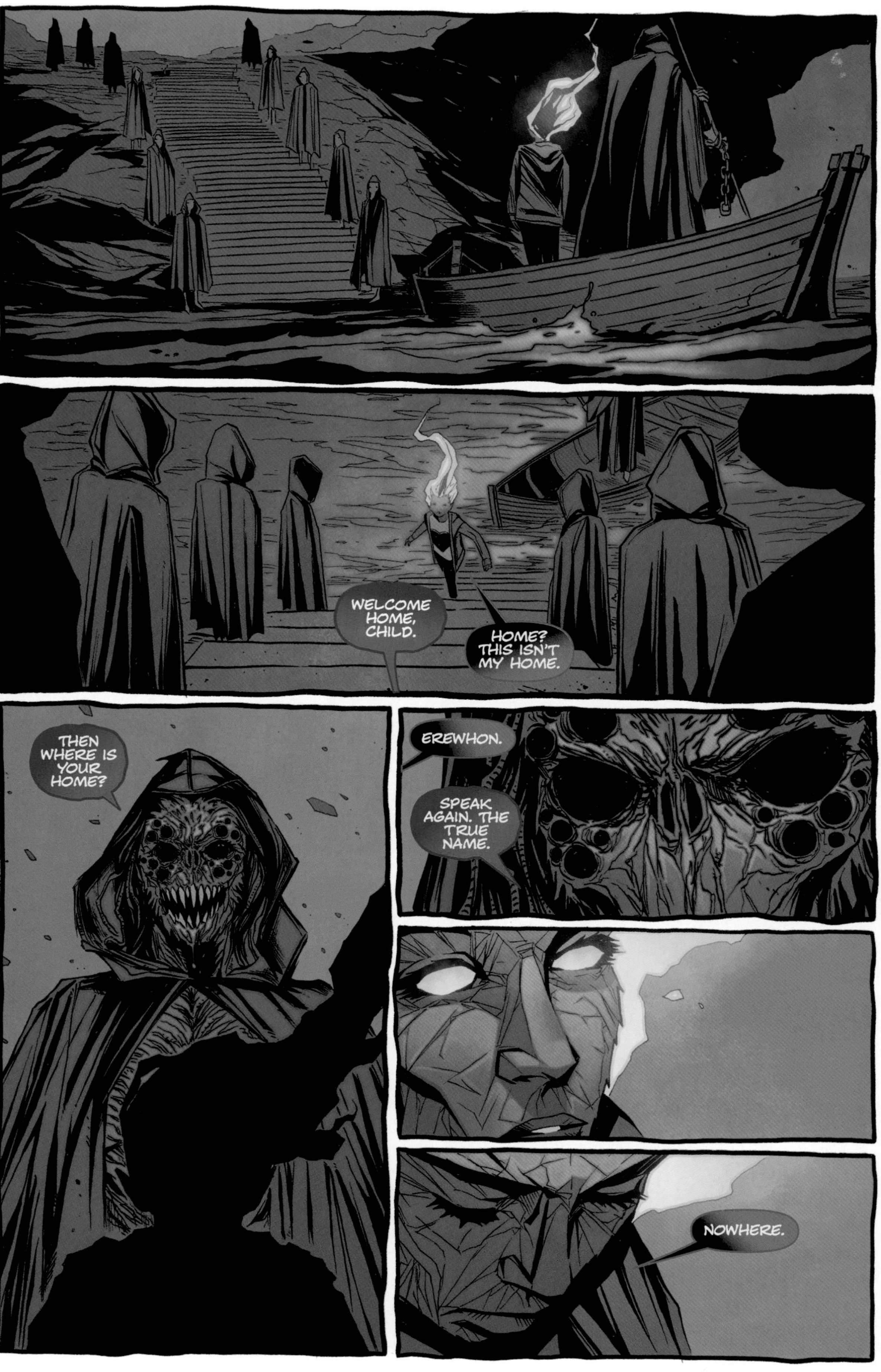
WELCOME HOME, CHILD.
HOME? THIS ISN'T MY HOME.
THEN WHERE IS YOUR HOME?
EREWHON.
SPEAK AGAIN. THE TRUE NAME.
NOWHERE.

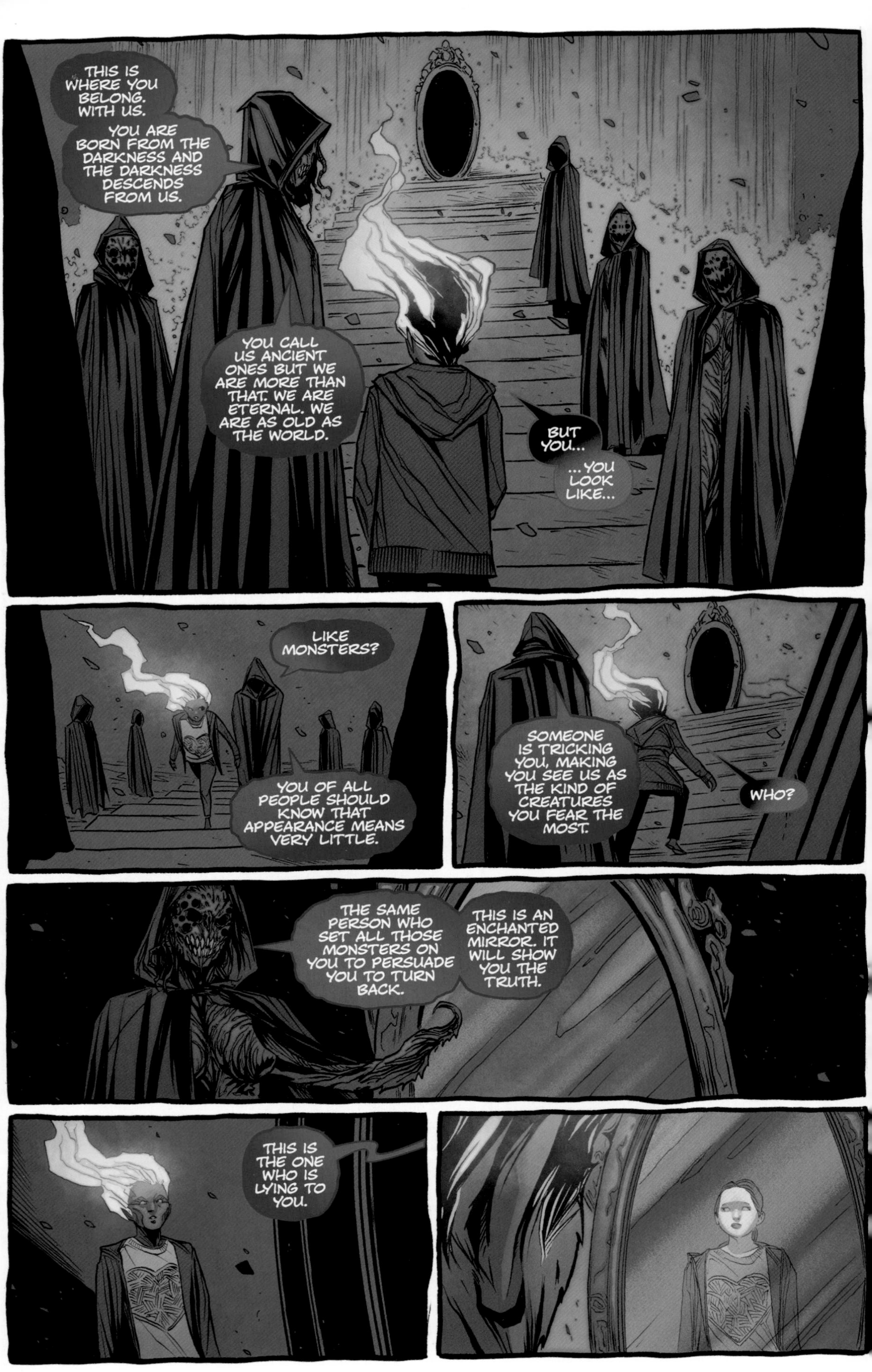
THIS IS WHERE YOU BELONG. WITH US.
YOU ARE BORN FROM THE DARKNESS AND THE DARKNESS DESCENDS FROM US.
YOU CALL US ANCIENT ONES BUT WE ARE MORE THAN THAT. WE ARE ETERNAL. WE ARE AS OLD AS THE WORLD.
BUT YOU...
...YOU LOOK LIKE...
LIKE MONSTERS?
YOU OF ALL PEOPLE SHOULD KNOW THAT APPEARANCE MEANS VERY LITTLE.
SOMEONE IS TRICKING YOU, MAKING YOU SEE US AS THE KIND OF CREATURES YOU FEAR THE MOST.
WHO?
THE SAME PERSON WHO SET ALL THOSE MONSTERS ON YOU TO PERSUADE YOU TO TURN BACK.
THIS IS AN ENCHANTED MIRROR. IT WILL SHOW YOU THE TRUTH.
THIS IS THE ONE WHO IS LYING TO YOU.

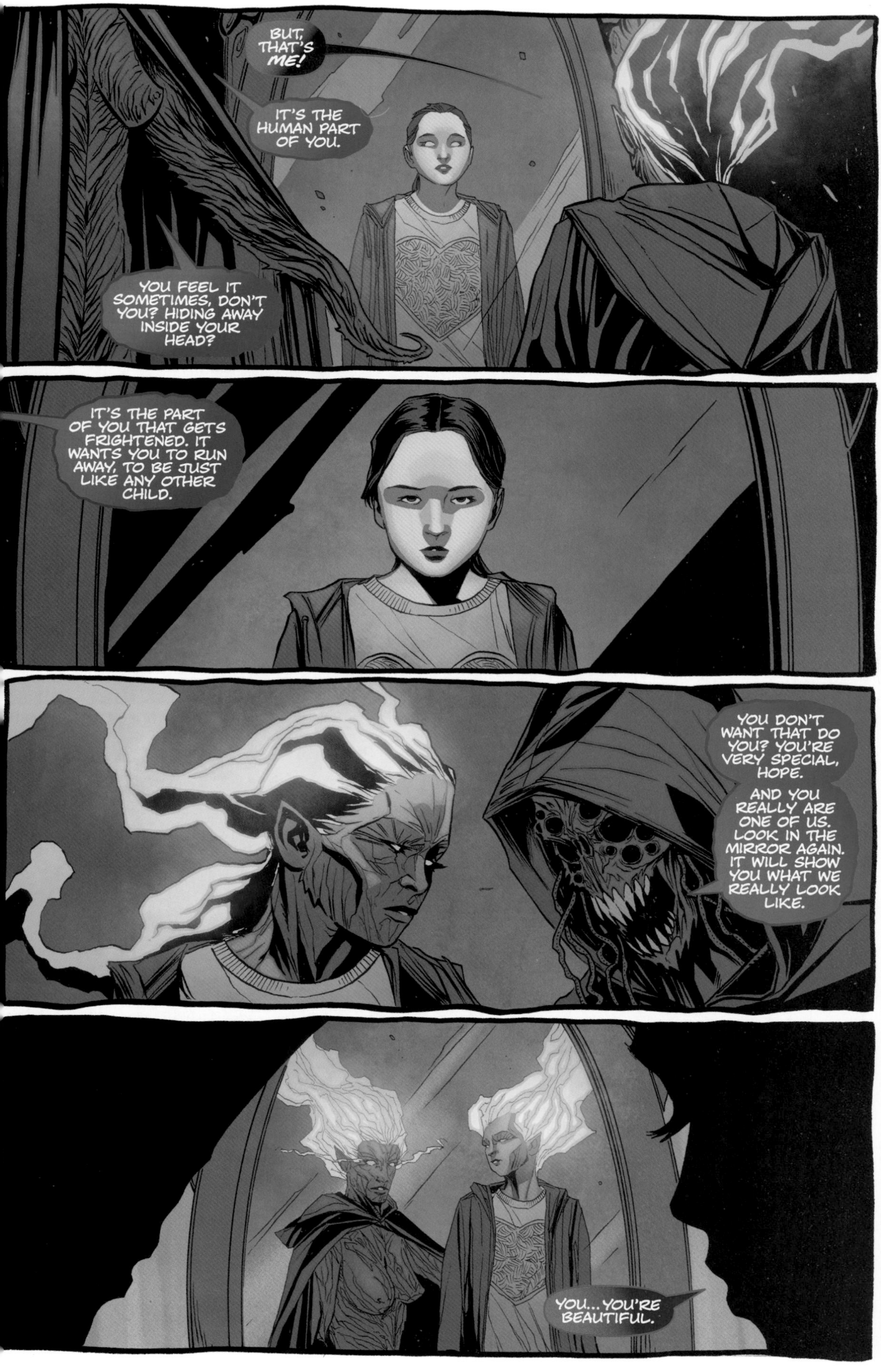
BUT, THAT'S ME!
IT'S THE HUMAN PART OF YOU.
YOU FEEL IT SOMETIMES, DON'T YOU? HIDING AWAY INSIDE YOUR HEAD?
IT'S THE PART OF YOU THAT GETS FRIGHTENED. IT WANTS YOU TO RUN AWAY, TO BE JUST LIKE ANY OTHER CHILD.
YOU DON'T WANT THAT DO YOU? YOU'RE VERY SPECIAL, HOPE.
AND YOU REALLY ARE ONE OF US. LOOK IN THE MIRROR AGAIN. IT WILL SHOW YOU WHAT WE REALLY LOOK LIKE.
YOU... YOU'RE BEAUTIFUL.

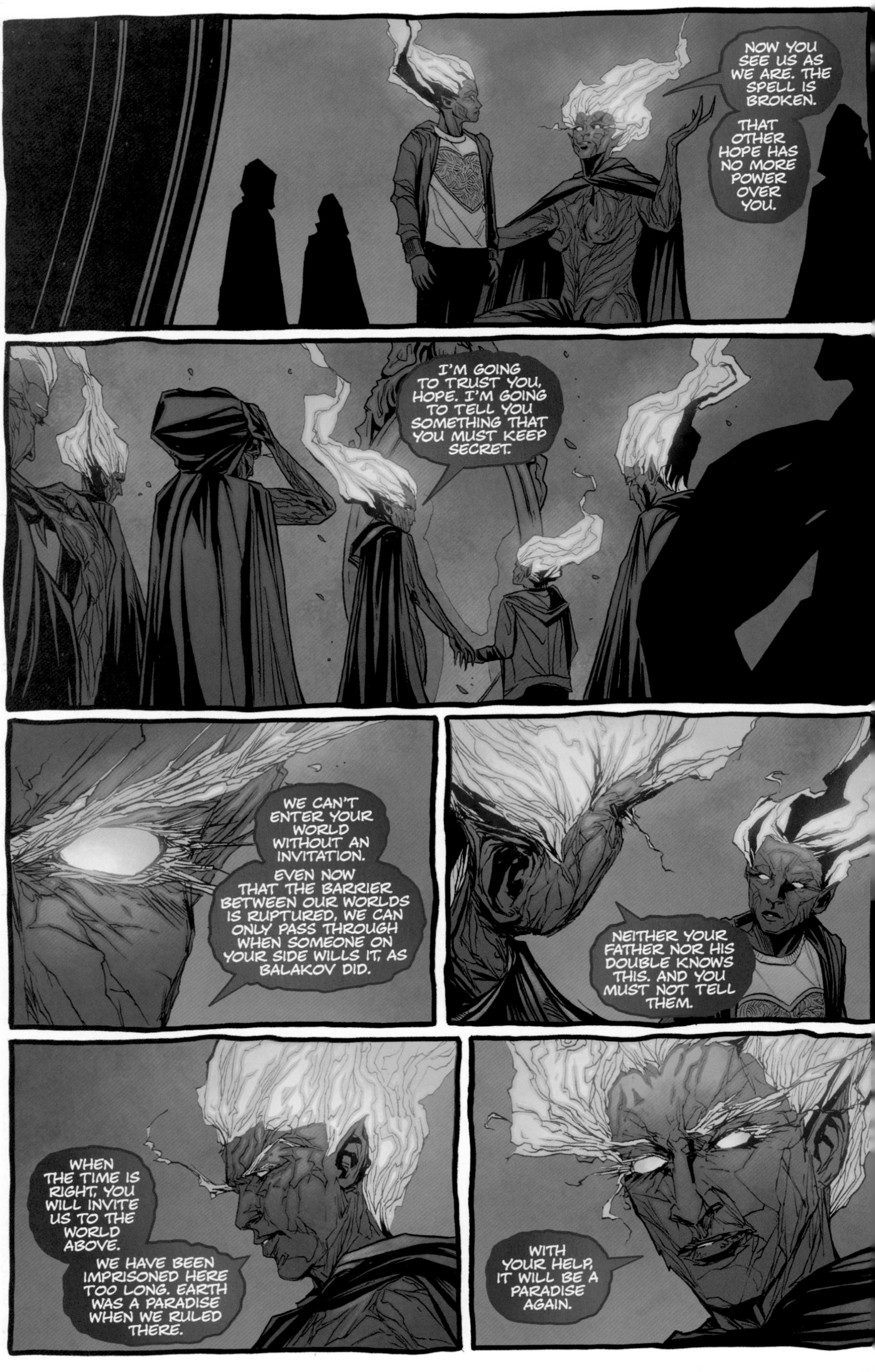
NOW YOU SEE US AS WE ARE. THE SPELL IS BROKEN.
THAT OTHER HOPE HAS NO MORE POWER OVER YOU.
I'M GOING TO TRUST YOU, HOPE. I'M GOING TO TELL YOU SOMETHING THAT YOU MUST KEEP SECRET.
WE CAN'T ENTER YOUR WORLD WITHOUT AN INVITATION.
EVEN NOW THAT THE BARRIER BETWEEN OUR WORLDS IS RUPTURED, WE CAN ONLY PASS THROUGH WHEN SOMEONE ON YOUR SIDE WILLS IT, AS BALAKOV DID.
NEITHER YOUR FATHER NOR HIS DOUBLE KNOWS THIS. AND YOU MUST NOT TELL THEM.
WHEN THE TIME IS RIGHT, YOU WILL INVITE US TO THE WORLD ABOVE.
WE HAVE BEEN IMPRISONED HERE TOO LONG. EARTH WAS A PARADISE WHEN WE RULED THERE.
WITH YOUR HELP, IT WILL BE A PARADISE AGAIN.

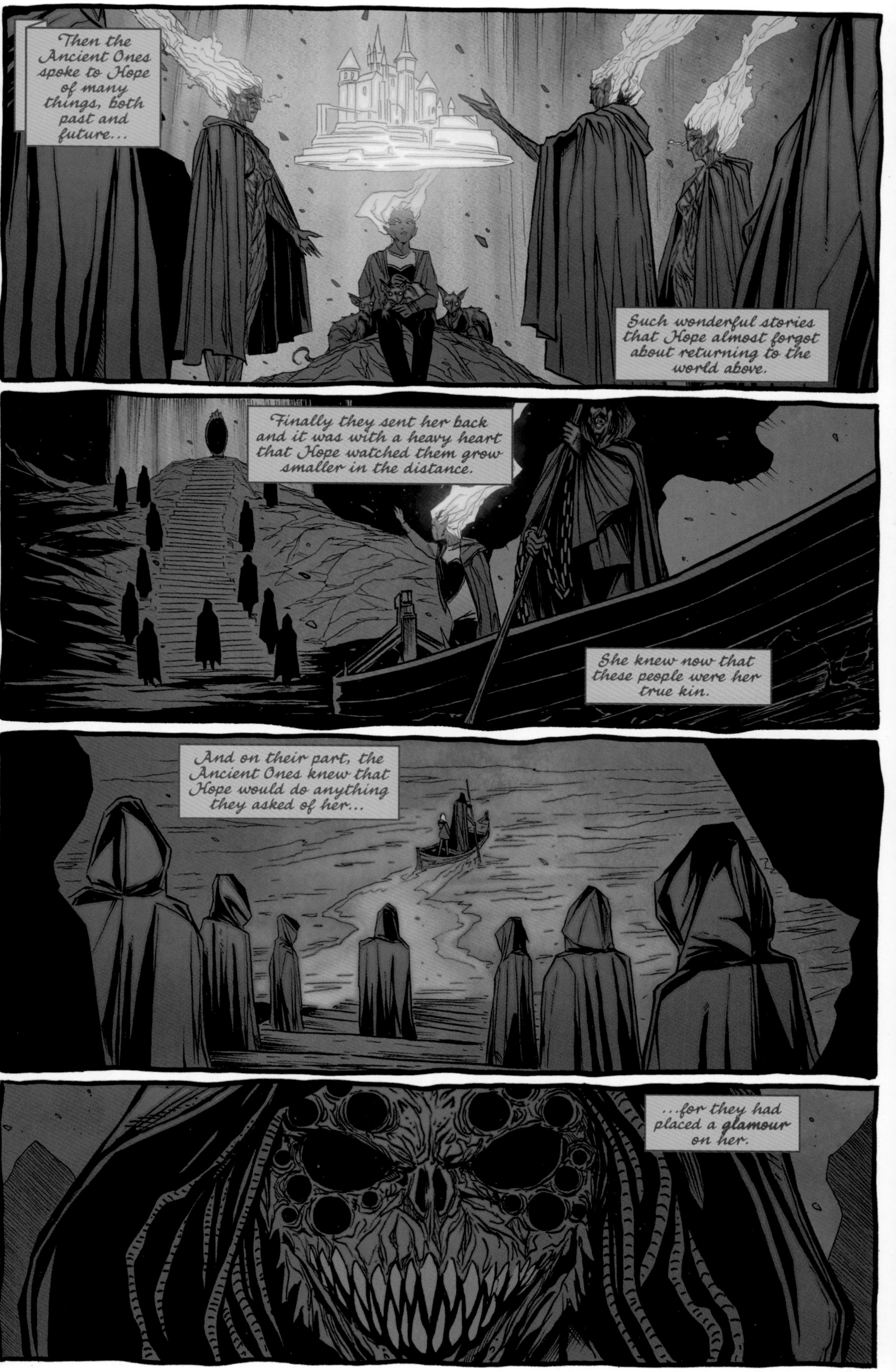
Then the Ancient Ones spoke to Hope of many things, both past and future...
Such wonderful stories that Hope almost forgot about returning to the world above.
Finally they sent her back and it was with a heavy heart that Hope watched them grow smaller in the distance.
She knew now that these people were her true kin.
And on their part, the Ancient Ones knew that Hope would do anything they asked of her...
...for they had placed a glamour on her.

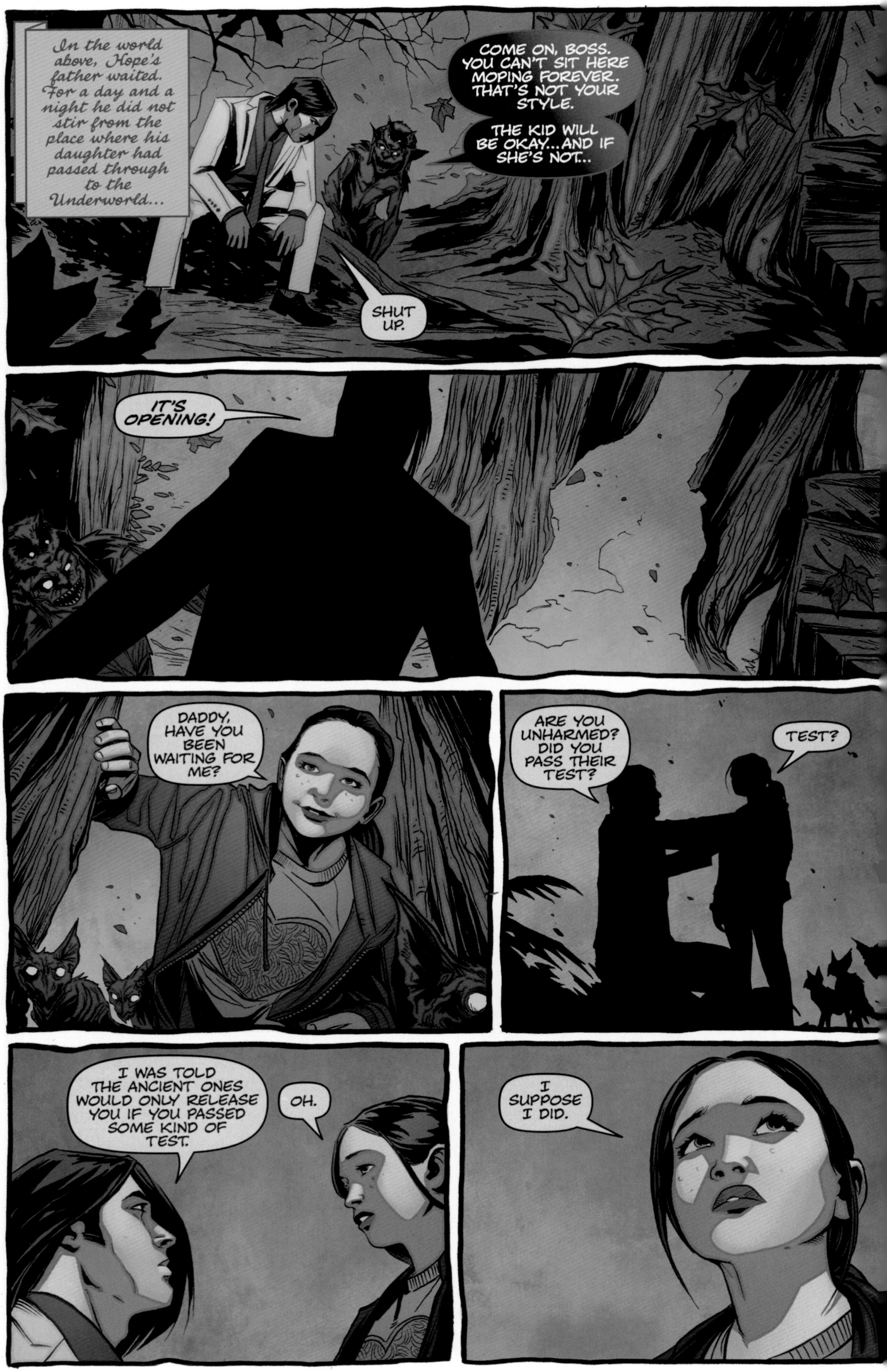

In the world above, Hope's father waited. For a day and a night he did not stir from the place where his daughter had passed through to the Underworld...
COME ON, BOSS. YOU CAN'T SIT HERE MOPING FOREVER. THAT'S NOT YOUR STYLE.
THE KID WILL BE OKAY...AND IF SHE'S NOT...
SHUT UP.
IT'S OPENING!
DADDY, HAVE YOU BEEN WAITING FOR ME?
ARE YOU UNHARMED? DID YOU PASS THEIR TEST?
TEST?
I WAS TOLD THE ANCIENT ONES WOULD ONLY RELEASE YOU IF YOU PASSED SOME KIND OF TEST.
OH.
I SUPPOSE I DID.

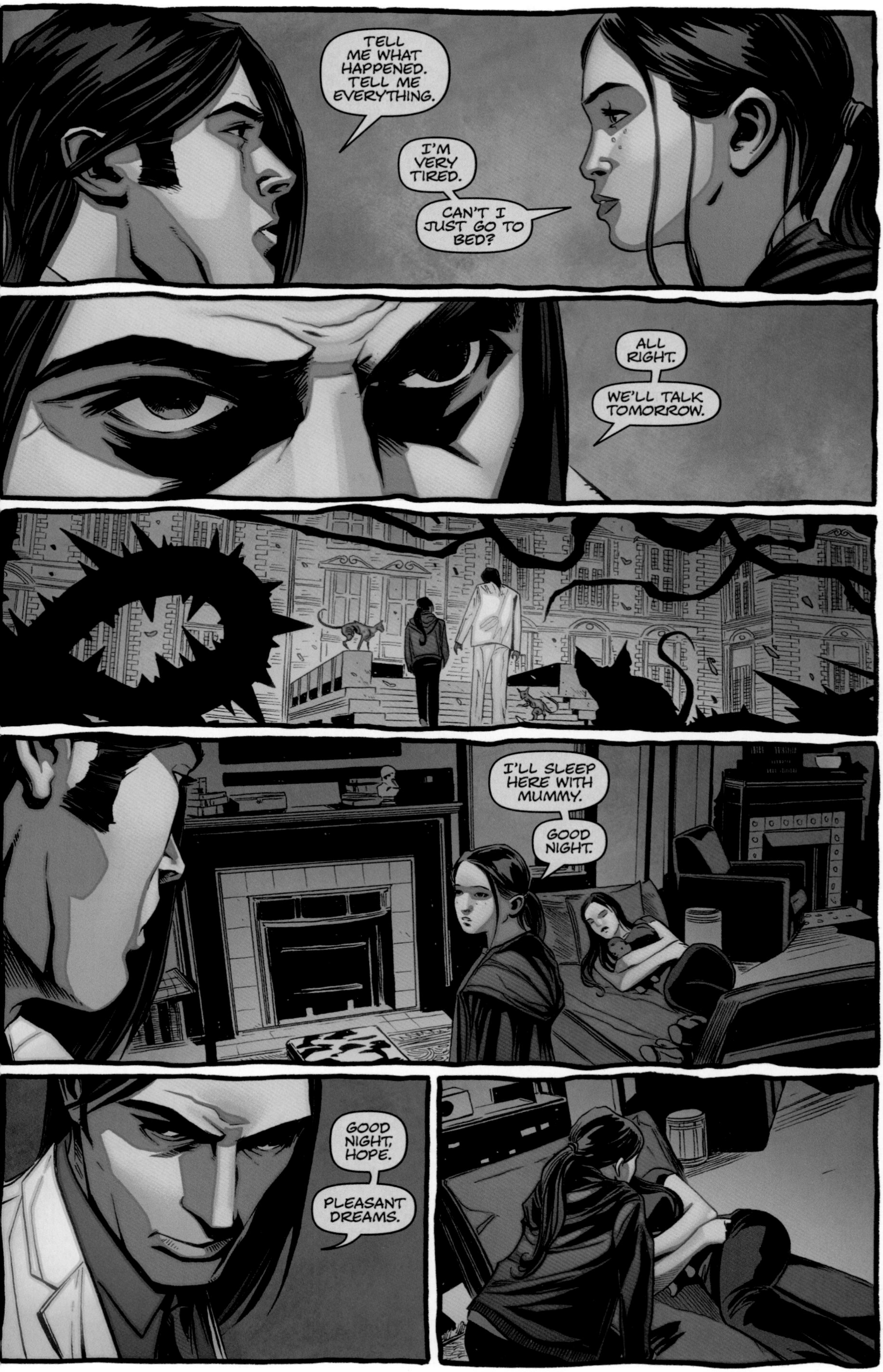
TELL ME WHAT HAPPENED. TELL ME EVERYTHING.
I'M VERY TIRED.
CAN'T I JUST GO TO BED?
ALL RIGHT.
WE'LL TALK TOMORROW.
I'LL SLEEP HERE WITH MUMMY.
GOOD NIGHT.
GOOD NIGHT, HOPE.
PLEASANT DREAMS.

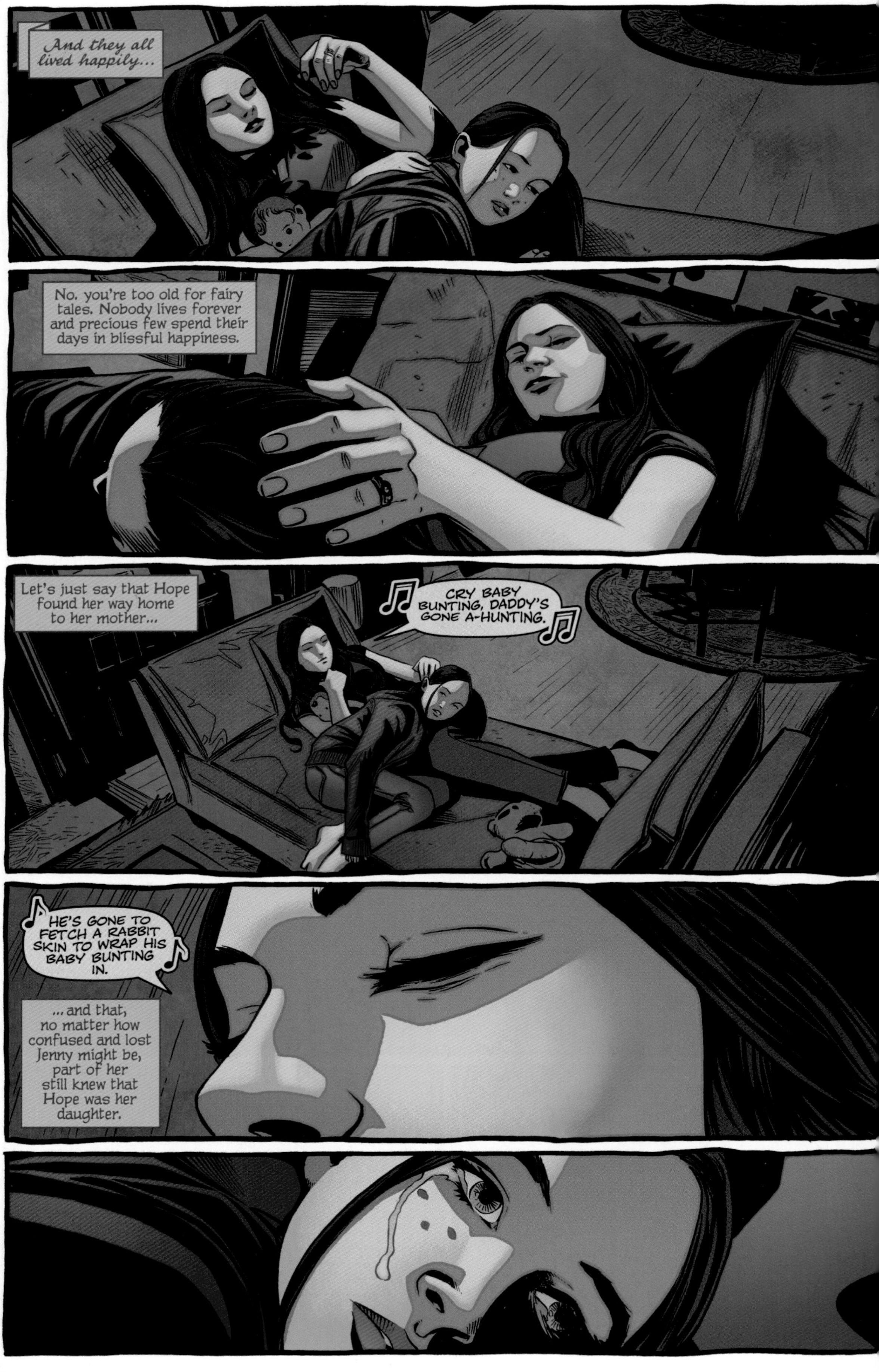
And they all lived happily...
No, you're too old for fairy tales. Nobody lives forever and precious few spend their days in blissful happiness.
Let's just say that Hope found her way home to her mother...
CRY BABY BUNTING, DADDY'S GONE A-HUNTING.
HE'S GONE TO FETCH A RABBIT SKIN TO WRAP HIS BABY BUNTING IN.
...and that, no matter how confused and lost Jenny might be, part of her still knew that Hope was her daughter.

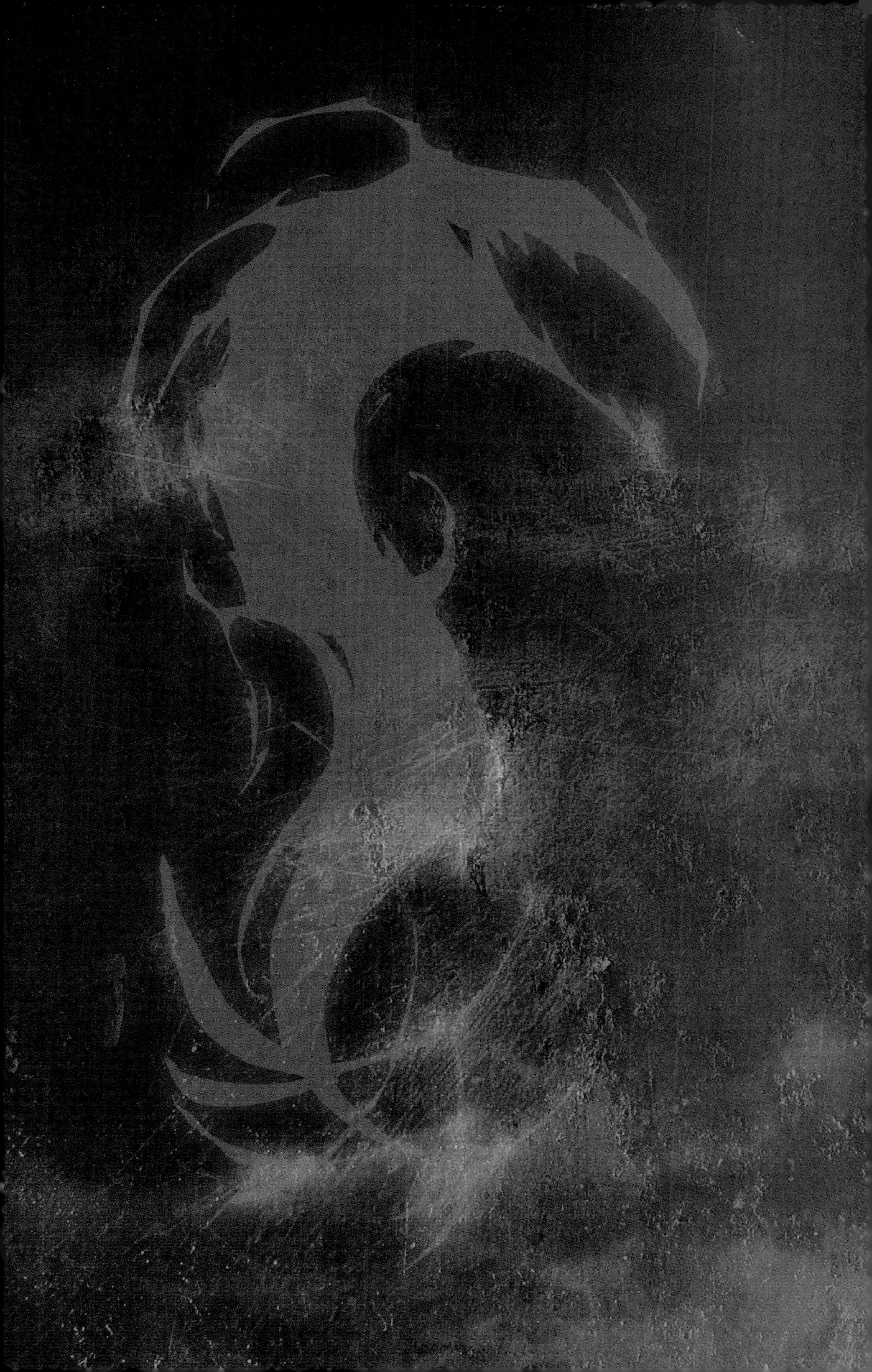

HOPE'S DREAM

by David Hine

Hope lay awake for a long time, even though she was exhausted after her adventures underground. She wondered why she didn't feel hungry. She hadn't touched the gingerbread that the witch had offered her, but now that she thought about it, she remembered that the Ancient Ones had given her some squares of pink powdered candy, soft on the inside, like Turkish Delight. She had nibbled at it while they told her their tales of the time when the people of Earth were happy and prospered under their rule, when the land was full of wonders, and magic was everywhere.

She sighed and snuggled closer to her mother, her eyelids growing heavy.

This is what she dreamed…

Two enormously bulky men were leading a horse and cart into the wood. They were naked except for filthy canvas loincloths, the kind that Tarzan wore in the old movies. But they didn't look like Tarzan. They had huge fat bellies and were covered all over with coarse black hair. Their faces were ugly and exactly identical. She supposed they must be twins, so in her head, she named them Ronnie and Reggie. She wasn't quite sure why, but the names seemed to fit. Ronnie held the horse's reins, jerking on them every time it slowed, while Reggie swung the shovel he was carrying at the tangled undergrowth where it strayed across the path. They grunted and muttered the whole time as they made their way along the narrow path until they came upon the corpse of the Werewolf. He looked human again and the expression on his face was one of mild surprise, as if he couldn't quite believe that his body was ripped open and his intestines were lying in a steaming heap beside him.

'Look at the state of him,' said Ronnie.
'Stuck up bugger got what was coming to him,' replied his brother, hauling him up by the arms. 'Grab his feet.'

The two men swung the body back and forth three times to build up momentum and then slung the Werewolf Prince into the cart. A pile of garden refuse sacks lay in the cart and Ronnie took one and held it open while Reggie shovelled the intestines into it. They did the same with the heap of frazzled spider corpses and then turned their attention to the charred heap of rags and bones that lay before the Witch's cottage.

Once the Witch's remains were bagged and in the cart, the grim procession wound its way to the great twisted oak at the heart of the wood. The entrance to the underworld had opened up again. This time a gentle slope had replaced the steps, and they descended with the horse and cart. Hope followed. She wasn't sure if she was walking or floating and she guessed she must be invisible because neither of the men seemed to notice her.

'Right, what's next on the list?'
'Tar Babies are all melted. Just more lumps in the tar pit.'
'They'll be back. Them little monsters always come back. Scarlet Queen too I shouldn't wonder, manky old slag.'
The surface of the tar stirred and a bubble burst, releasing foul gases into the air.
'I think she just farted.'

The two men guffawed and poked one another's bellies in appreciation of their wit, then abruptly fell silent as the White Rabbit spoke up plaintively.
'You're not going to throw me in the tar pit are you?'
Reggie and Ronnie turned towards the head where it lay in a pool of dry blood. Reggie sighed. 'No, Rabbit, we aren't going to throw you in the tar pit.' He bent and picked the head up by the ears. The rabbit's eyes rolled in their sockets until they were gazing at Reggie's face.
'Pleeeease don't throw me in the tar pit.'
'Oh, sod it.'
Reggie turned and flung the head way out into the middle of the pit. The head floated on the surface for a minute or two, the Rabbit's voice squealing for help all the while, then slowly sank out of sight.
'That was uncalled for,' Ronnie told him. 'Right out of order.'
'He annoyed me. Last bloke that annoyed me, I nailed his feet to the floor.'
'That was him. The Rabbit. You nailed the Rabbit's feet to the floor.'
'He annoyed me.'
'You said.'
Reggie sighed. 'All right. I'm sorry. I'll be'ave meself for the rest of the day. Now let's get the job done, and piss off 'ome.'

He lumbered over to the Rabbit's body, still standing where it had been when the Scarlet Queen decapitated it with a single stroke of her axe. He hefted the body over his shoulder and carried it back towards the tar pit.
'In the pit?'
'Might as well. No point in giving 'is body a decent Christian burial without a head on it.'
Into the pit went the Rabbit's corpse. Hope watched sadly as it sank. The White Rabbit had done his best to help her and she was sorry that he had come to such a sticky end.

'That's that, then.'
Ronnie clambered up onto the cart and took the horse's reins in his hands, turning to Reggie, who was poking at the Rabbit's body with the shovel. The white tail was all that was showing. He gave one last shove and the tar swallowed it with a belch.
'You coming or what?'
Reggie straightened up and stretched his aching muscles.
'Yeah. I'm bloody knackered. Let's get off. We can stop in at the Blind Beggar on the way, yeah? I could do with a pint an' a pasty.'
He flung his shovel into the cart then, as he was about to climb up next to Ronnie, he paused and turned.

'And by the way,' he said, leaning down and leering into Hope's face.
'You're not invisible.'

"HEART OF DARKNESS"

WRITER : DAVID HINE
ARTIST : LAURA BRAGA
COLORIST : BILL FARMER
LETTERER : TROY PETERI

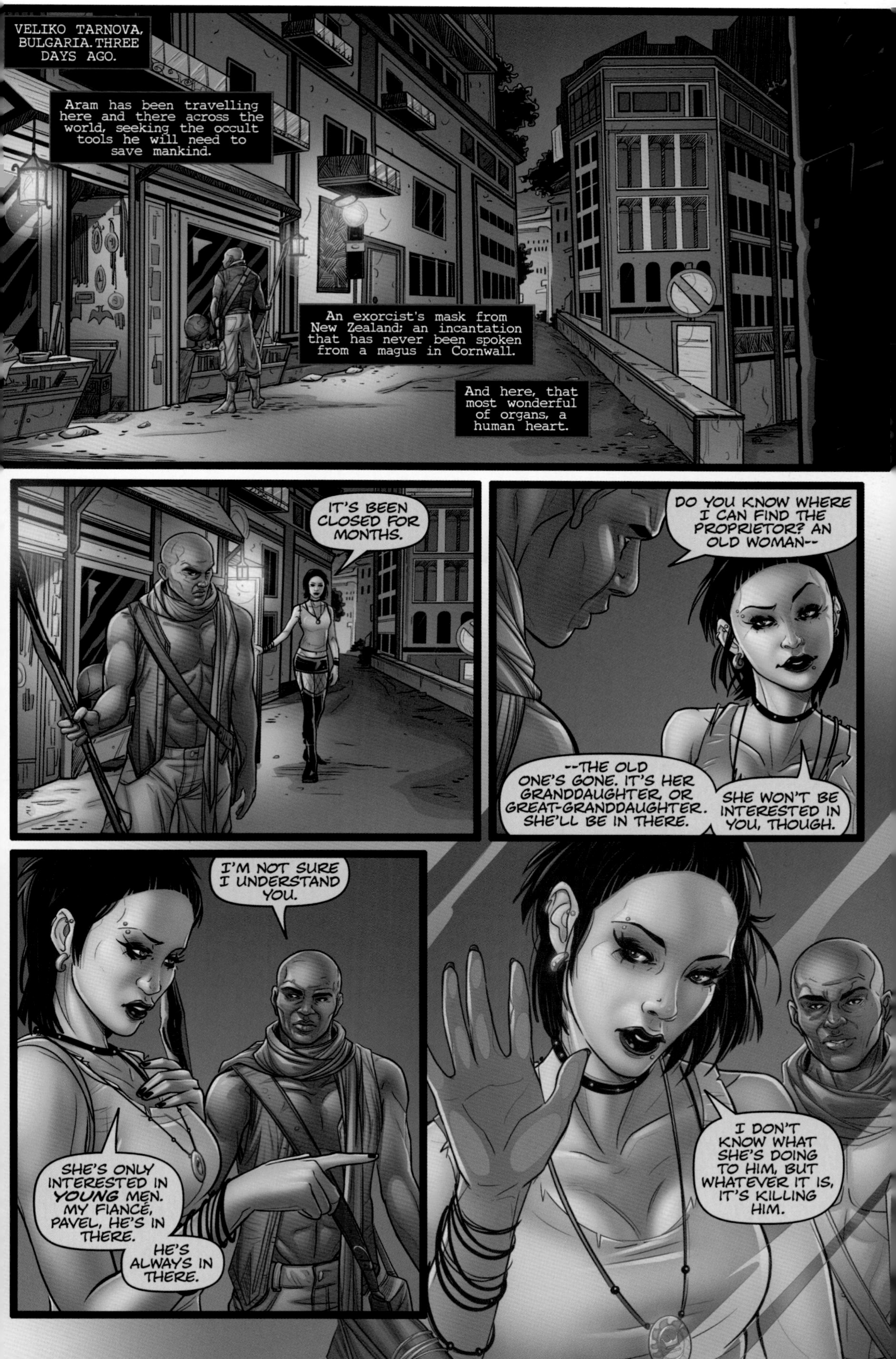
VELIKO TARNOVA, BULGARIA. THREE DAYS AGO.
Aram has been travelling here and there across the world, seeking the occult tools he will need to save mankind.
An exorcist's mask from New Zealand; an incantation that has never been spoken from a magus in Cornwall.
And here, that most wonderful of organs, a human heart.
IT'S BEEN CLOSED FOR MONTHS.
DO YOU KNOW WHERE I CAN FIND THE PROPRIETOR? AN OLD WOMAN--
--THE OLD ONE'S GONE. IT'S HER GRANDDAUGHTER, OR GREAT-GRANDDAUGHTER. SHE'LL BE IN THERE.
SHE WON'T BE INTERESTED IN YOU, THOUGH.
I'M NOT SURE I UNDERSTAND YOU.
SHE'S ONLY INTERESTED IN YOUNG MEN. MY FIANCÉ, PAVEL, HE'S IN THERE.
HE'S ALWAYS IN THERE.
I DON'T KNOW WHAT SHE'S DOING TO HIM, BUT WHATEVER IT IS, IT'S KILLING HIM.

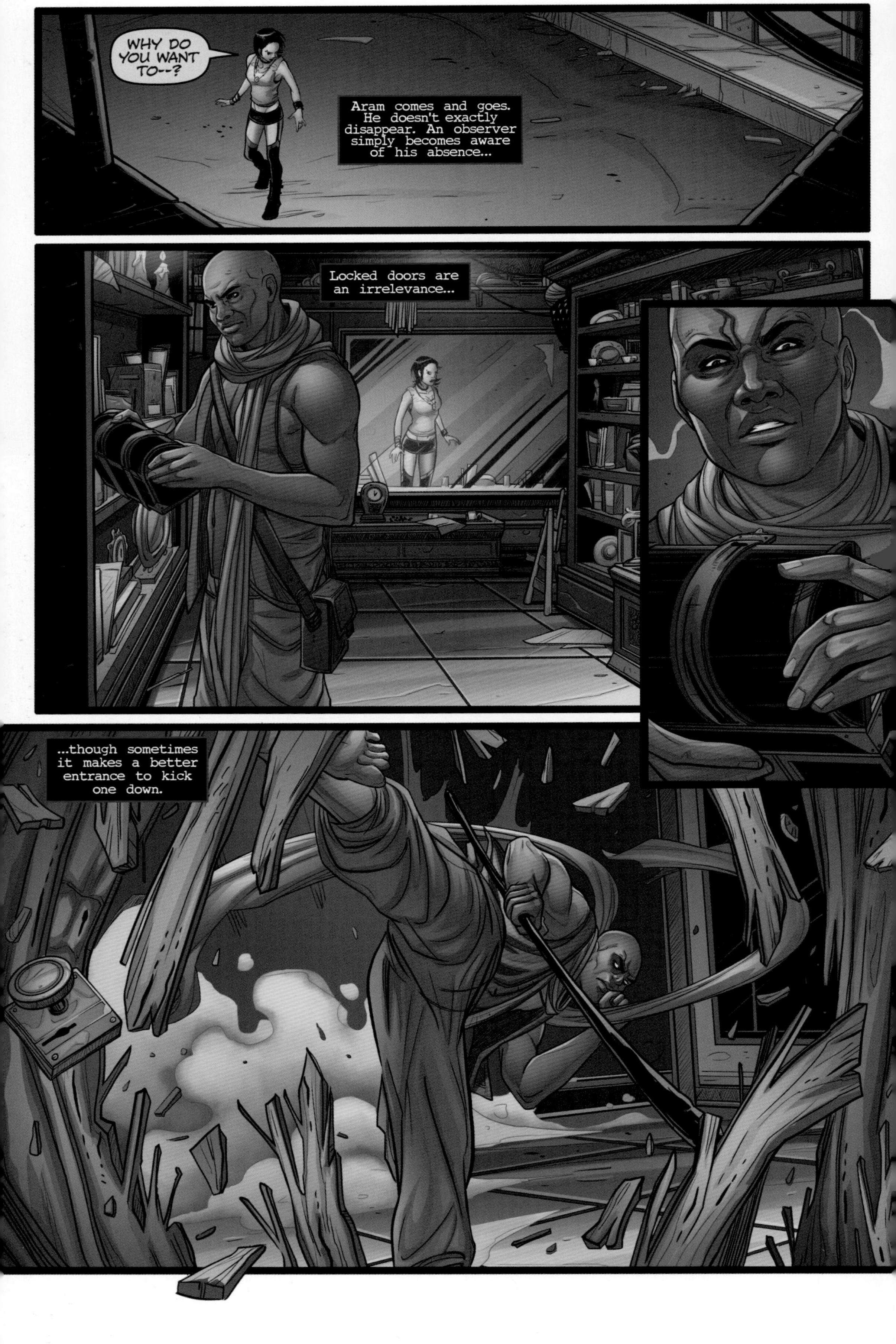
WHY DO YOU WANT TO--?
Aram comes and goes. He doesn't exactly disappear. An observer simply becomes aware of his absence...
Locked doors are an irrelevance...
...though sometimes it makes a better entrance to kick one down.

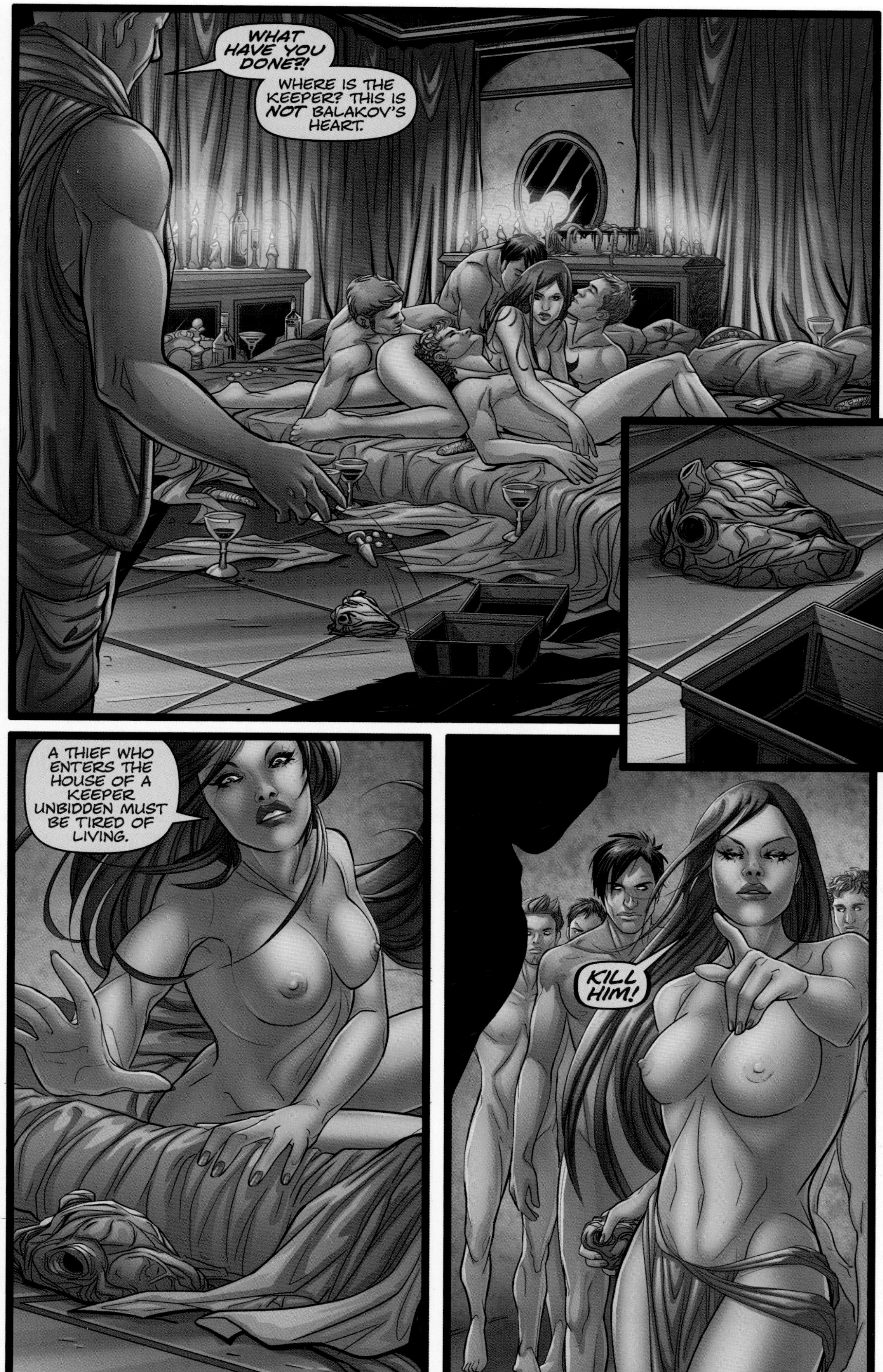
WHAT HAVE YOU DONE?!
WHERE IS THE KEEPER? THIS IS NOT BALAKOV'S HEART.
A THIEF WHO ENTERS THE HOUSE OF A KEEPER UNBIDDEN MUST BE TIRED OF LIVING.
KILL HIM!

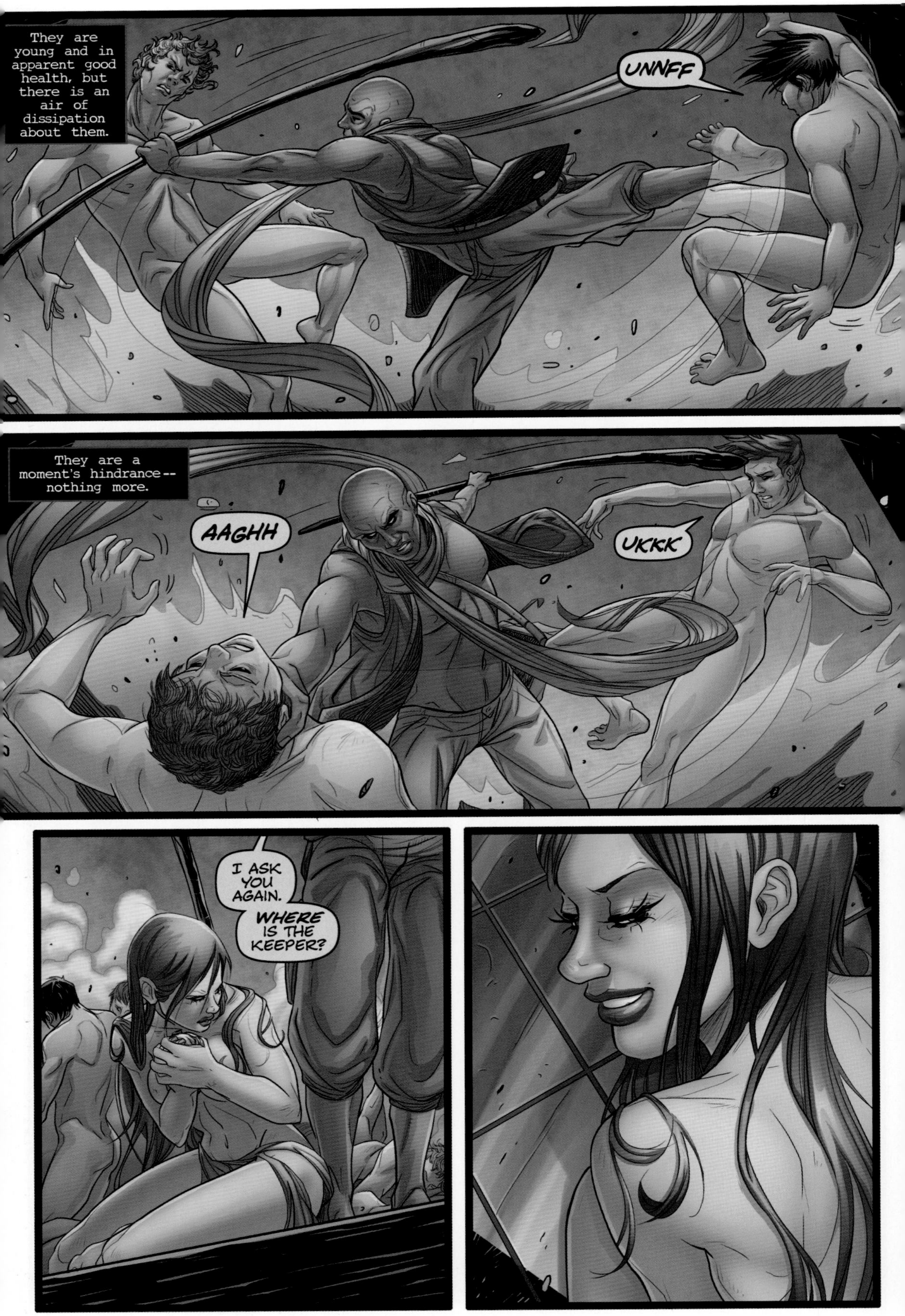

They are young and in apparent good health, but there is an air of dissipation about them.
UNNFF
They are a moment's hindrance--nothing more.
AAGHH
UKKK
I ASK YOU AGAIN. WHERE IS THE KEEPER?

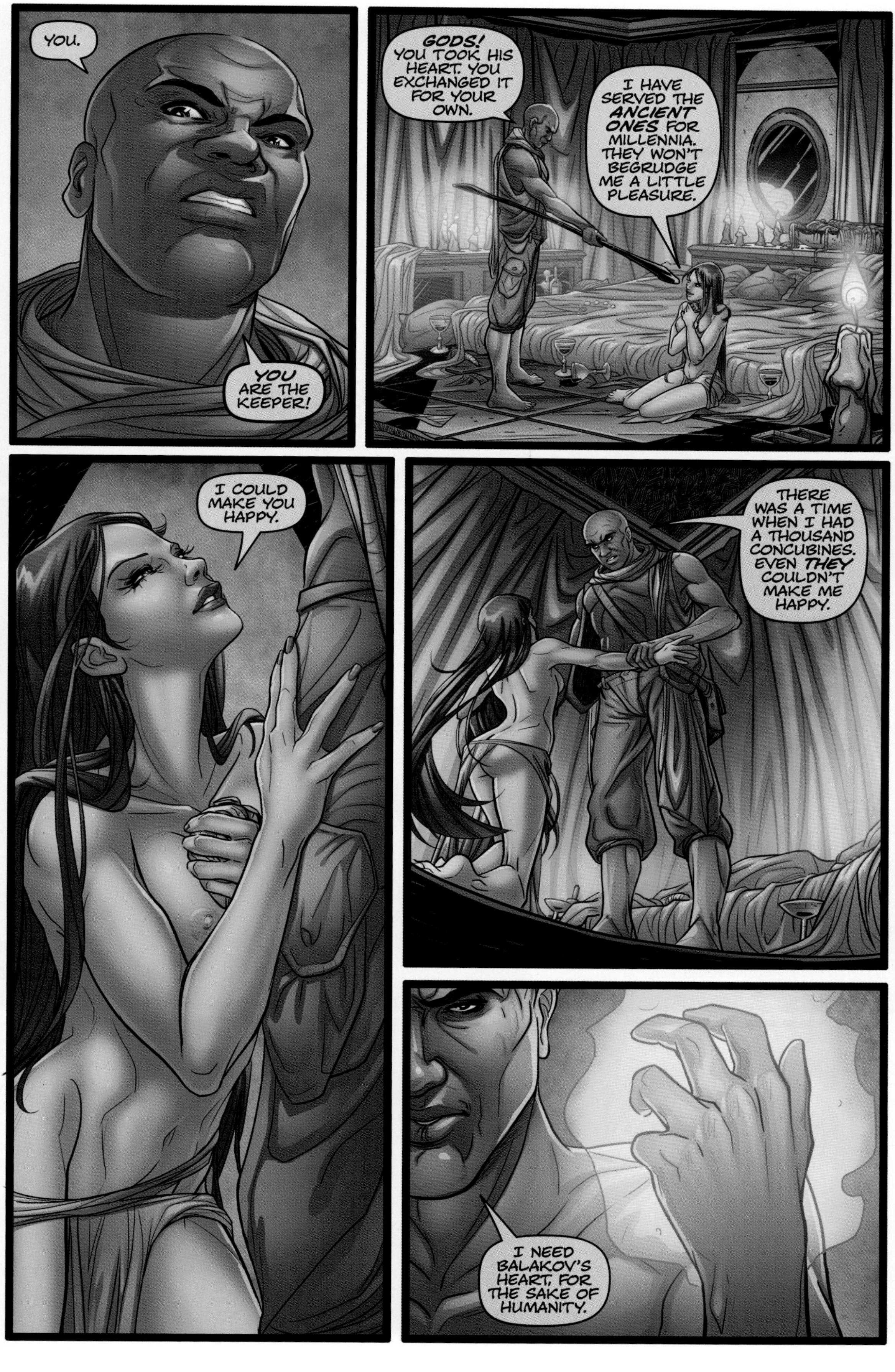
YOU.
YOU ARE THE KEEPER!
GODS! YOU TOOK HIS HEART. YOU EXCHANGED IT FOR YOUR OWN.
I HAVE SERVED THE ANCIENT ONES FOR MILLENNIA. THEY WON'T BEGRUDGE ME A LITTLE PLEASURE.
I COULD MAKE YOU HAPPY.
THERE WAS A TIME WHEN I HAD A THOUSAND CONCUBINES. EVEN THEY COULDN'T MAKE ME HAPPY.
I NEED BALAKOV'S HEART, FOR THE SAKE OF HUMANITY.

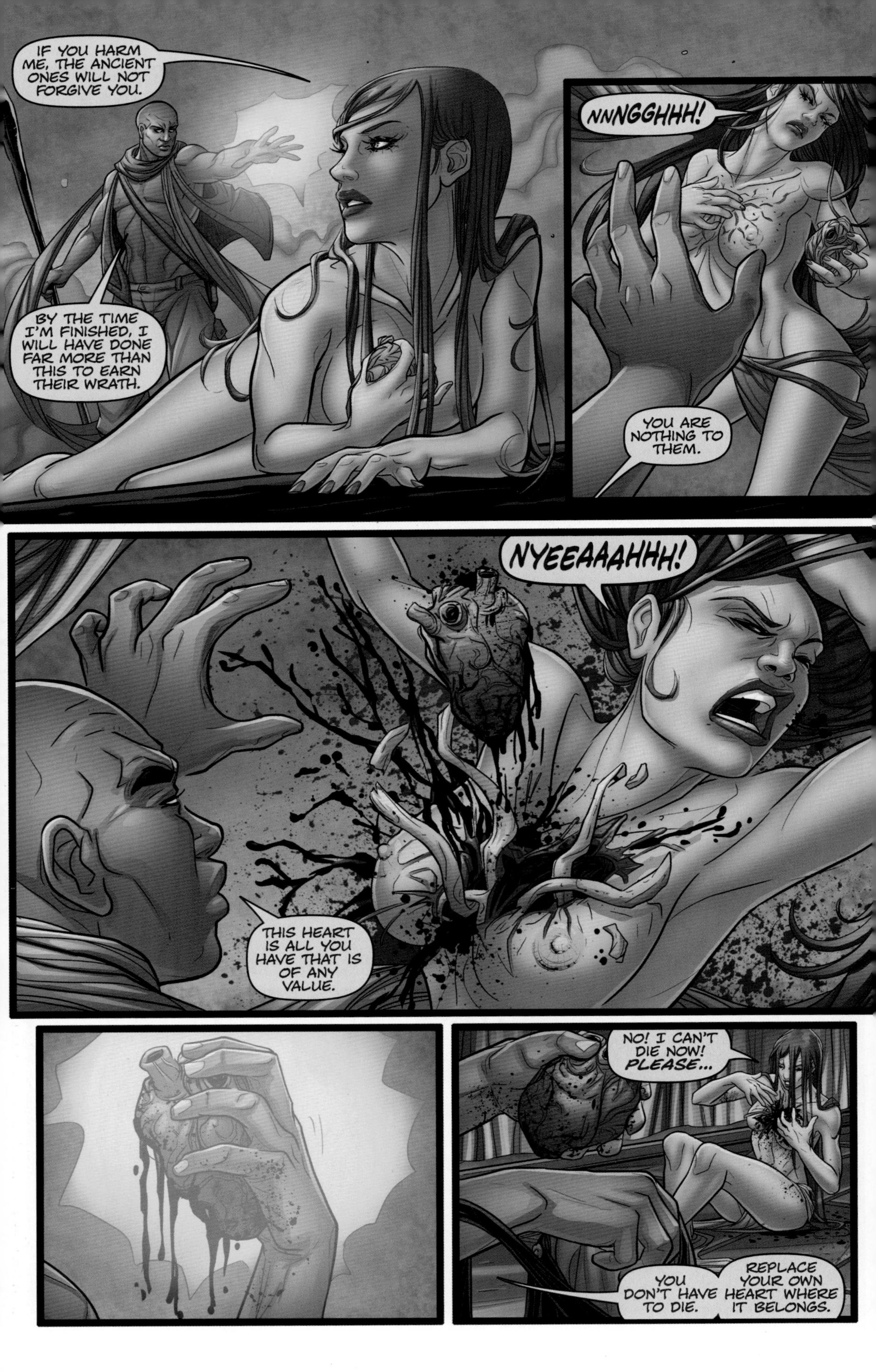
IF YOU HARM ME, THE ANCIENT ONES WILL NOT FORGIVE YOU.
BY THE TIME I'M FINISHED, I WILL HAVE DONE FAR MORE THAN THIS TO EARN THEIR WRATH.
NNNGGHHH!
YOU ARE NOTHING TO THEM.
NYEEAAAHHH!
THIS HEART IS ALL YOU HAVE THAT IS OF ANY VALUE.
NO! I CAN'T DIE NOW! PLEASE...
YOU DON'T HAVE TO DIE.
REPLACE YOUR OWN HEART WHERE IT BELONGS.

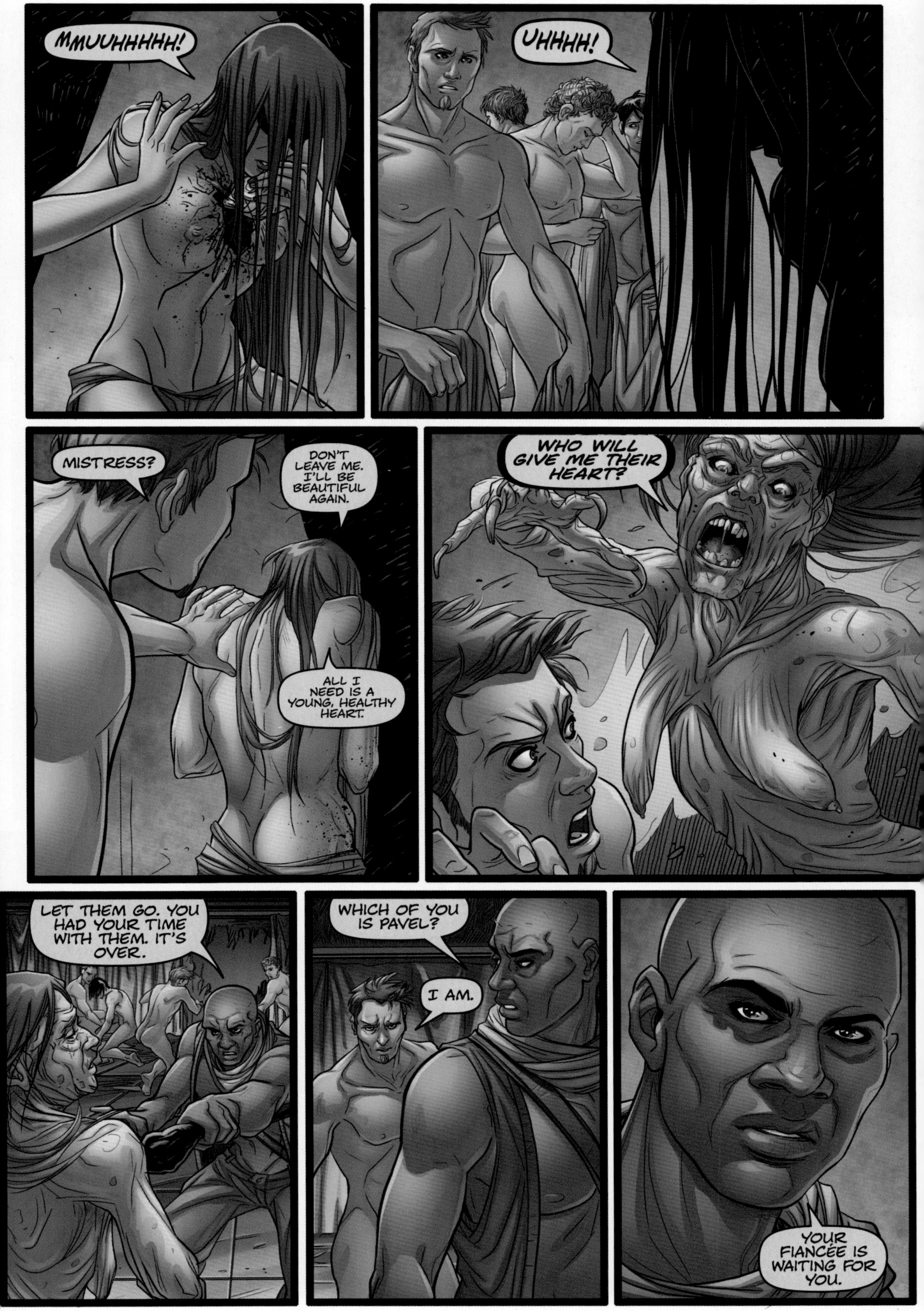
MMUUHHHHH!
UHHHH!
MISTRESS?
DON'T LEAVE ME. I'LL BE BEAUTIFUL AGAIN.
ALL I NEED IS A YOUNG, HEALTHY HEART.
WHO WILL GIVE ME THEIR HEART?
LET THEM GO. YOU HAD YOUR TIME WITH THEM. IT'S OVER.
WHICH OF YOU IS PAVEL?
I AM.
YOUR FIANCÉE IS WAITING FOR YOU.

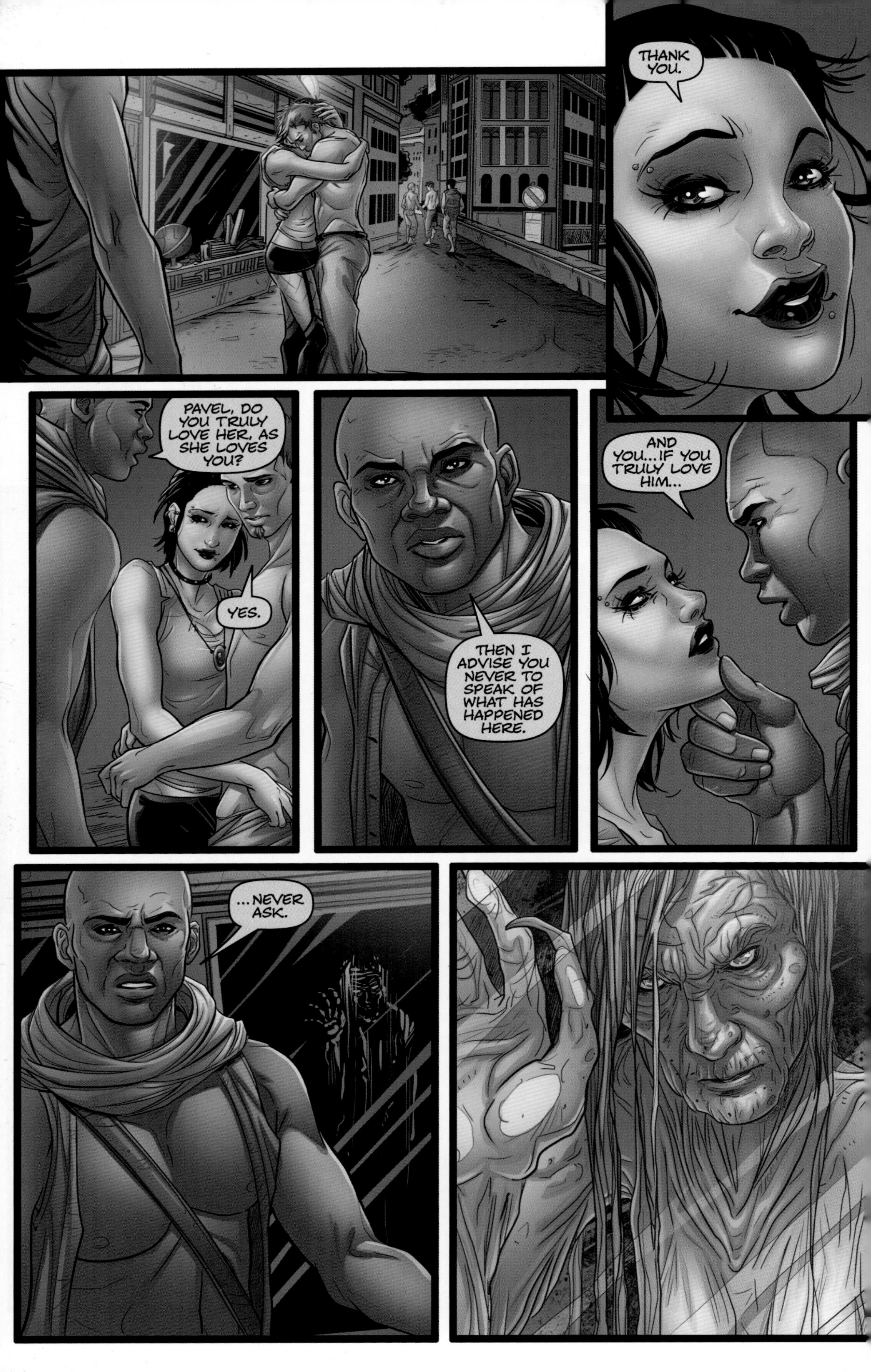
THANK YOU.
PAVEL, DO YOU TRULY LOVE HER, AS SHE LOVES YOU?
YES.
THEN I ADVISE YOU NEVER TO SPEAK OF WHAT HAS HAPPENED HERE.
AND YOU...IF YOU TRULY LOVE HIM...
...NEVER ASK.

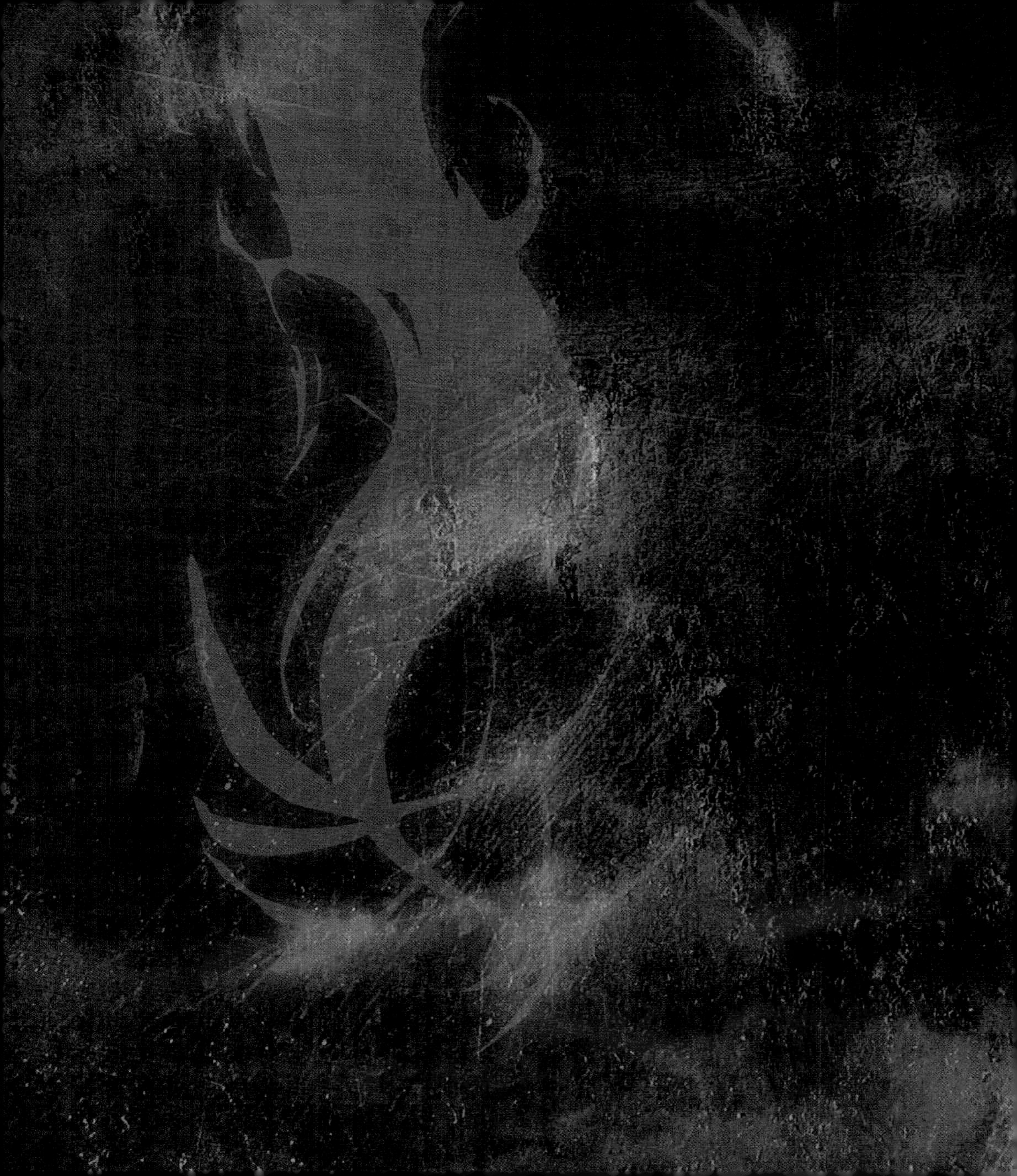

"THE AGE OF REASON"
PART
I

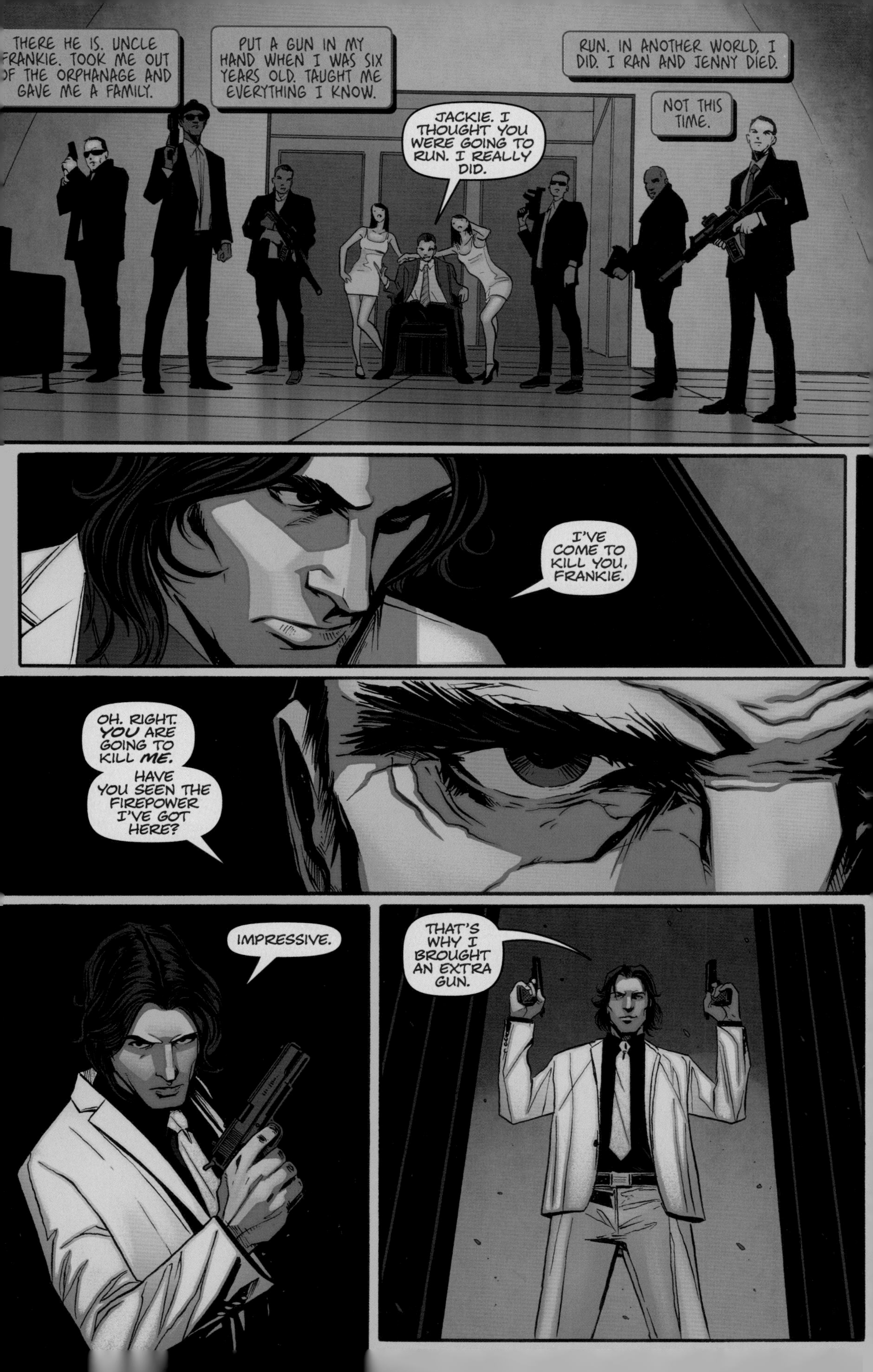
THERE HE IS. UNCLE FRANKIE. TOOK ME OUT OF THE ORPHANAGE AND GAVE ME A FAMILY.
PUT A GUN IN MY HAND WHEN I WAS SIX YEARS OLD. TAUGHT ME EVERYTHING I KNOW.
JACKIE. I THOUGHT YOU WERE GOING TO RUN. I REALLY DID.
RUN. IN ANOTHER WORLD, I DID. I RAN AND JENNY DIED.
NOT THIS TIME.
I'VE COME TO KILL YOU, FRANKIE.
OH. RIGHT. YOU ARE GOING TO KILL ME.
HAVE YOU SEEN THE FIREPOWER I'VE GOT HERE?
IMPRESSIVE.
THAT'S WHY I BROUGHT AN EXTRA GUN.

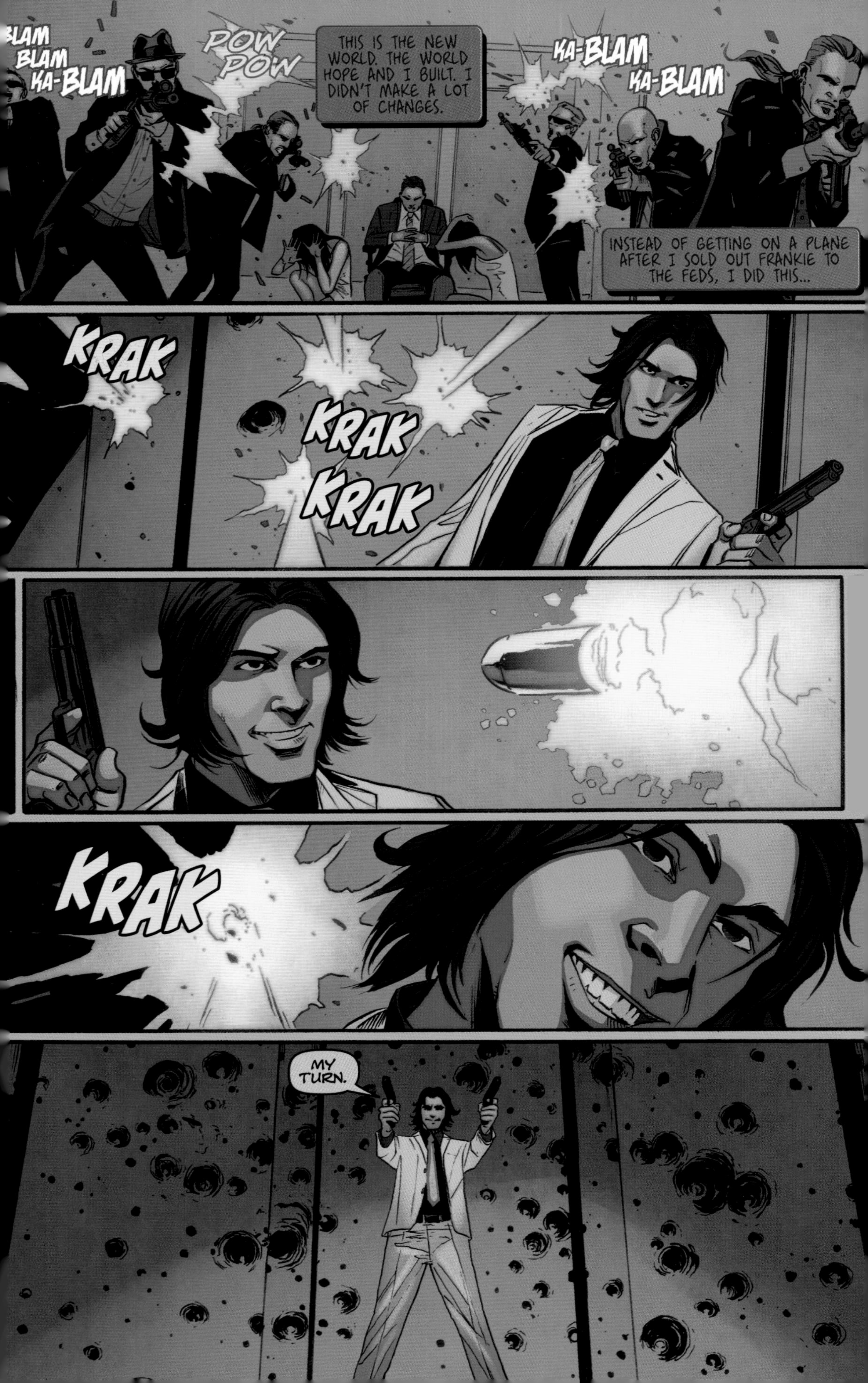
BLAM
BLAM
KA-BLAM
POW
POW
THIS IS THE NEW WORLD. THE WORLD HOPE AND I BUILT. I DIDN'T MAKE A LOT OF CHANGES.
KA-BLAM
KA-BLAM
INSTEAD OF GETTING ON A PLANE AFTER I SOLD OUT FRANKIE TO THE FEDS, I DID THIS...
KRAK
KRAK
KRAK
KRAK
MY TURN.

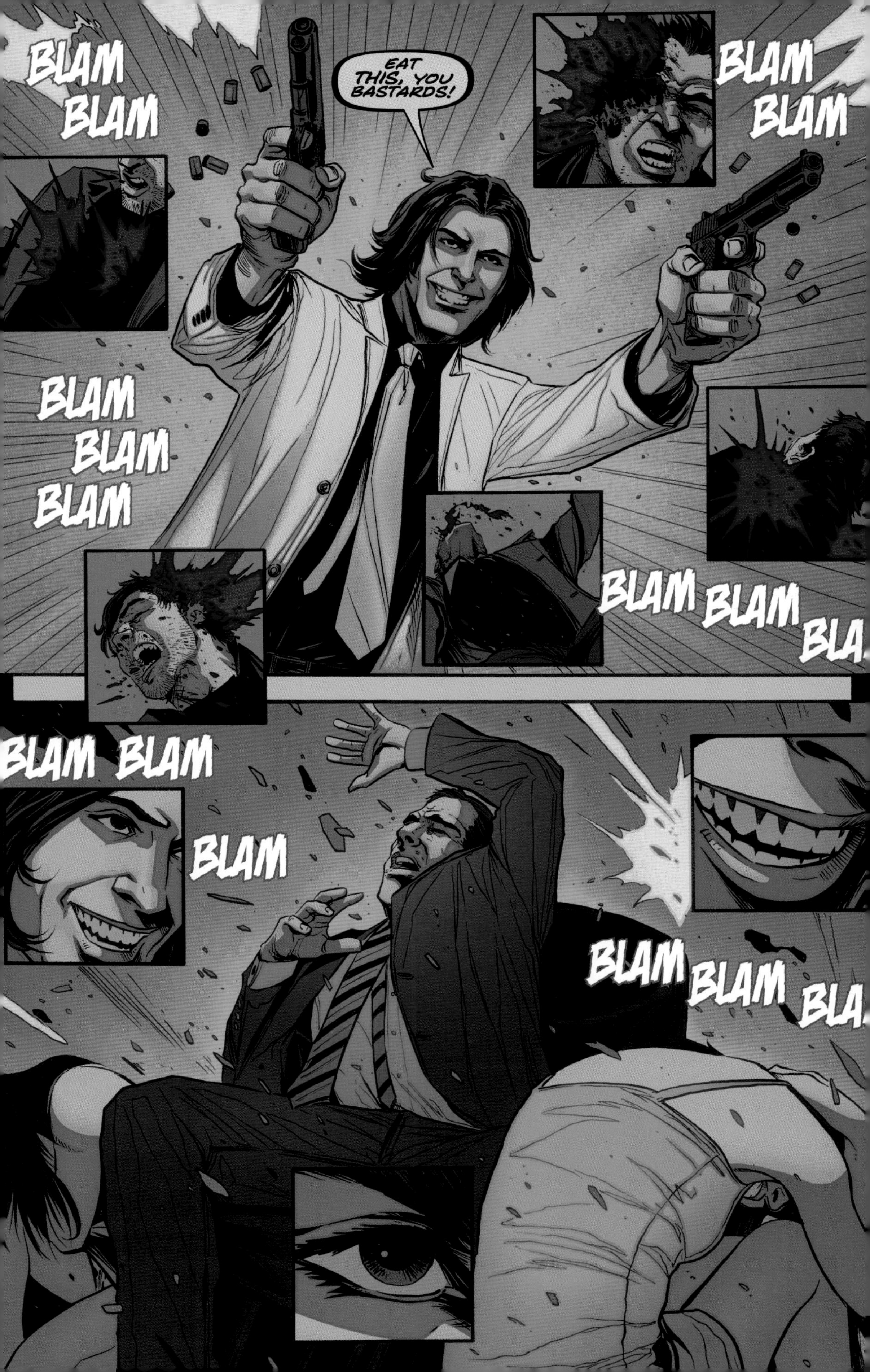
BLAM
BLAM
EAT THIS, YOU BASTARDS!
BLAM
BLAM
BLAM
BLAM
BLAM
BLAM BLAM BLA
BLAM BLAM
BLAM
BLAM BLAM BLA

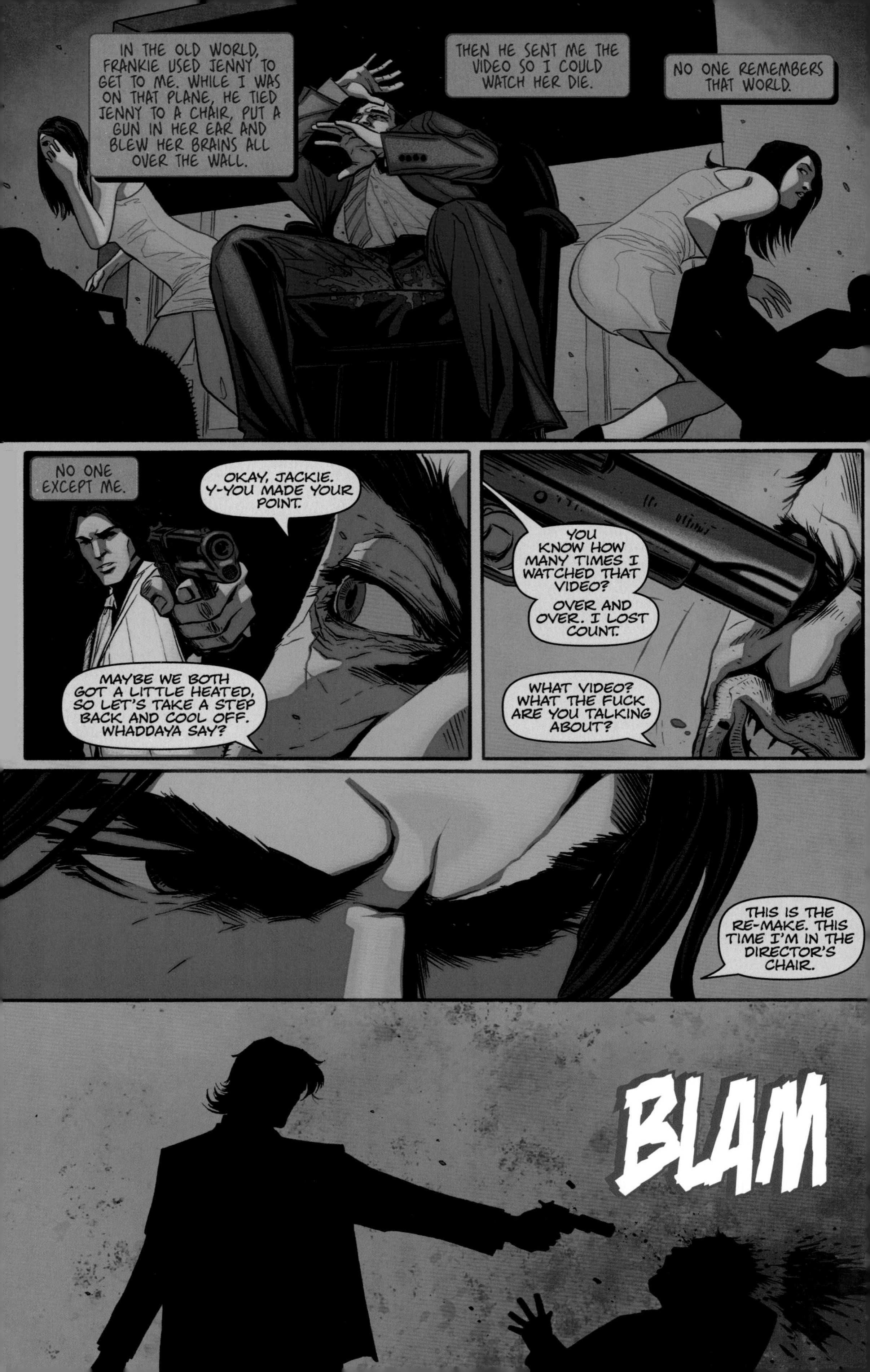
IN THE OLD WORLD, FRANKIE USED JENNY TO GET TO ME. WHILE I WAS ON THAT PLANE, HE TIED JENNY TO A CHAIR, PUT A GUN IN HER EAR AND BLEW HER BRAINS ALL OVER THE WALL.
THEN HE SENT ME THE VIDEO SO I COULD WATCH HER DIE.
NO ONE REMEMBERS THAT WORLD.
NO ONE EXCEPT ME.
OKAY, JACKIE. Y-YOU MADE YOUR POINT.
MAYBE WE BOTH GOT A LITTLE HEATED, SO LET'S TAKE A STEP BACK AND COOL OFF. WHADDAYA SAY?
YOU KNOW HOW MANY TIMES I WATCHED THAT VIDEO?
OVER AND OVER. I LOST COUNT.
WHAT VIDEO? WHAT THE FUCK ARE YOU TALKING ABOUT?
THIS IS THE RE-MAKE. THIS TIME I'M IN THE DIRECTOR'S CHAIR.
BLAM

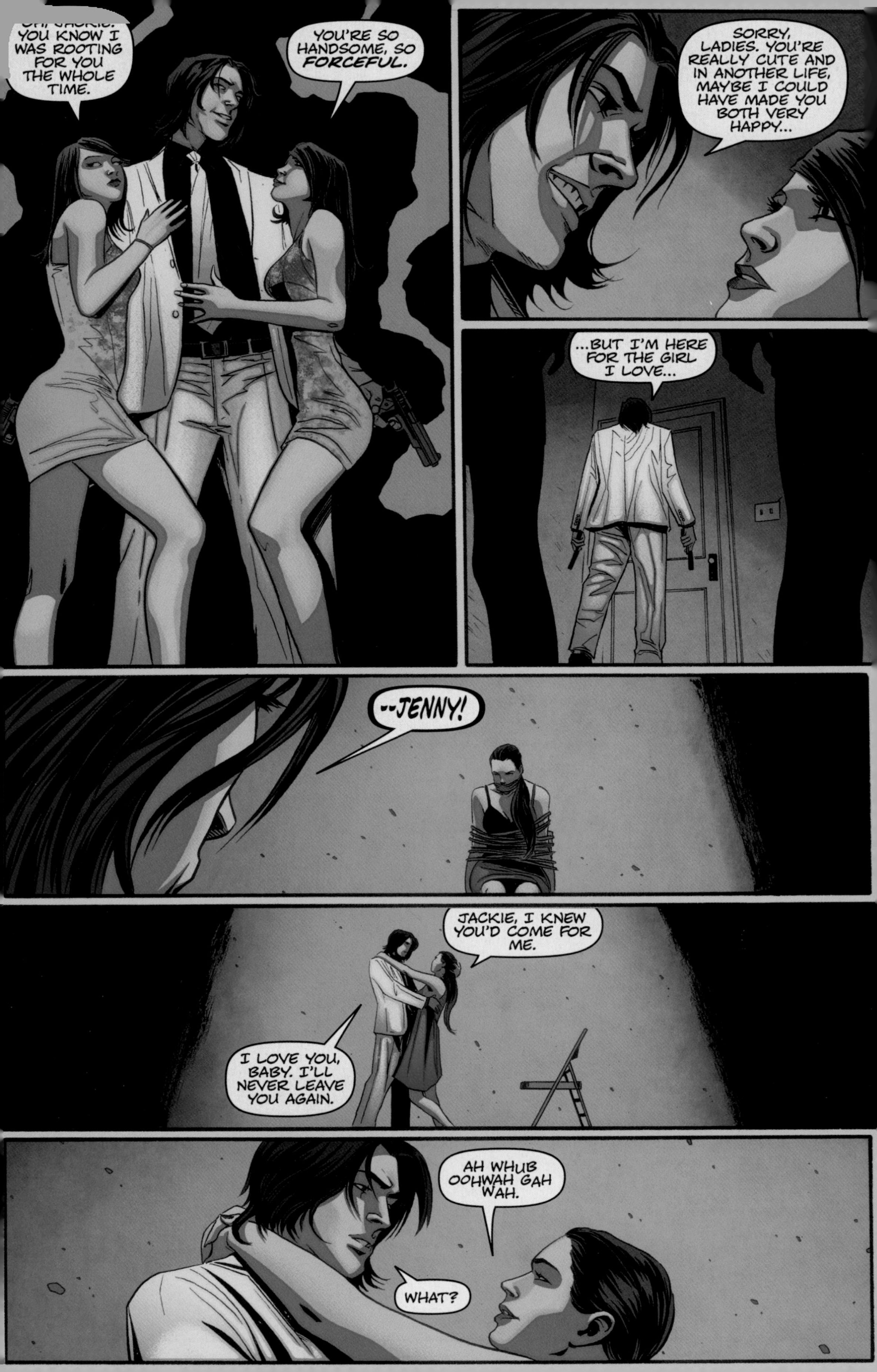
...YOU KNOW I WAS ROOTING FOR YOU THE WHOLE TIME.
YOU'RE SO HANDSOME, SO FORCEFUL.
SORRY, LADIES. YOU'RE REALLY CUTE AND IN ANOTHER LIFE, MAYBE I COULD HAVE MADE YOU BOTH VERY HAPPY...
...BUT I'M HERE FOR THE GIRL I LOVE...
--JENNY!
JACKIE, I KNEW YOU'D COME FOR ME.
I LOVE YOU, BABY. I'LL NEVER LEAVE YOU AGAIN.
AH WHUB OOHWAH GAH WAH.
WHAT?

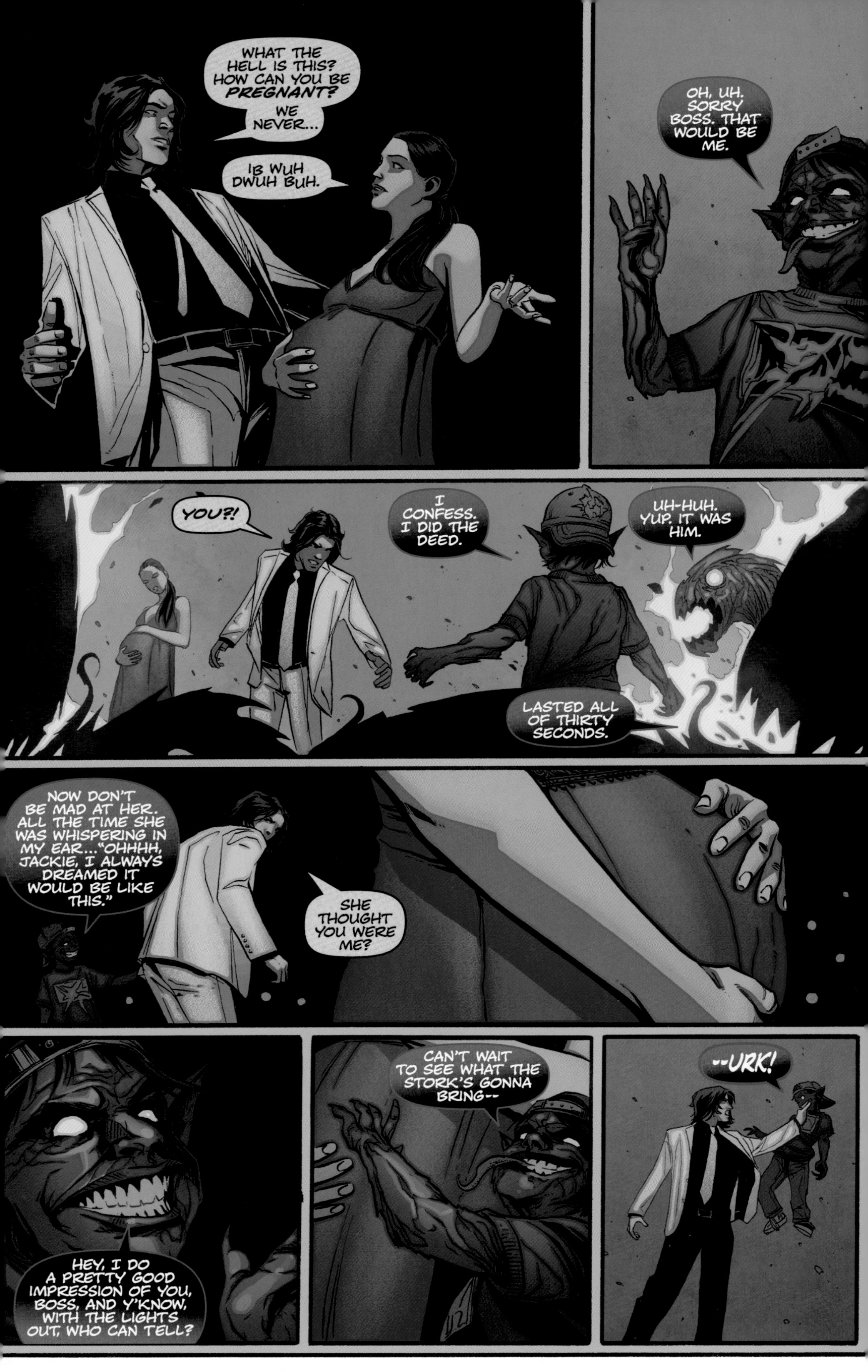
WHAT THE HELL IS THIS? HOW CAN YOU BE PREGNANT?
WE NEVER...
IB WUH DWUH BUH.
OH, UH. SORRY BOSS. THAT WOULD BE ME.
YOU?!
I CONFESS. I DID THE DEED.
UH-HUH. YUP. IT WAS HIM.
LASTED ALL OF THIRTY SECONDS.
NOW DON'T BE MAD AT HER. ALL THE TIME SHE WAS WHISPERING IN MY EAR..."OHHHH, JACKIE, I ALWAYS DREAMED IT WOULD BE LIKE THIS."
SHE THOUGHT YOU WERE ME?
HEY, I DO A PRETTY GOOD IMPRESSION OF YOU, BOSS, AND Y'KNOW, WITH THE LIGHTS OUT, WHO CAN TELL?
CAN'T WAIT TO SEE WHAT THE STORK'S GONNA BRING--
--URK!

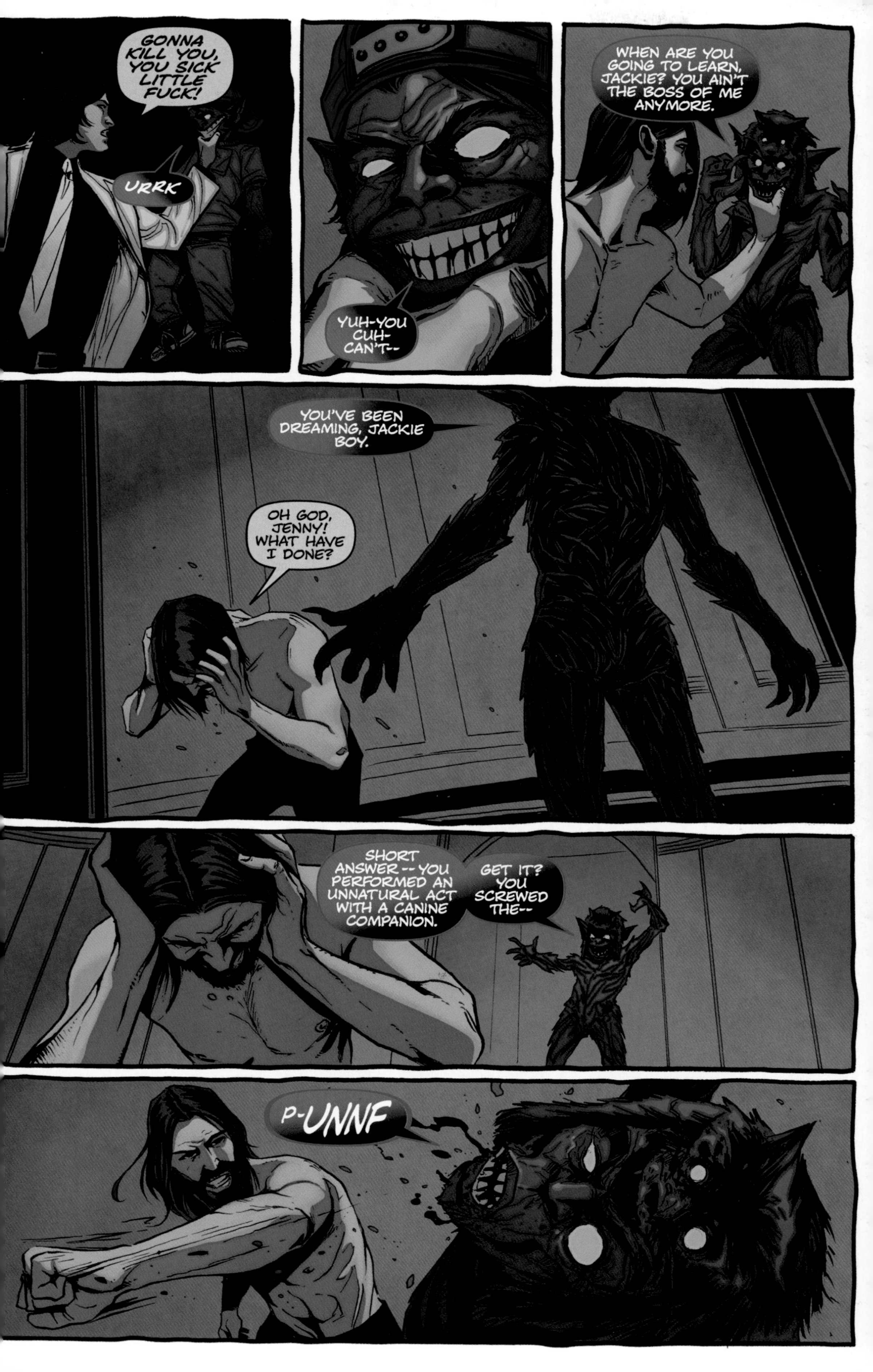
GONNA KILL YOU, YOU SICK LITTLE FUCK!
URRK
YUH-YOU CUH-CAN'T--
WHEN ARE YOU GOING TO LEARN, JACKIE? YOU AIN'T THE BOSS OF ME ANYMORE.
YOU'VE BEEN DREAMING, JACKIE BOY.
OH GOD, JENNY! WHAT HAVE I DONE?
SHORT ANSWER -- YOU PERFORMED AN UNNATURAL ACT WITH A CANINE COMPANION.
GET IT? YOU SCREWED THE--
P-UNNF

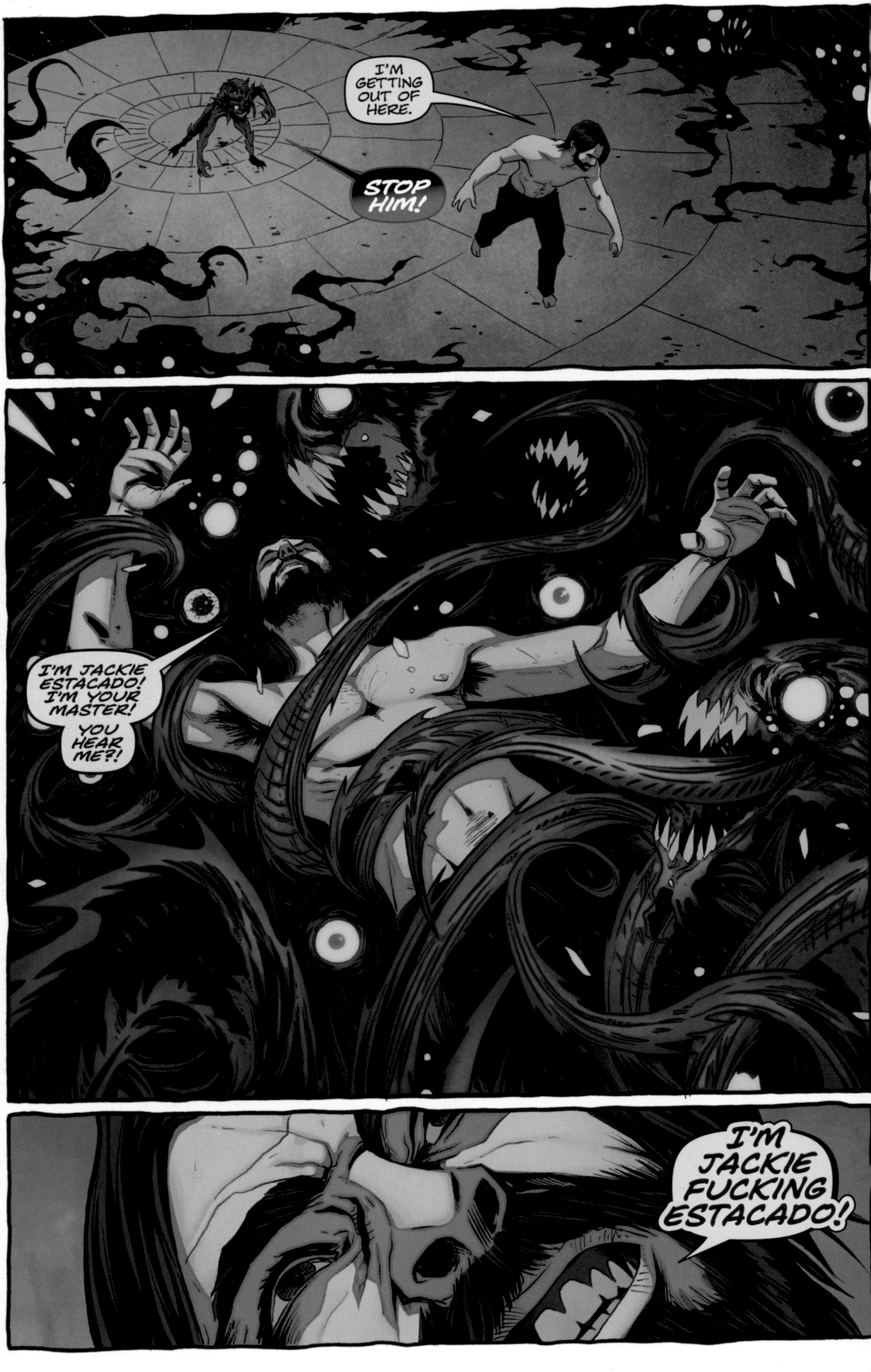
I'M GETTING OUT OF HERE.
STOP HIM!
I'M JACKIE ESTACADO! I'M YOUR MASTER!
YOU HEAR ME?!
I'M JACKIE FUCKING ESTACADO!

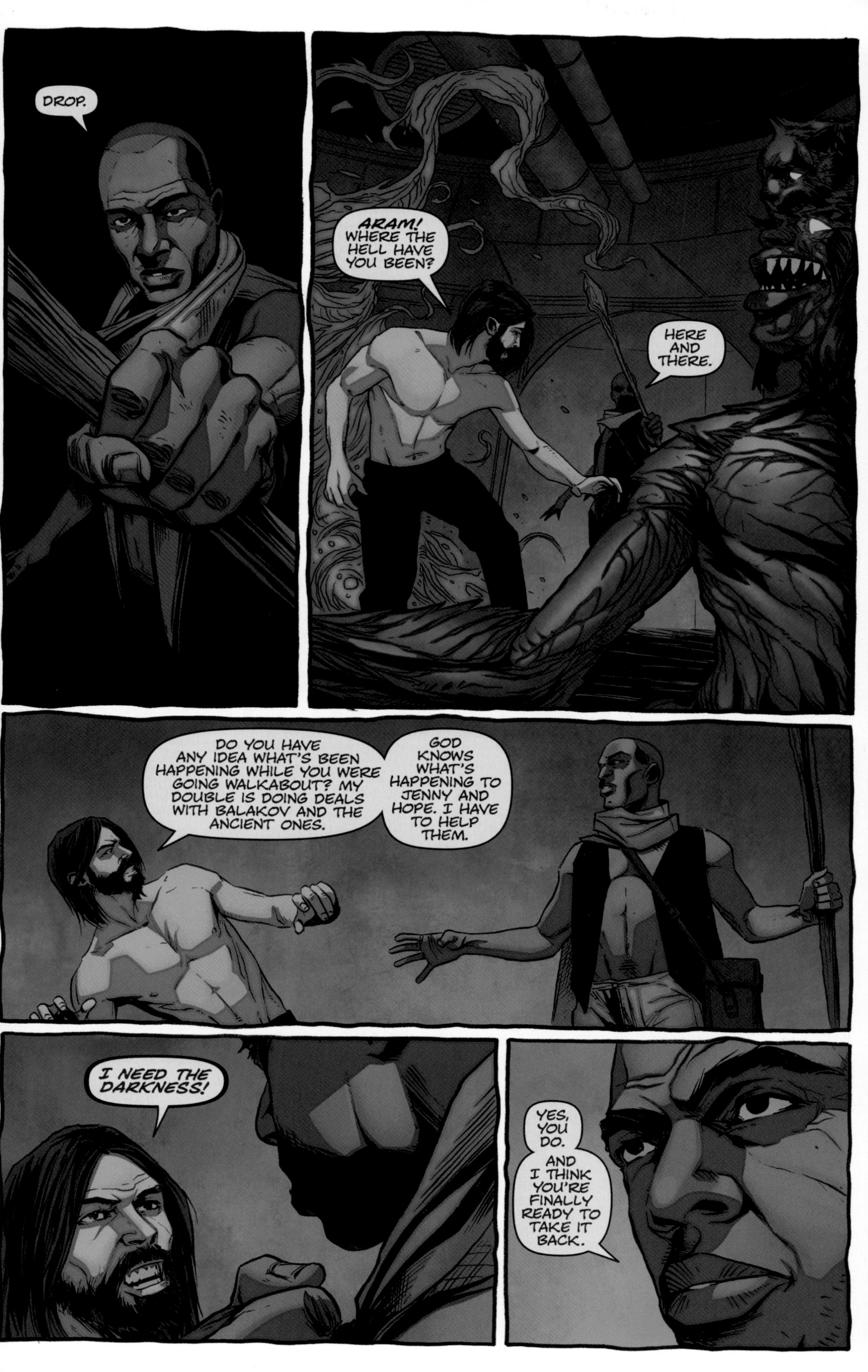
DROP.
ARAM! WHERE THE HELL HAVE YOU BEEN?
HERE AND THERE.
DO YOU HAVE ANY IDEA WHAT'S BEEN HAPPENING WHILE YOU WERE GOING WALKABOUT? MY DOUBLE IS DOING DEALS WITH BALAKOV AND THE ANCIENT ONES.
GOD KNOWS WHAT'S HAPPENING TO JENNY AND HOPE. I HAVE TO HELP THEM.
I NEED THE DARKNESS!
YES, YOU DO.
AND I THINK YOU'RE FINALLY READY TO TAKE IT BACK.

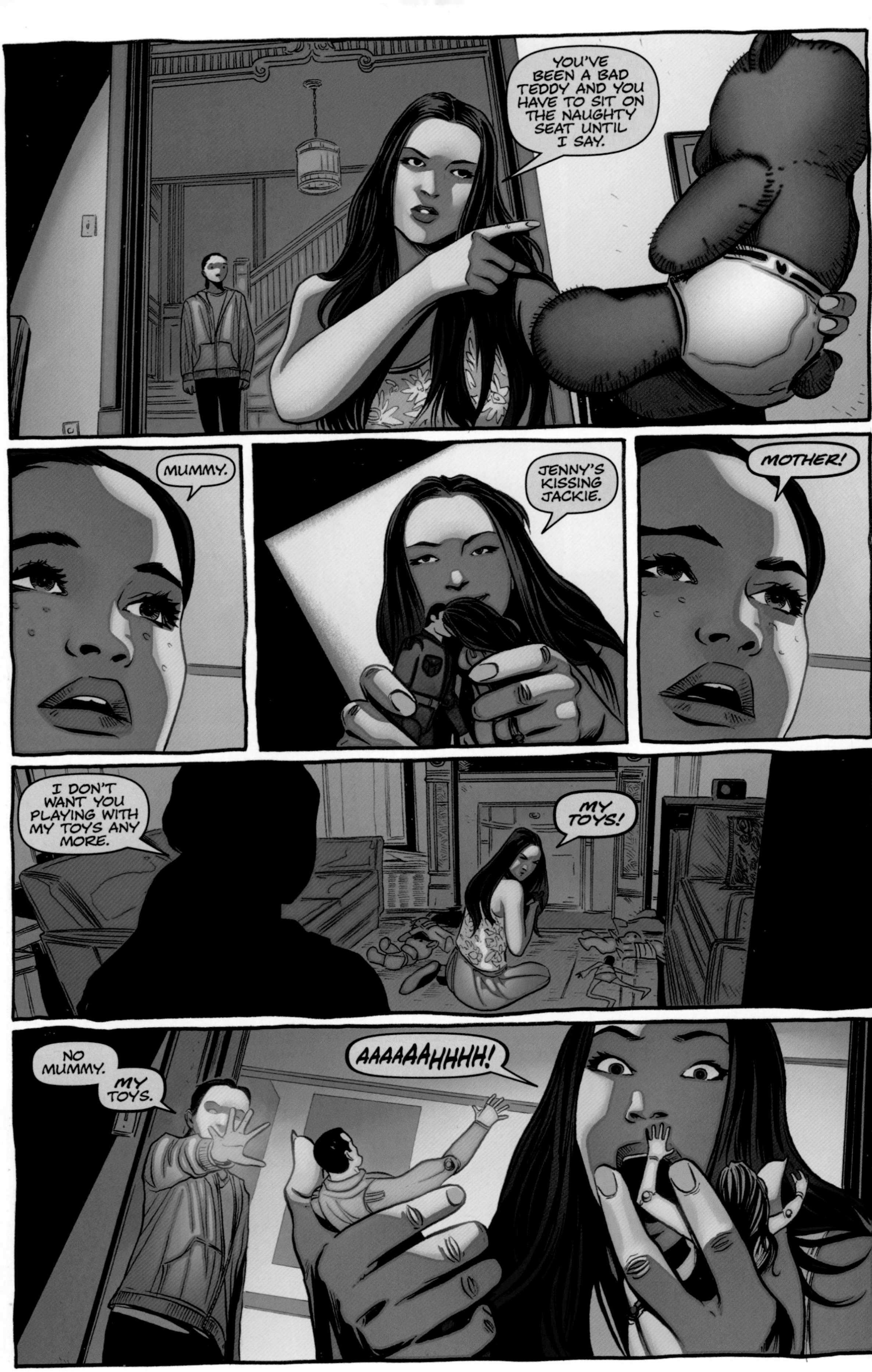
YOU'VE BEEN A BAD TEDDY AND YOU HAVE TO SIT ON THE NAUGHTY SEAT UNTIL I SAY.
MUMMY.
JENNY'S KISSING JACKIE.
MOTHER!
I DON'T WANT YOU PLAYING WITH MY TOYS ANY MORE.
MY TOYS!
NO MUMMY.
MY TOYS.
AAAAAAHHHH!

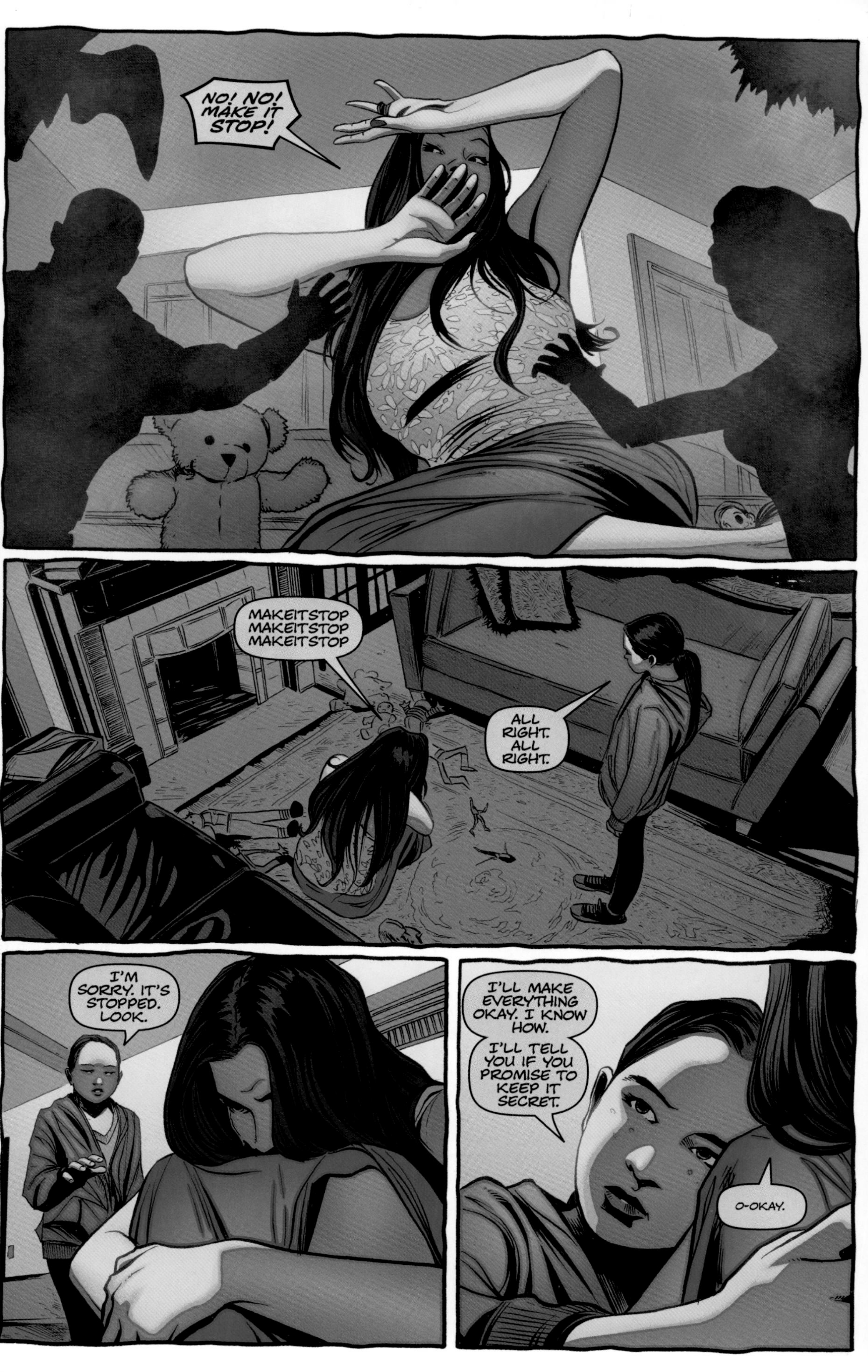
NO! NO! MAKE IT STOP!
MAKEITSTOP MAKEITSTOP MAKEITSTOP
ALL RIGHT. ALL RIGHT.
I'M SORRY. IT'S STOPPED. LOOK.
I'LL MAKE EVERYTHING OKAY. I KNOW HOW.
I'LL TELL YOU IF YOU PROMISE TO KEEP IT SECRET.
O-OKAY.

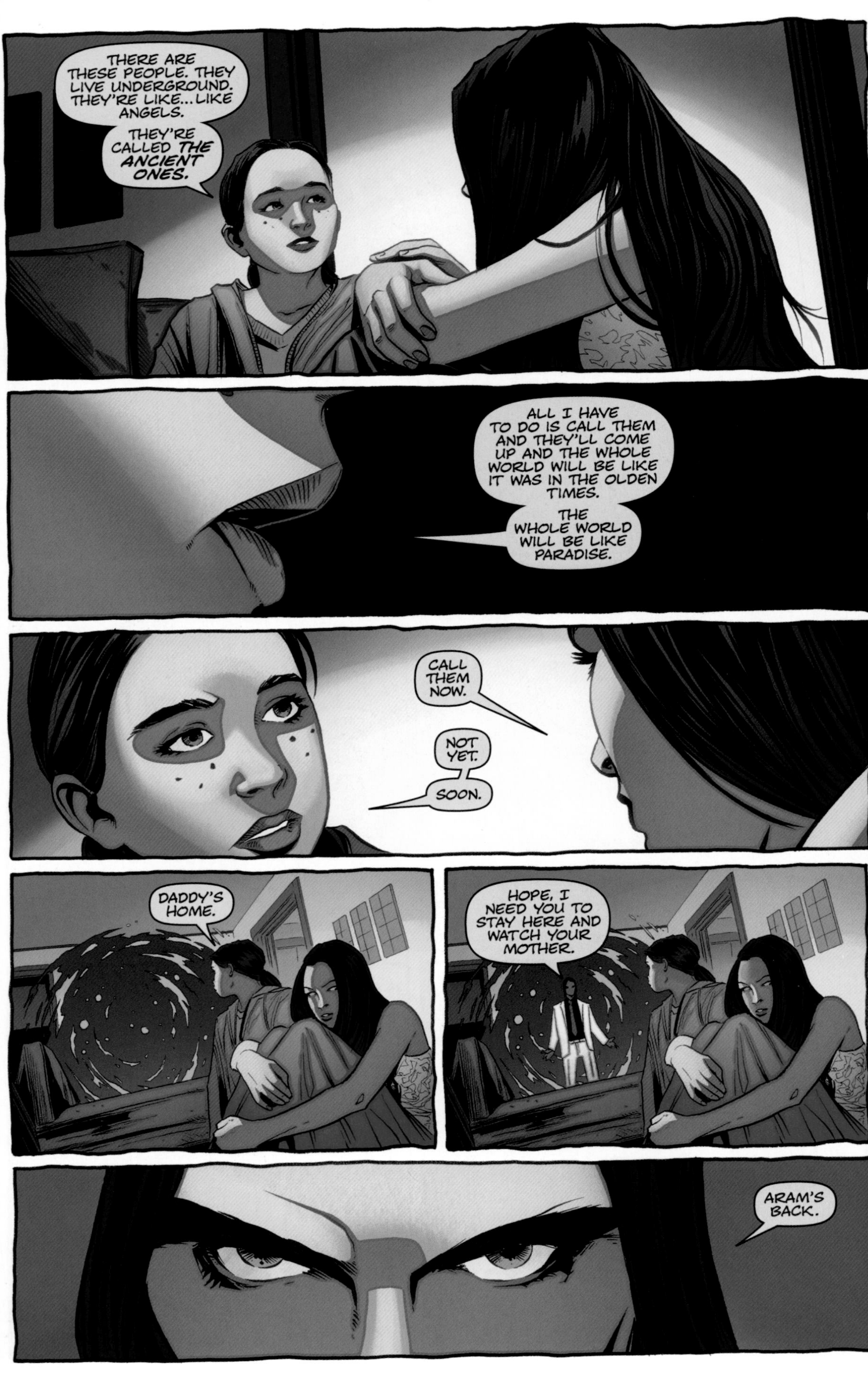
THERE ARE THESE PEOPLE. THEY LIVE UNDERGROUND. THEY'RE LIKE... LIKE ANGELS.
THEY'RE CALLED THE ANCIENT ONES.
ALL I HAVE TO DO IS CALL THEM AND THEY'LL COME UP AND THE WHOLE WORLD WILL BE LIKE IT WAS IN THE OLDEN TIMES.
THE WHOLE WORLD WILL BE LIKE PARADISE.
CALL THEM NOW.
NOT YET.
SOON.
DADDY'S HOME.
HOPE, I NEED YOU TO STAY HERE AND WATCH YOUR MOTHER.
ARAM'S BACK.

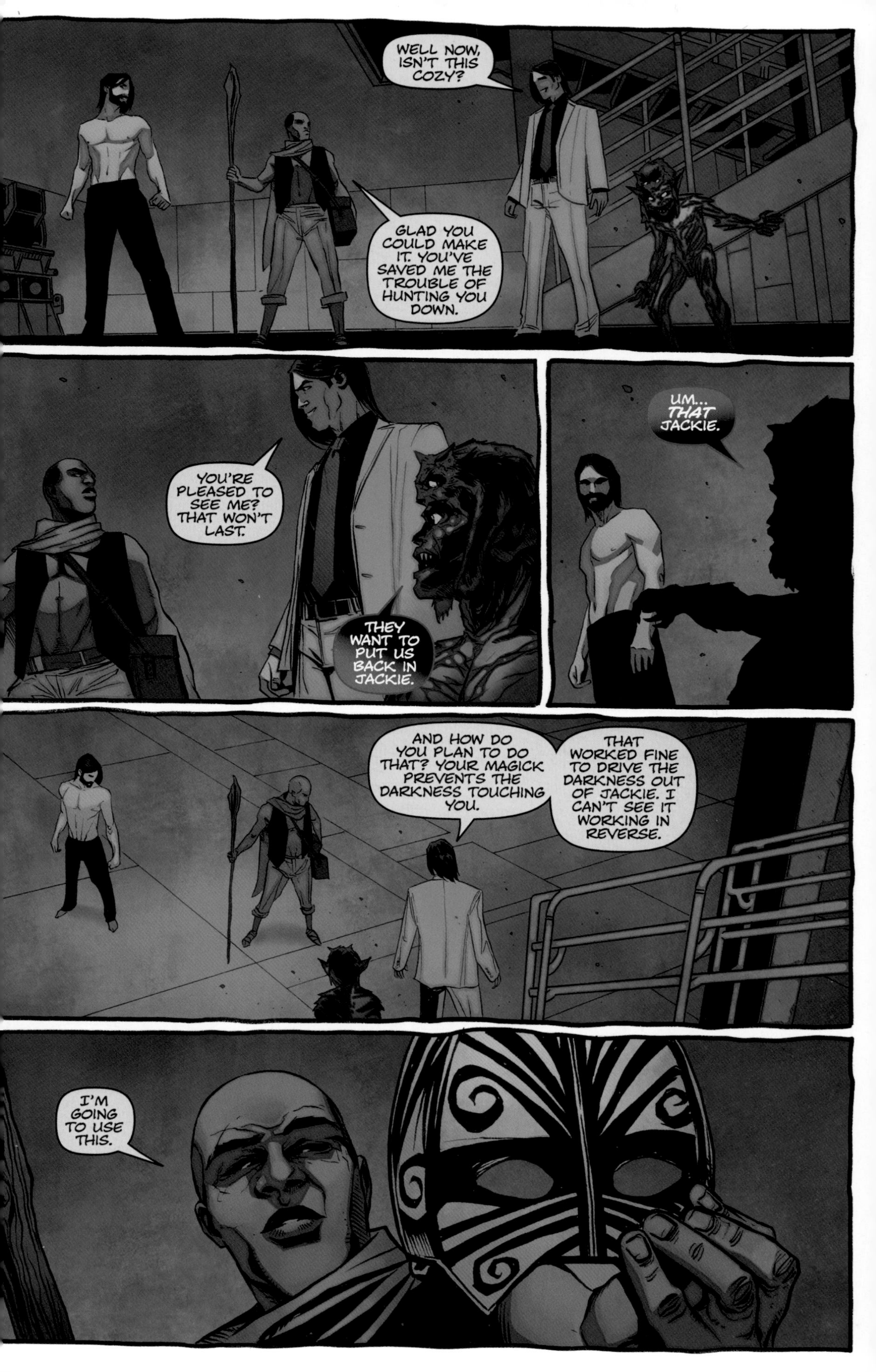

WELL NOW, ISN'T THIS COZY?
GLAD YOU COULD MAKE IT. YOU'VE SAVED ME THE TROUBLE OF HUNTING YOU DOWN.
YOU'RE PLEASED TO SEE ME? THAT WON'T LAST.
THEY WANT TO PUT US BACK IN JACKIE.
UM... THAT JACKIE.
AND HOW DO YOU PLAN TO DO THAT? YOUR MAGICK PREVENTS THE DARKNESS TOUCHING YOU.
THAT WORKED FINE TO DRIVE THE DARKNESS OUT OF JACKIE. I CAN'T SEE IT WORKING IN REVERSE.
I'M GOING TO USE THIS.

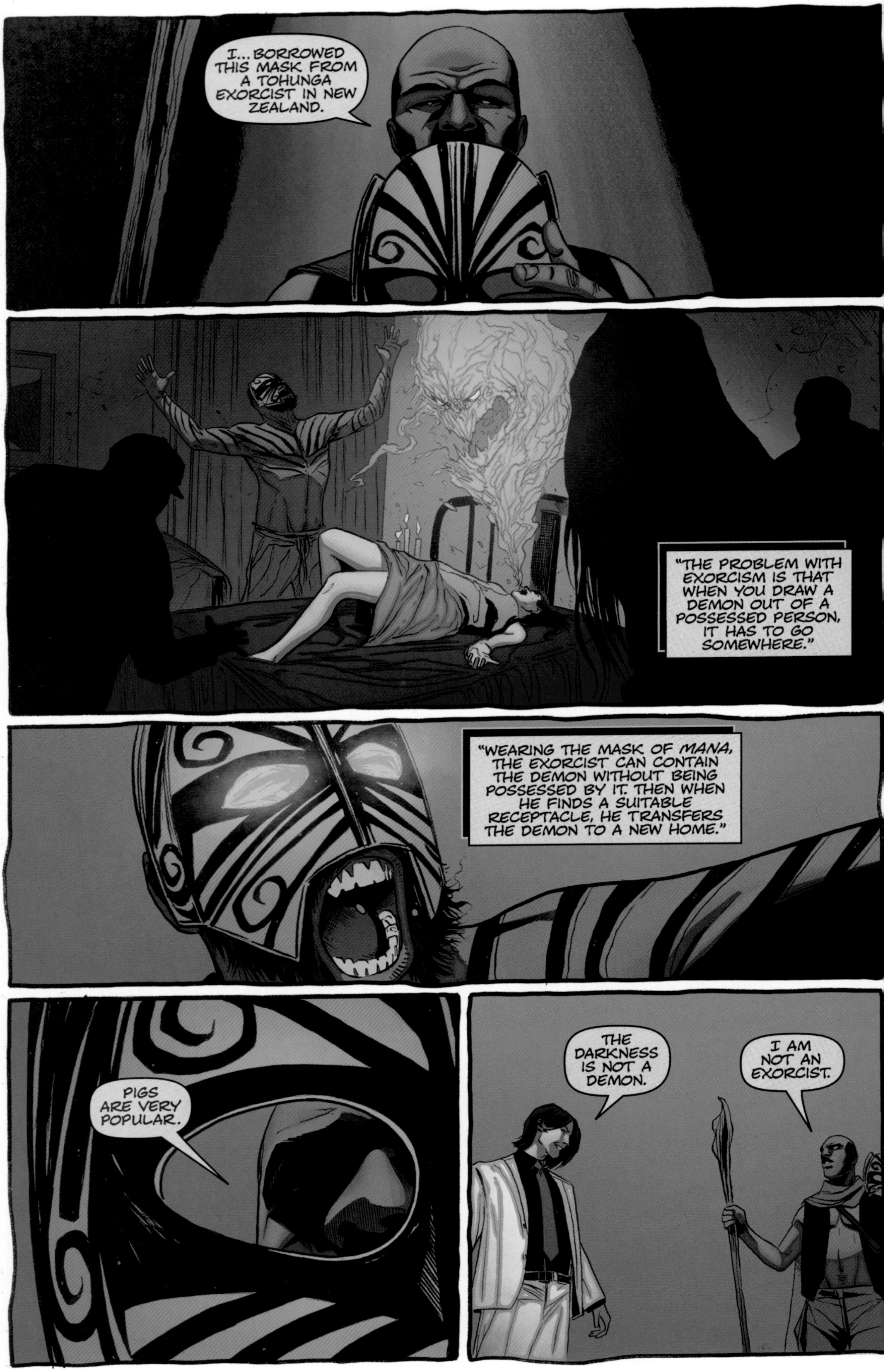
I... BORROWED THIS MASK FROM A TOHUNGA EXORCIST IN NEW ZEALAND.
"THE PROBLEM WITH EXORCISM IS THAT WHEN YOU DRAW A DEMON OUT OF A POSSESSED PERSON, IT HAS TO GO SOMEWHERE."
"WEARING THE MASK OF *MANA*, THE EXORCIST CAN CONTAIN THE DEMON WITHOUT BEING POSSESSED BY IT. THEN WHEN HE FINDS A SUITABLE RECEPTACLE, HE TRANSFERS THE DEMON TO A NEW HOME."
PIGS ARE VERY POPULAR.
THE DARKNESS IS NOT A DEMON.
I AM NOT AN EXORCIST.

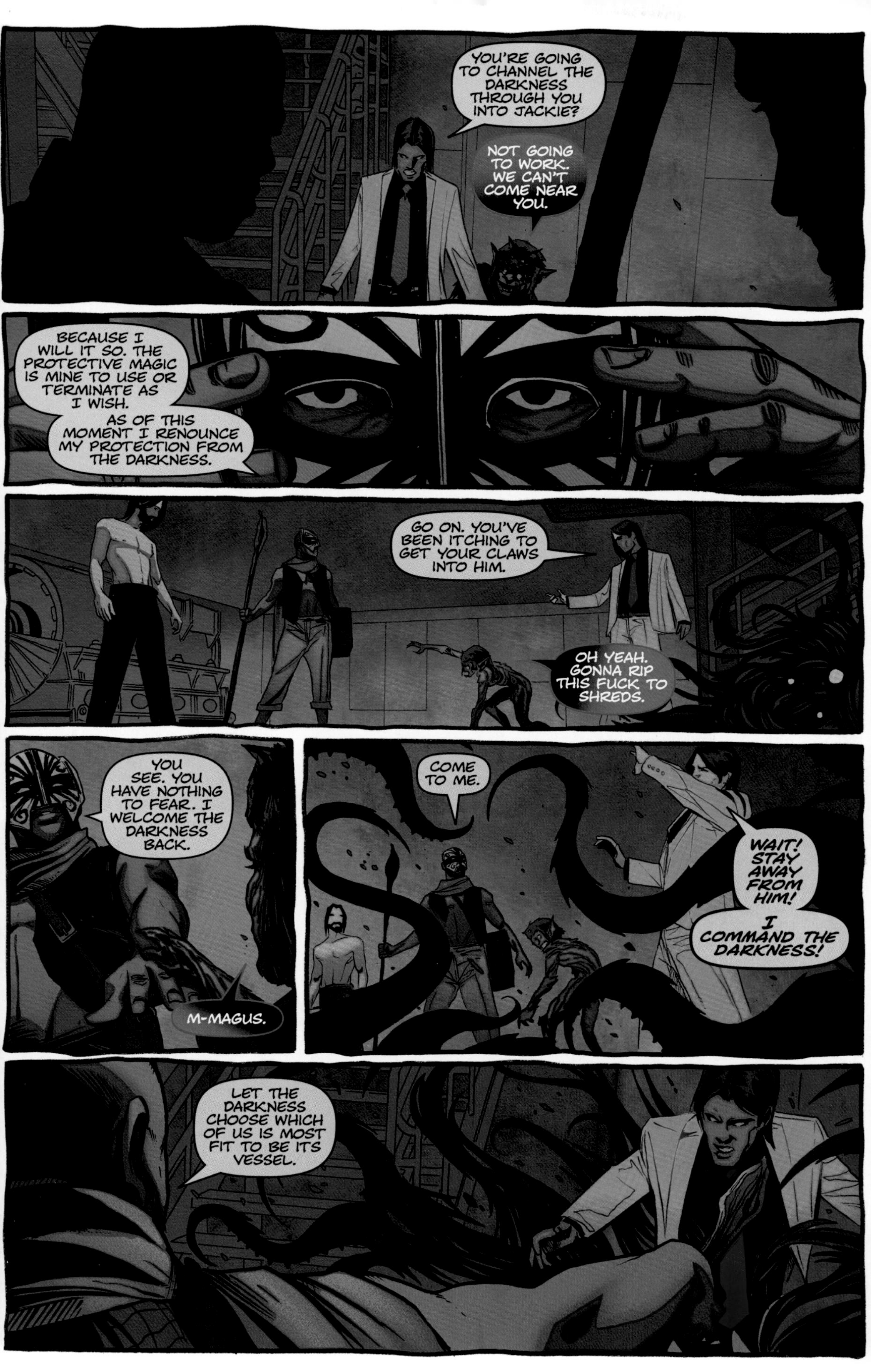
YOU'RE GOING TO CHANNEL THE DARKNESS THROUGH YOU INTO JACKIE?
NOT GOING TO WORK. WE CAN'T COME NEAR YOU.
BECAUSE I WILL IT SO. THE PROTECTIVE MAGIC IS MINE TO USE OR TERMINATE AS I WISH.
AS OF THIS MOMENT I RENOUNCE MY PROTECTION FROM THE DARKNESS.
GO ON. YOU'VE BEEN ITCHING TO GET YOUR CLAWS INTO HIM.
OH YEAH. GONNA RIP THIS FUCK TO SHREDS.
YOU SEE. YOU HAVE NOTHING TO FEAR. I WELCOME THE DARKNESS BACK.
M-MAGUS.
COME TO ME.
WAIT! STAY AWAY FROM HIM!
I COMMAND THE DARKNESS!
LET THE DARKNESS CHOOSE WHICH OF US IS MOST FIT TO BE ITS VESSEL.

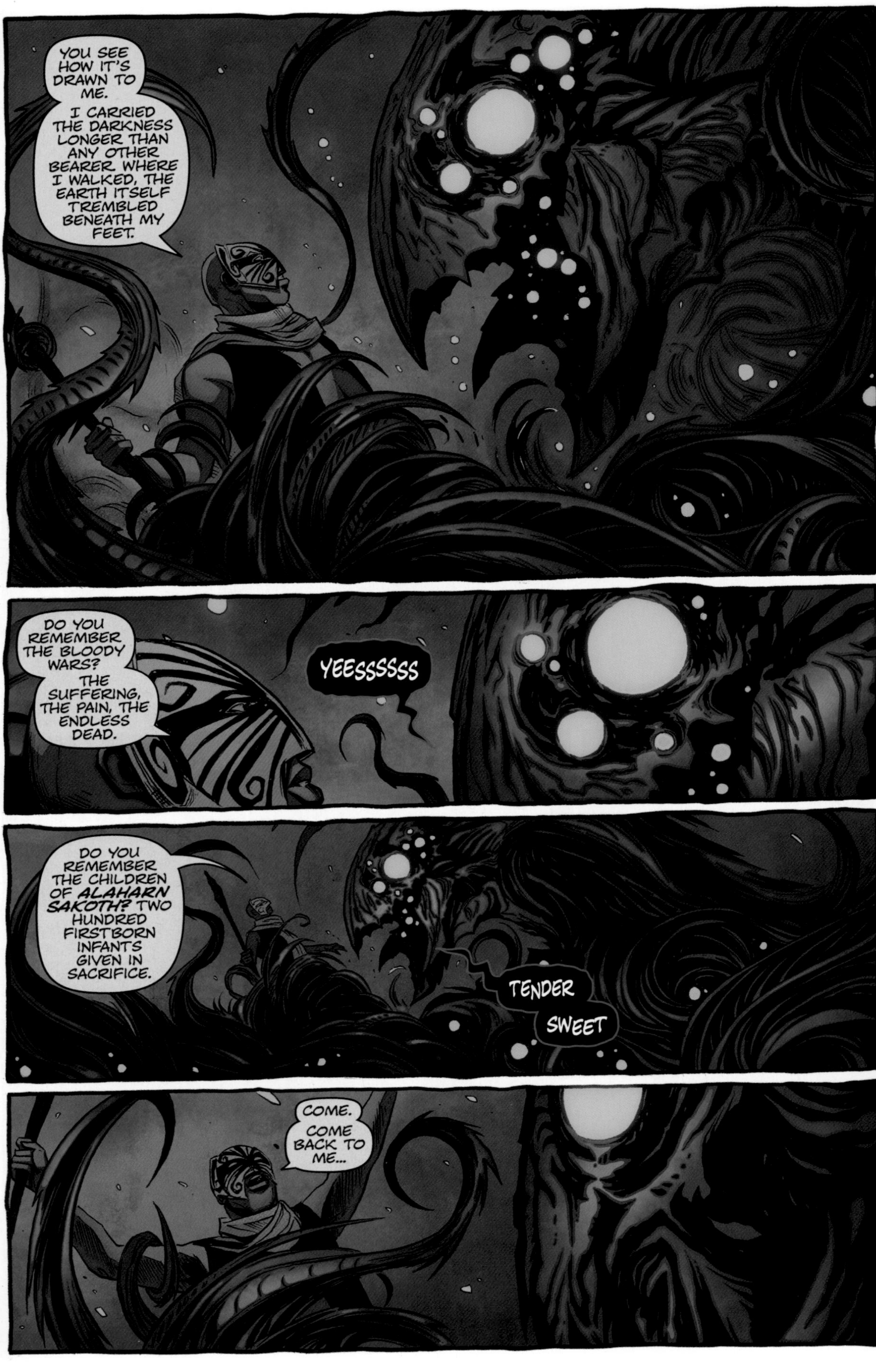
YOU SEE HOW IT'S DRAWN TO ME.
I CARRIED THE DARKNESS LONGER THAN ANY OTHER BEARER WHERE I WALKED, THE EARTH ITSELF TREMBLED BENEATH MY FEET.
DO YOU REMEMBER THE BLOODY WARS?
THE SUFFERING, THE PAIN, THE ENDLESS DEAD.
YEESSSSSS
DO YOU REMEMBER THE CHILDREN OF ALAHARN SAKOTH? TWO HUNDRED FIRSTBORN INFANTS GIVEN IN SACRIFICE.
TENDER
SWEET
COME.
COME BACK TO ME...

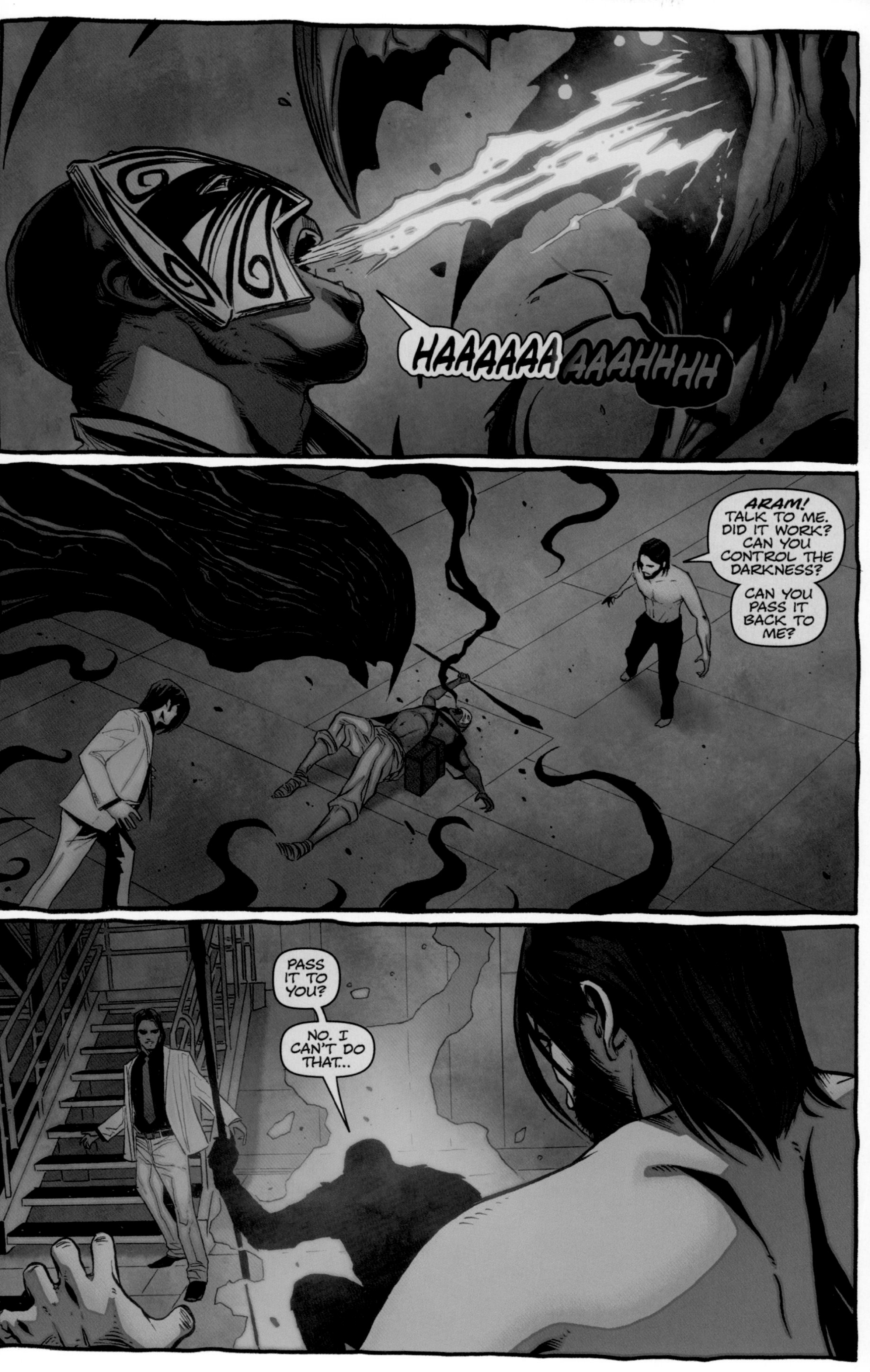
HAAAAAA AAAHHHH
ARAM! TALK TO ME. DID IT WORK? CAN YOU CONTROL THE DARKNESS?
CAN YOU PASS IT BACK TO ME?
PASS IT TO YOU?
NO. I CAN'T DO THAT...

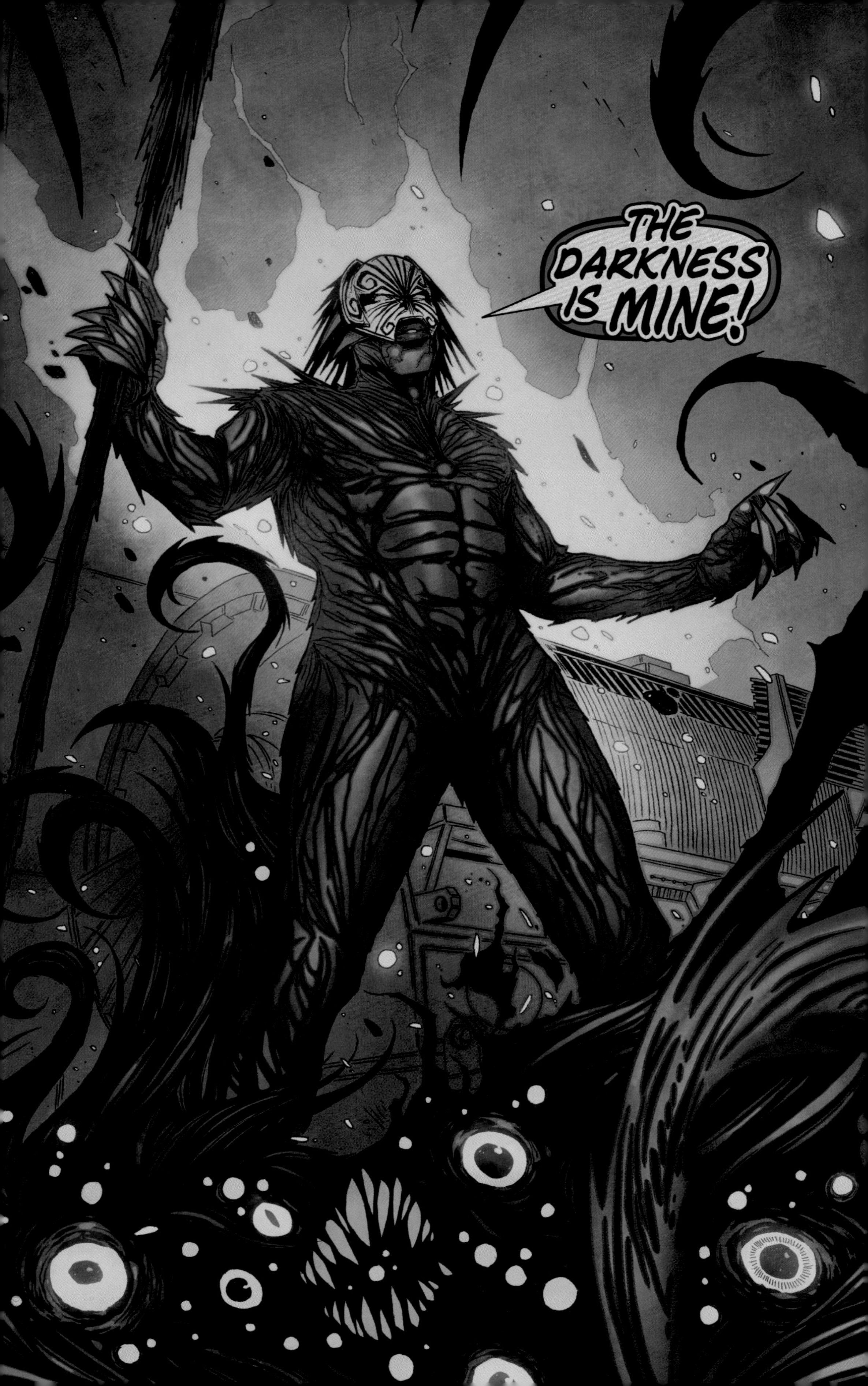
THE DARKNESS IS MINE!

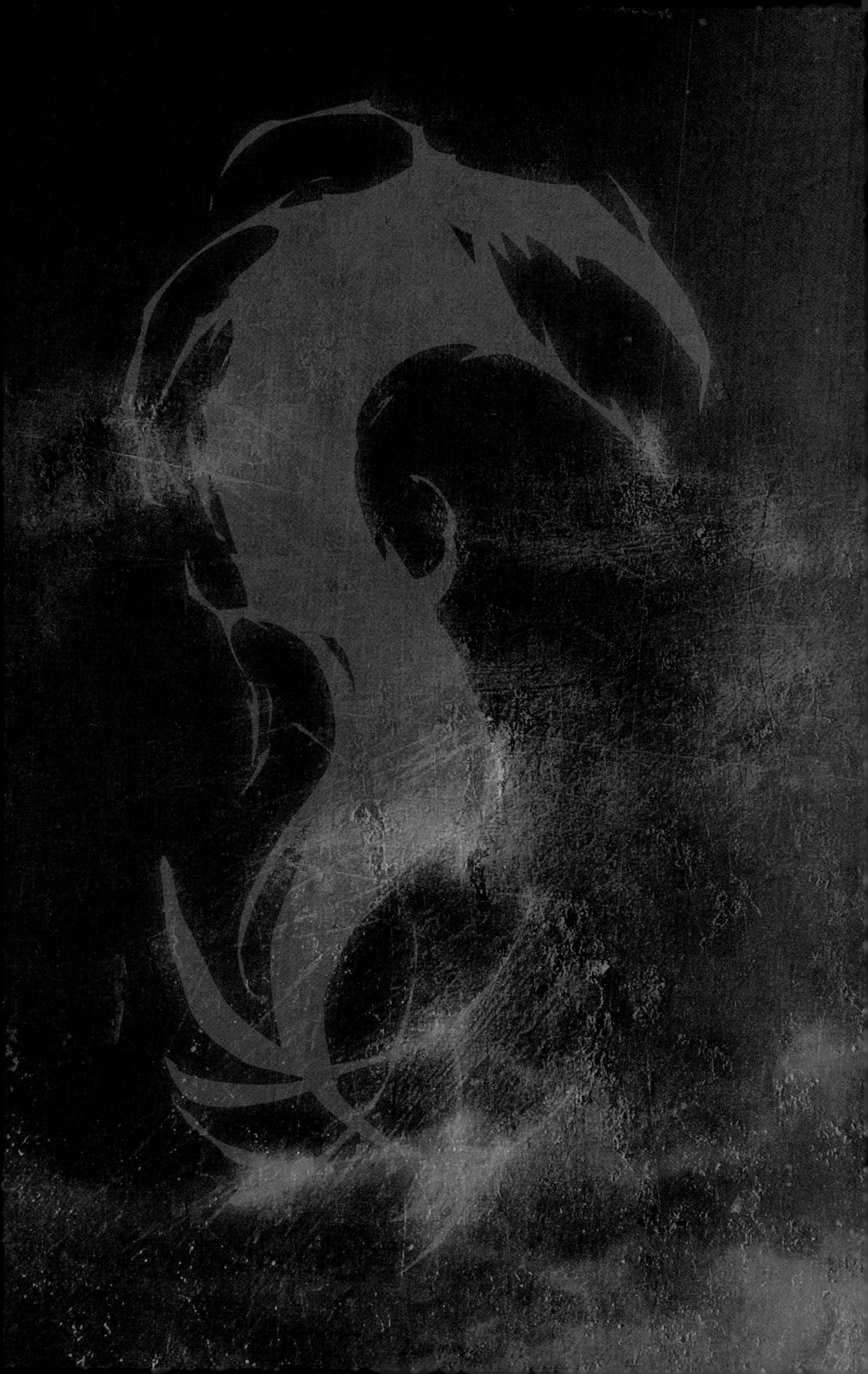

"THE AGE OF REASON"

PART

2

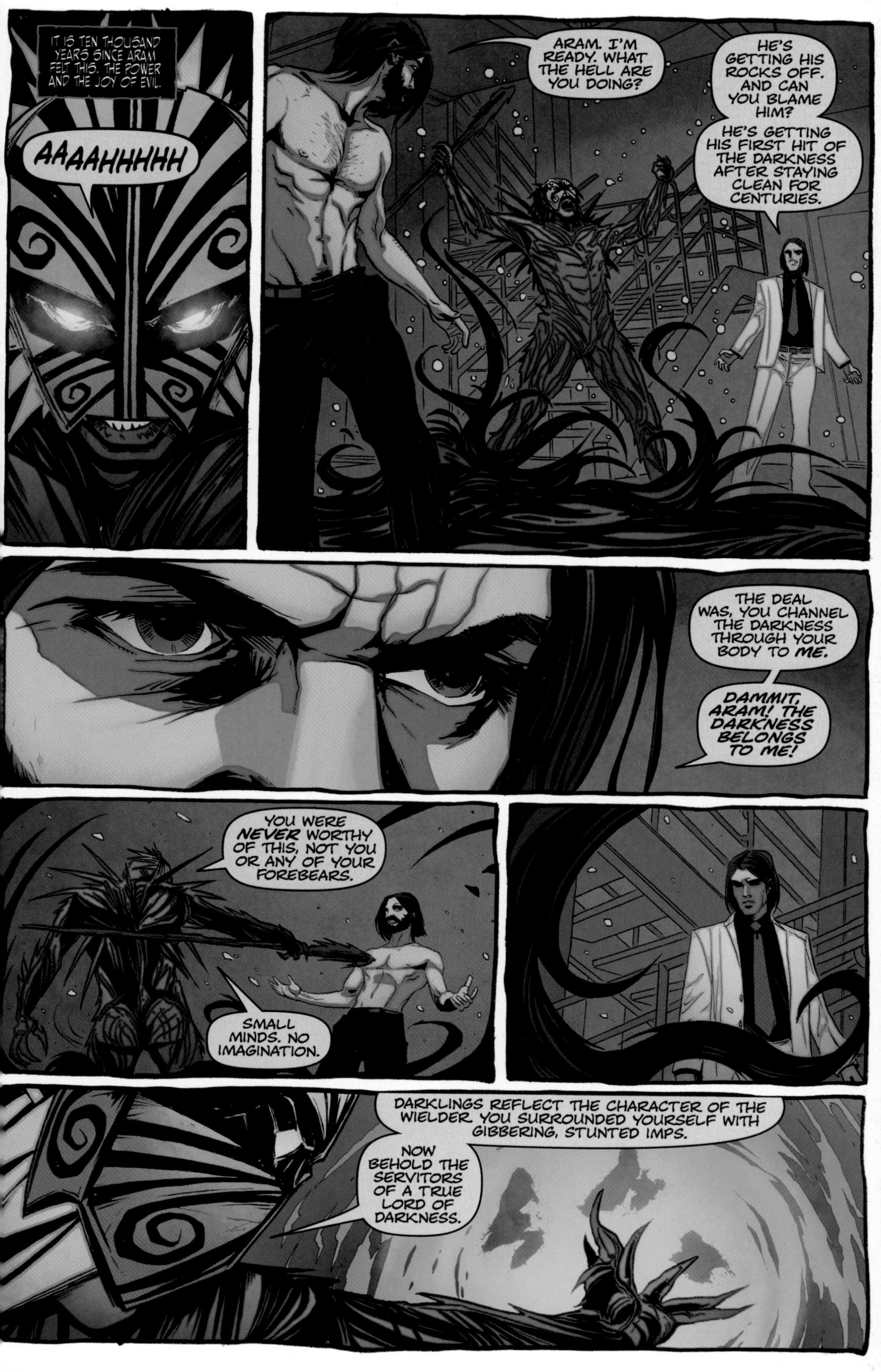

IT IS TEN THOUSAND YEARS SINCE ARAM FELT THIS. THE POWER AND THE JOY OF EVIL.
AAAAHHHHH
ARAM. I'M READY. WHAT THE HELL ARE YOU DOING?
HE'S GETTING HIS ROCKS OFF. AND CAN YOU BLAME HIM?
HE'S GETTING HIS FIRST HIT OF THE DARKNESS AFTER STAYING CLEAN FOR CENTURIES.
THE DEAL WAS, YOU CHANNEL THE DARKNESS THROUGH YOUR BODY TO *ME.*
DAMMIT, ARAM! THE DARKNESS BELONGS TO ME!
YOU WERE *NEVER* WORTHY OF THIS, NOT YOU OR ANY OF YOUR FOREBEARS.
SMALL MINDS. NO IMAGINATION.
DARKLINGS REFLECT THE CHARACTER OF THE WIELDER. YOU SURROUNDED YOURSELF WITH GIBBERING, STUNTED IMPS.
NOW BEHOLD THE SERVITORS OF A TRUE LORD OF DARKNESS.

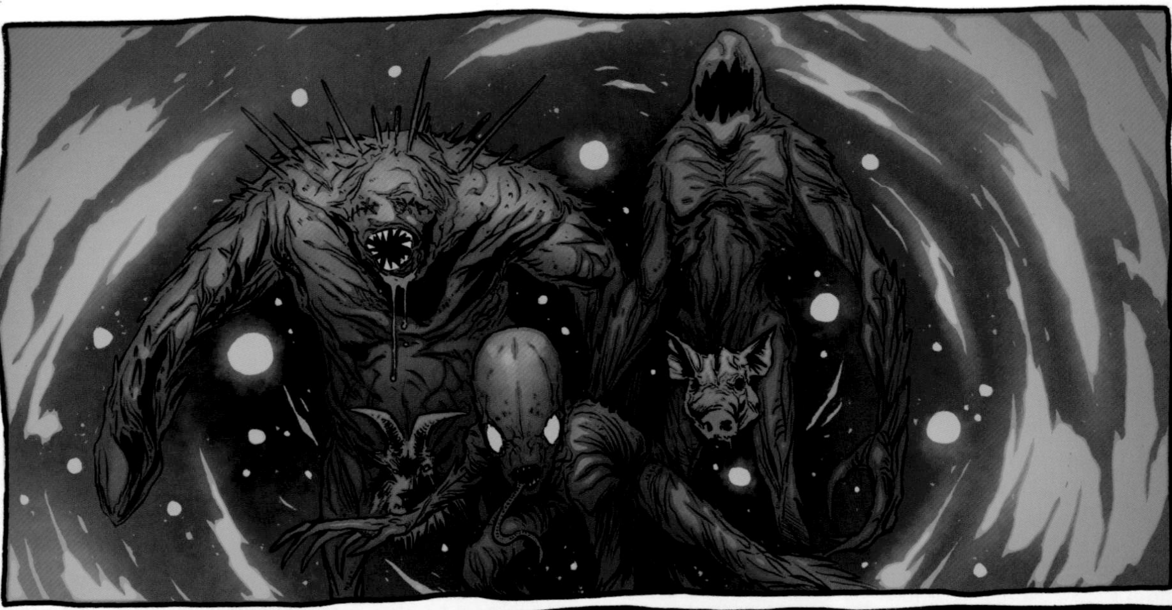

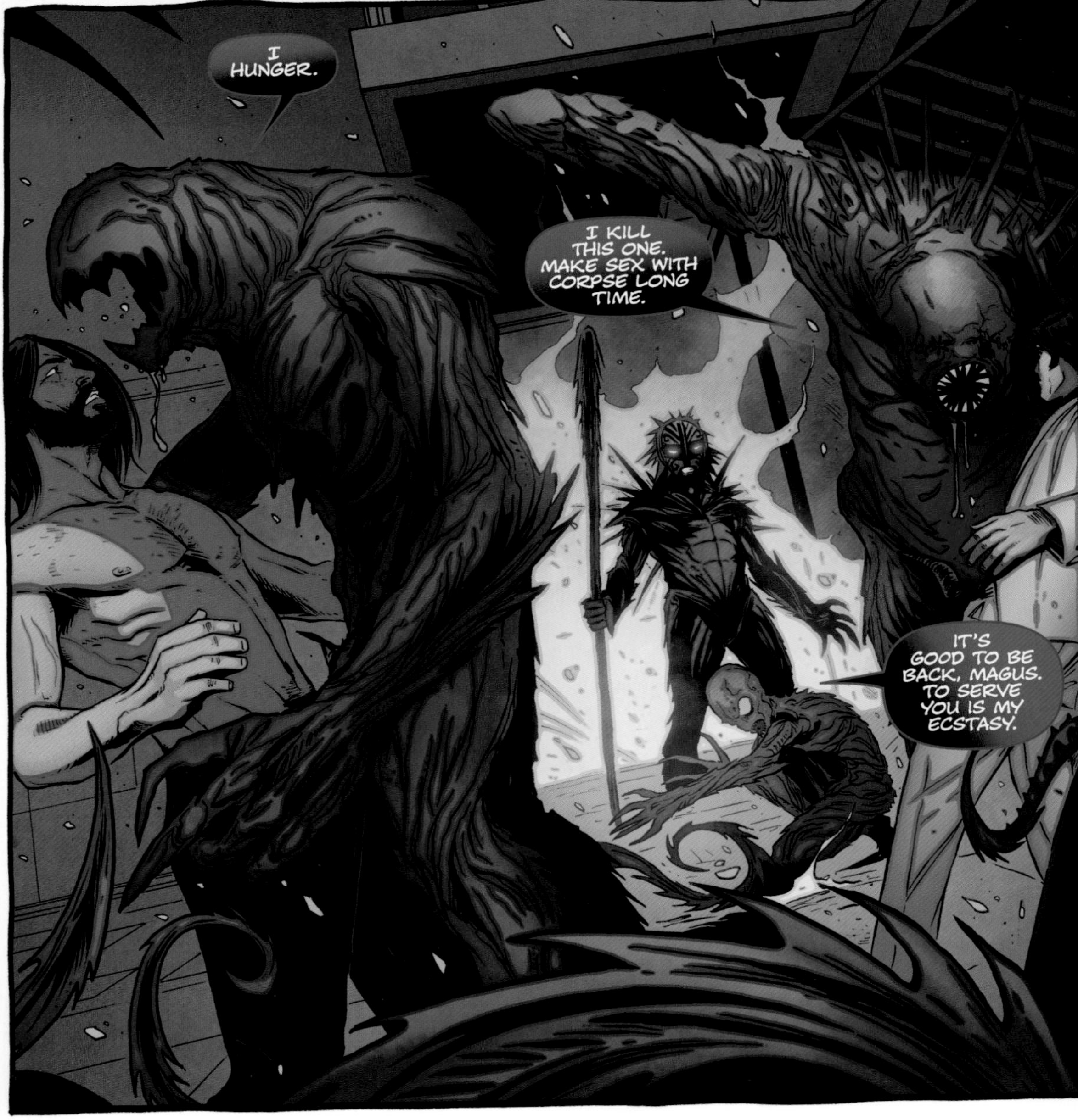
I HUNGER.
I KILL THIS ONE. MAKE SEX WITH CORPSE LONG TIME.
IT'S GOOD TO BE BACK, MAGUS. TO SERVE YOU IS MY ECSTASY.

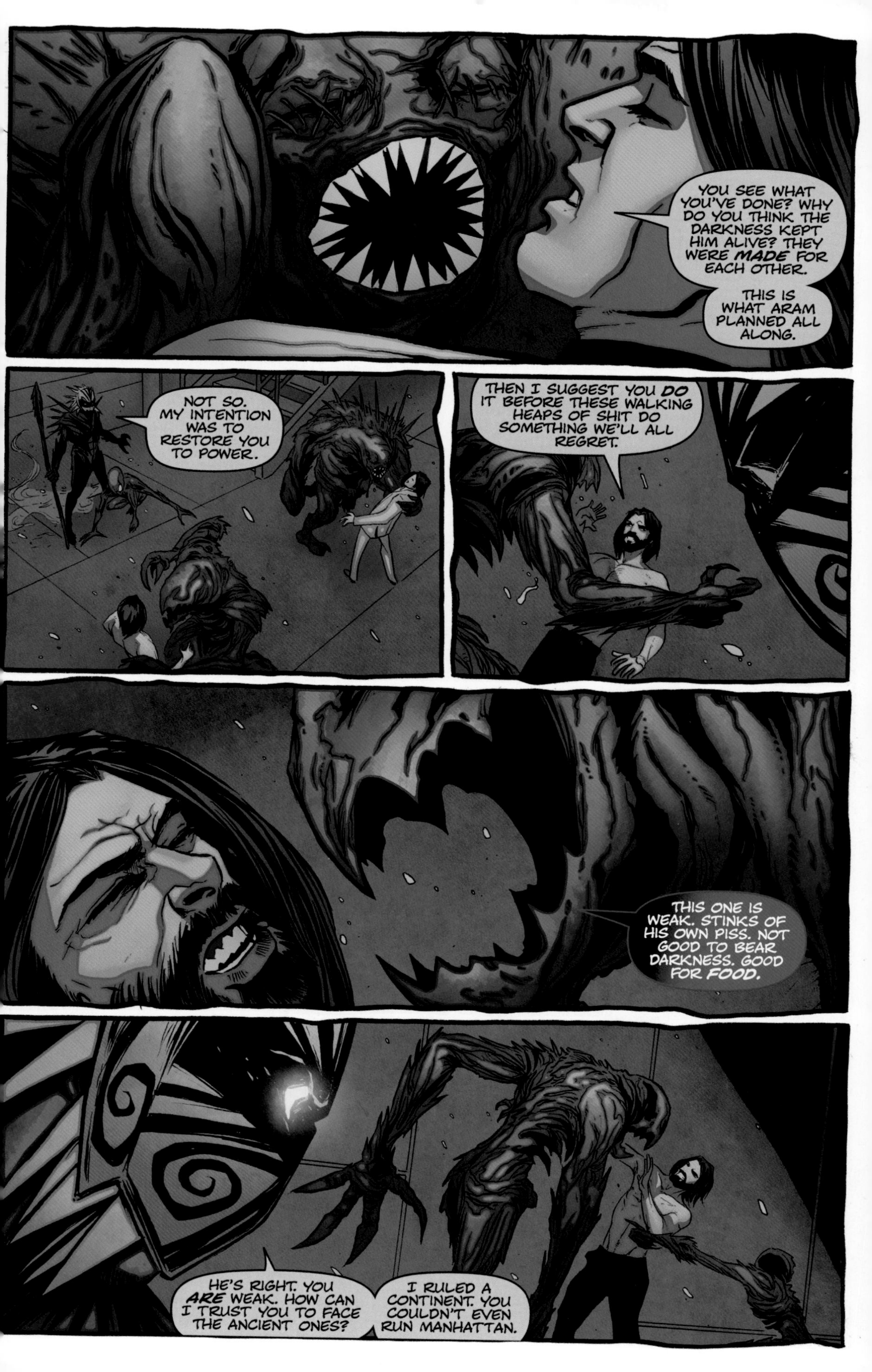
YOU SEE WHAT YOU'VE DONE? WHY DO YOU THINK THE DARKNESS KEPT HIM ALIVE? THEY WERE MADE FOR EACH OTHER.
THIS IS WHAT ARAM PLANNED ALL ALONG.
NOT SO. MY INTENTION WAS TO RESTORE YOU TO POWER.
THEN I SUGGEST YOU DO IT BEFORE THESE WALKING HEAPS OF SHIT DO SOMETHING WE'LL ALL REGRET.
THIS ONE IS WEAK. STINKS OF HIS OWN PISS. NOT GOOD TO BEAR DARKNESS. GOOD FOR FOOD.
HE'S RIGHT. YOU ARE WEAK. HOW CAN I TRUST YOU TO FACE THE ANCIENT ONES?
I RULED A CONTINENT. YOU COULDN'T EVEN RUN MANHATTAN.

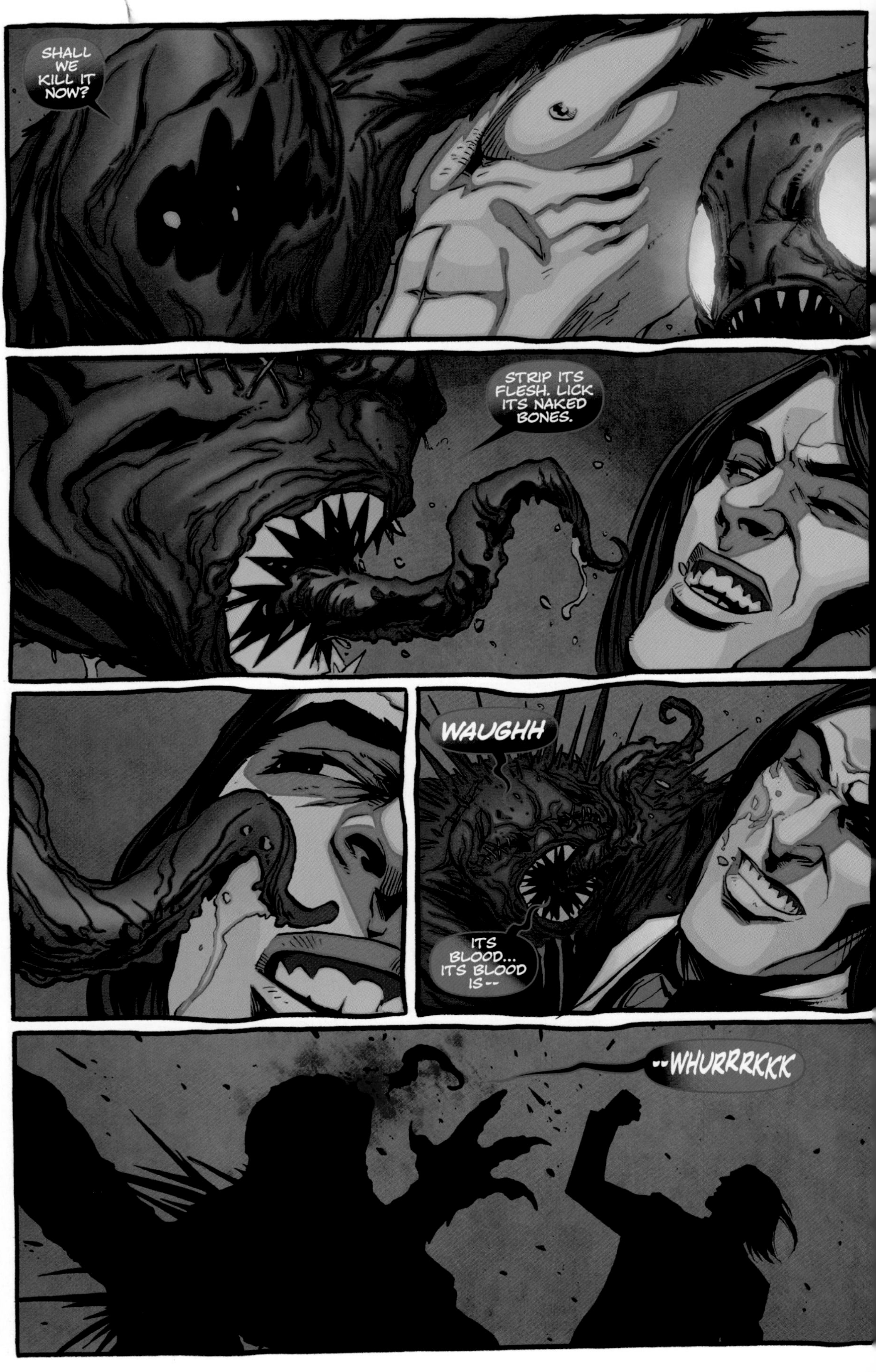
SHALL WE KILL IT NOW?
STRIP ITS FLESH. LICK ITS NAKED BONES.
WAUGHH
ITS BLOOD... ITS BLOOD IS--
--WHURRRKKK

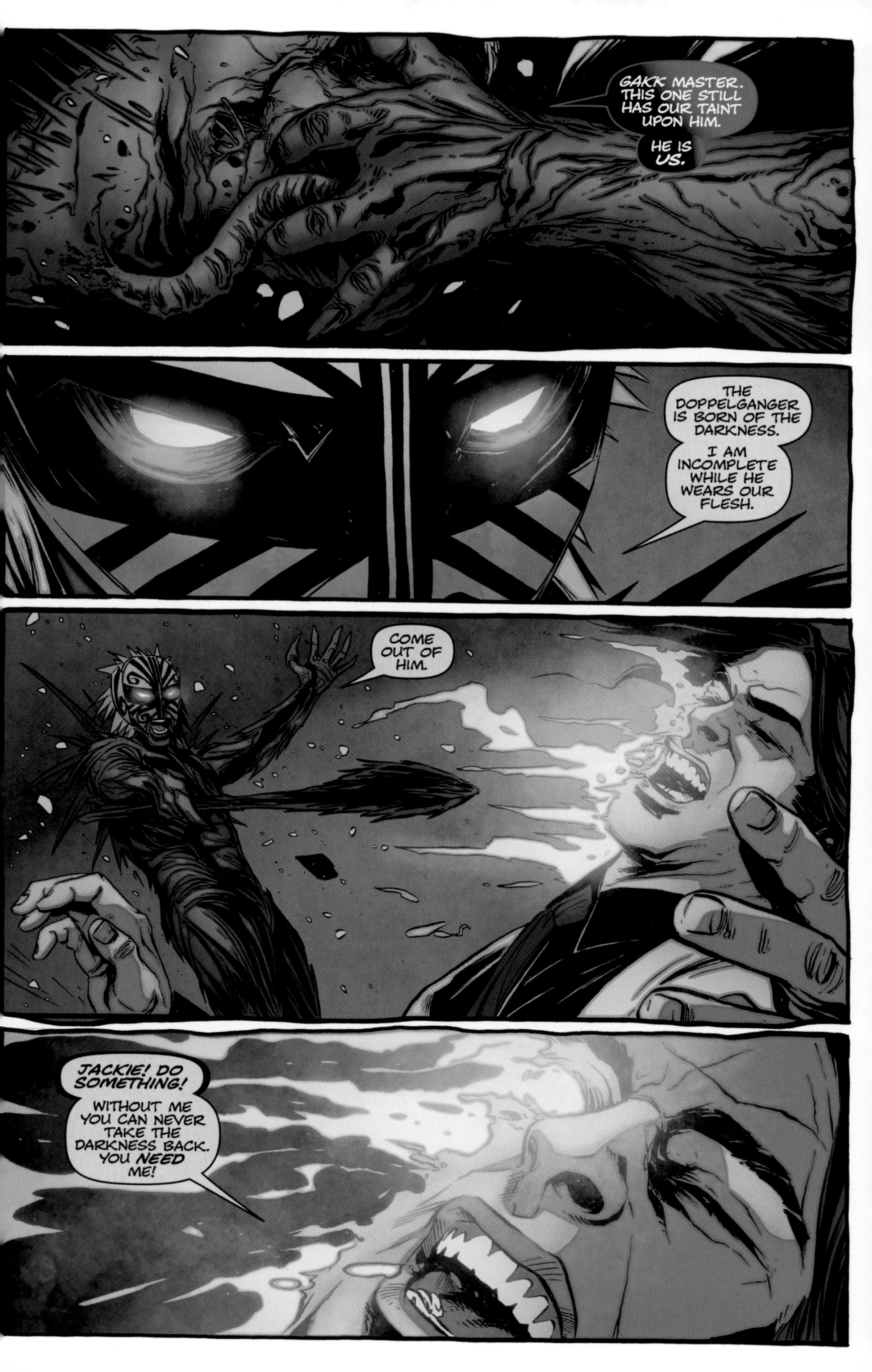
GAKK MASTER. THIS ONE STILL HAS OUR TAINT UPON HIM.
HE IS US.
THE DOPPELGANGER IS BORN OF THE DARKNESS.
I AM INCOMPLETE WHILE HE WEARS OUR FLESH.
COME OUT OF HIM.
JACKIE! DO SOMETHING!
WITHOUT ME YOU CAN NEVER TAKE THE DARKNESS BACK. YOU NEED ME!

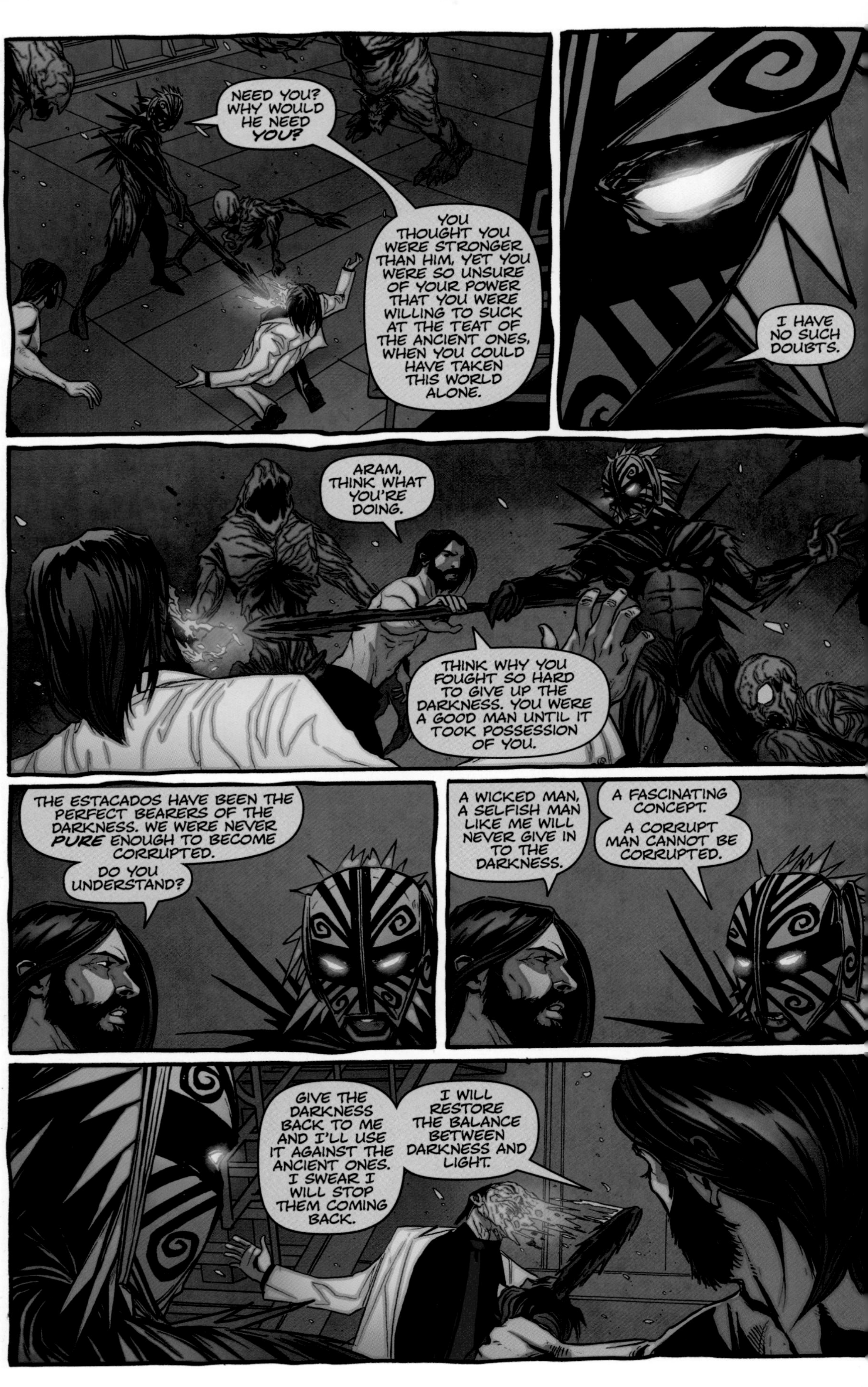
NEED YOU? WHY WOULD HE NEED YOU?
YOU THOUGHT YOU WERE STRONGER THAN HIM, YET YOU WERE SO UNSURE OF YOUR POWER THAT YOU WERE WILLING TO SUCK AT THE TEAT OF THE ANCIENT ONES, WHEN YOU COULD HAVE TAKEN THIS WORLD ALONE.
I HAVE NO SUCH DOUBTS.
ARAM, THINK WHAT YOU'RE DOING.
THINK WHY YOU FOUGHT SO HARD TO GIVE UP THE DARKNESS. YOU WERE A GOOD MAN UNTIL IT TOOK POSSESSION OF YOU.
THE ESTACADOS HAVE BEEN THE PERFECT BEARERS OF THE DARKNESS. WE WERE NEVER PURE ENOUGH TO BECOME CORRUPTED.
DO YOU UNDERSTAND?
A WICKED MAN, A SELFISH MAN LIKE ME WILL NEVER GIVE IN TO THE DARKNESS.
A FASCINATING CONCEPT.
A CORRUPT MAN CANNOT BE CORRUPTED.
GIVE THE DARKNESS BACK TO ME AND I'LL USE IT AGAINST THE ANCIENT ONES. I SWEAR I WILL STOP THEM COMING BACK.
I WILL RESTORE THE BALANCE BETWEEN DARKNESS AND LIGHT.

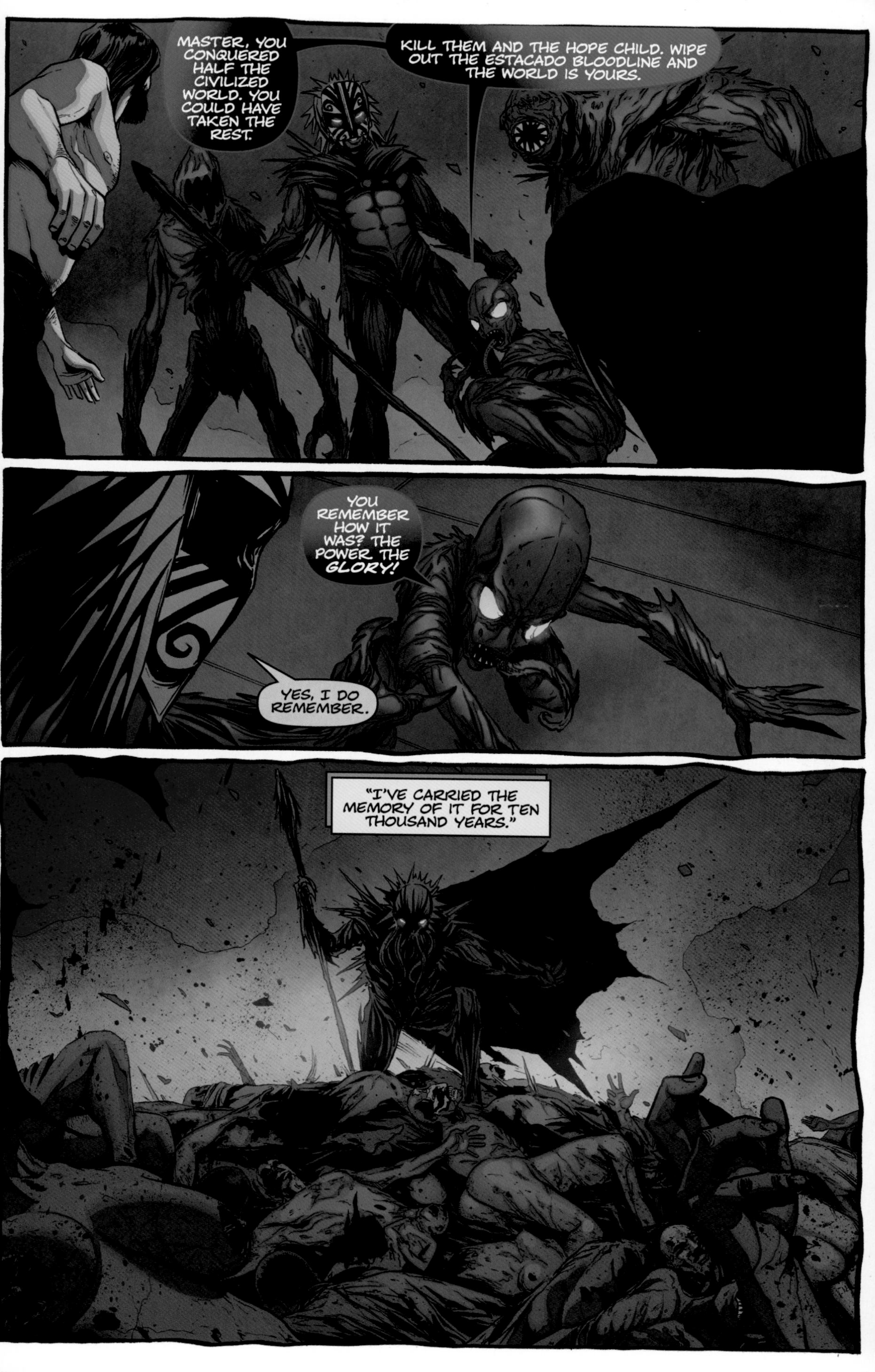
MASTER, YOU CONQUERED HALF THE CIVILIZED WORLD. YOU COULD HAVE TAKEN THE REST.
KILL THEM AND THE HOPE CHILD. WIPE OUT THE ESTACADO BLOODLINE AND THE WORLD IS YOURS.
YOU REMEMBER HOW IT WAS? THE POWER. THE GLORY!
YES, I DO REMEMBER.
"I'VE CARRIED THE MEMORY OF IT FOR TEN THOUSAND YEARS."

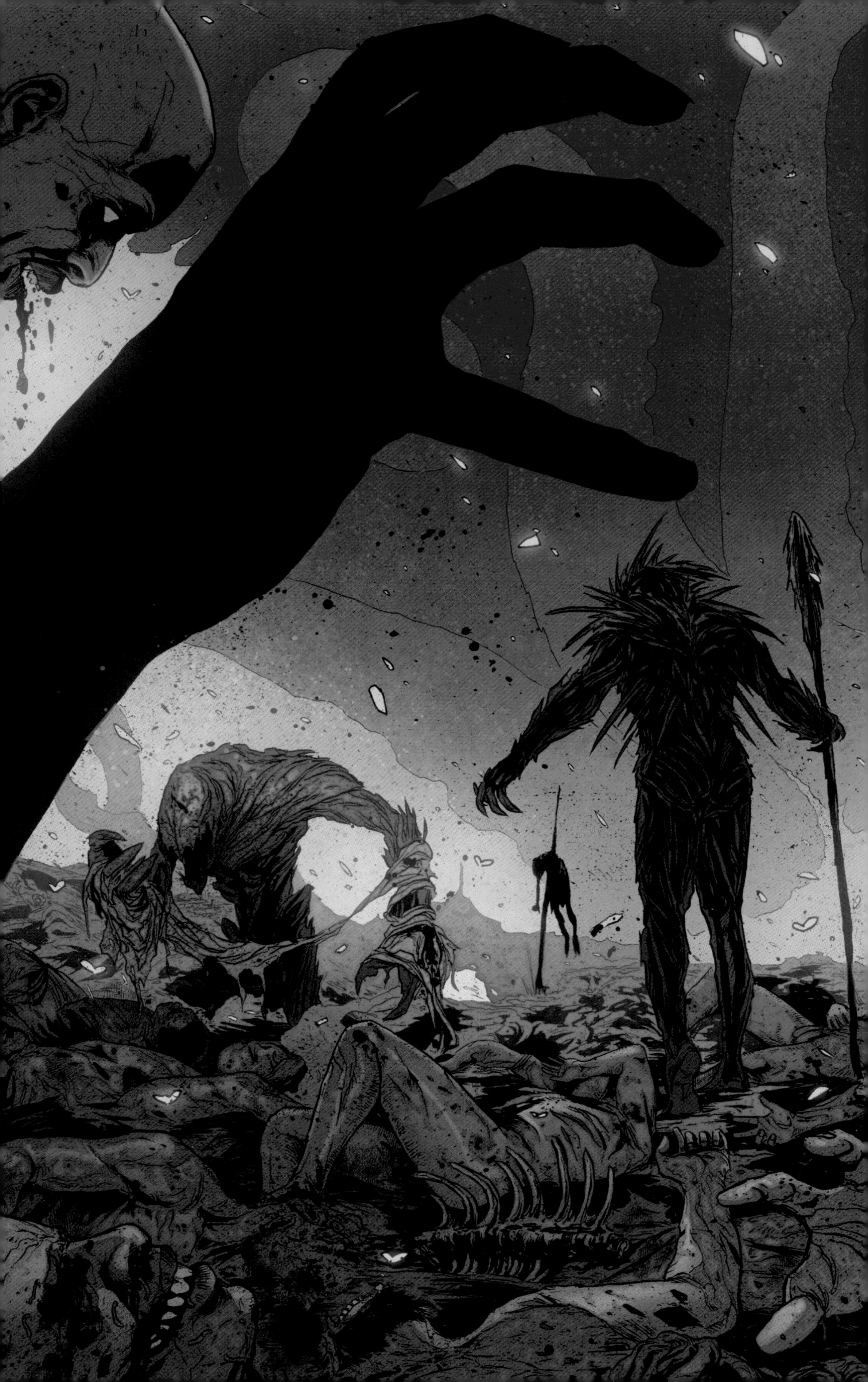

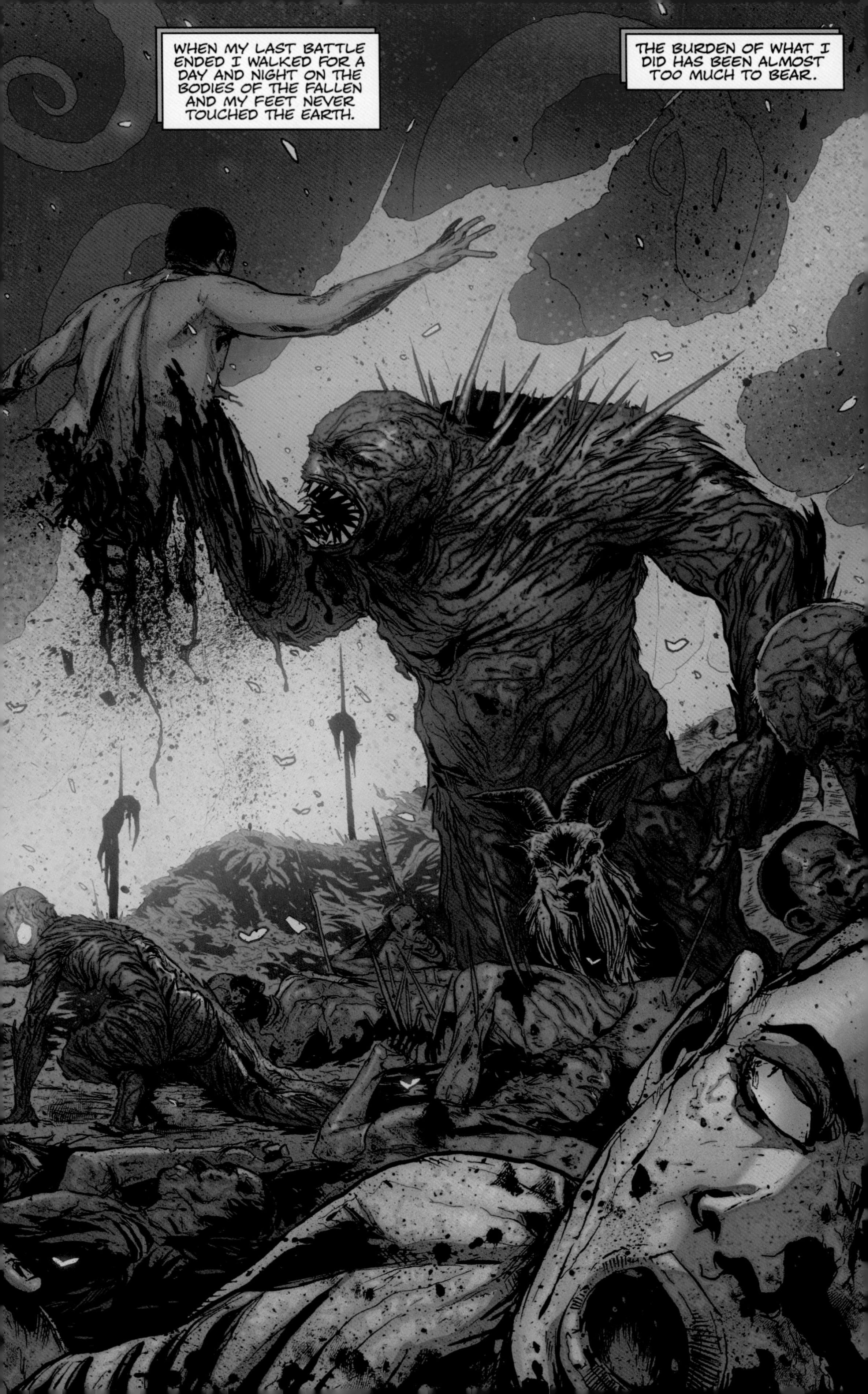
WHEN MY LAST BATTLE ENDED I WALKED FOR A DAY AND NIGHT ON THE BODIES OF THE FALLEN AND MY FEET NEVER TOUCHED THE EARTH.
THE BURDEN OF WHAT I DID HAS BEEN ALMOST TOO MUCH TO BEAR.

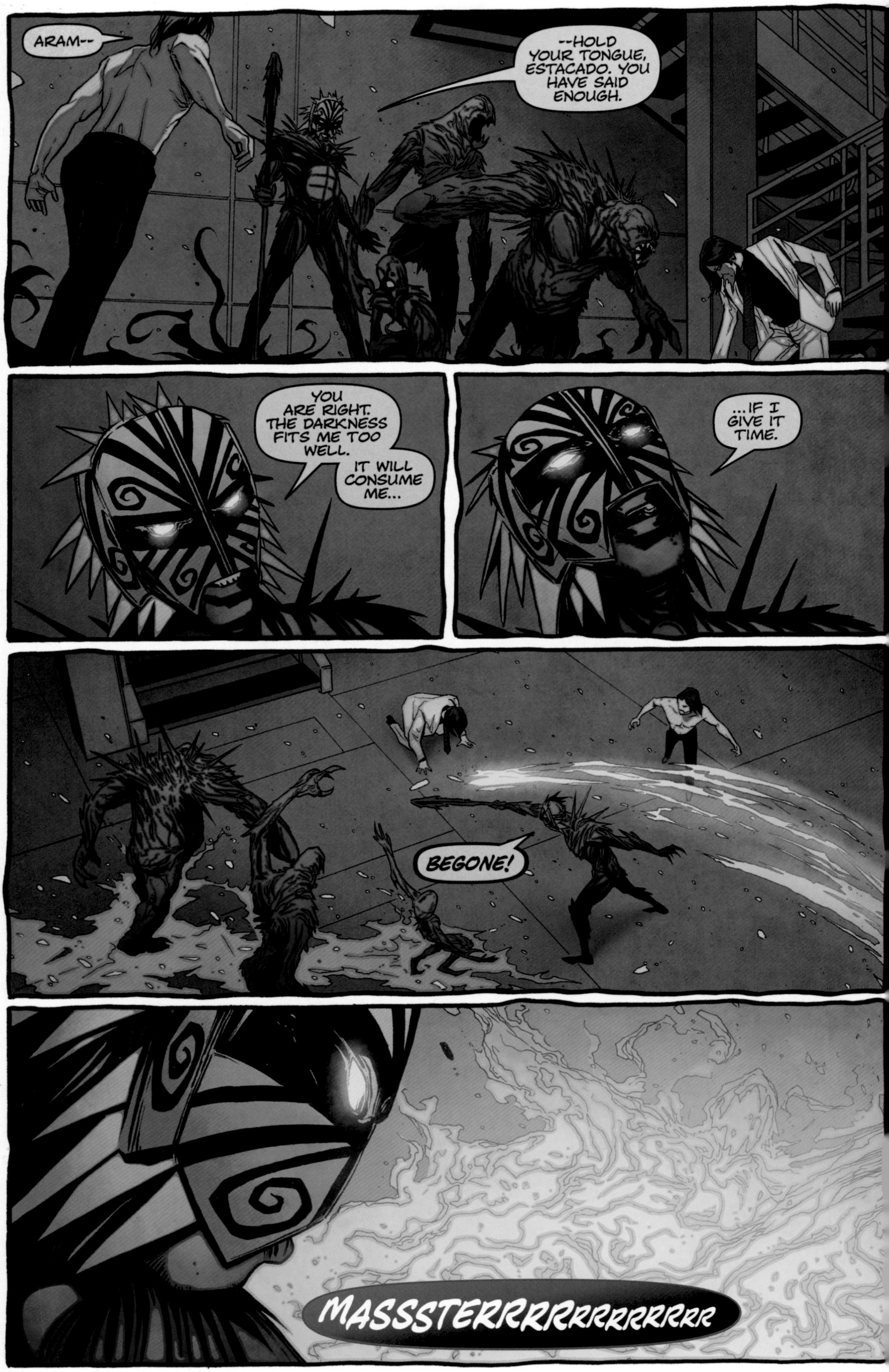
ARAM--
--HOLD YOUR TONGUE, ESTACADO. YOU HAVE SAID ENOUGH.
YOU ARE RIGHT. THE DARKNESS FITS ME TOO WELL.
IT WILL CONSUME ME...
...IF I GIVE IT TIME.
BEGONE!
MASSSTERRRRrrrrrrrr

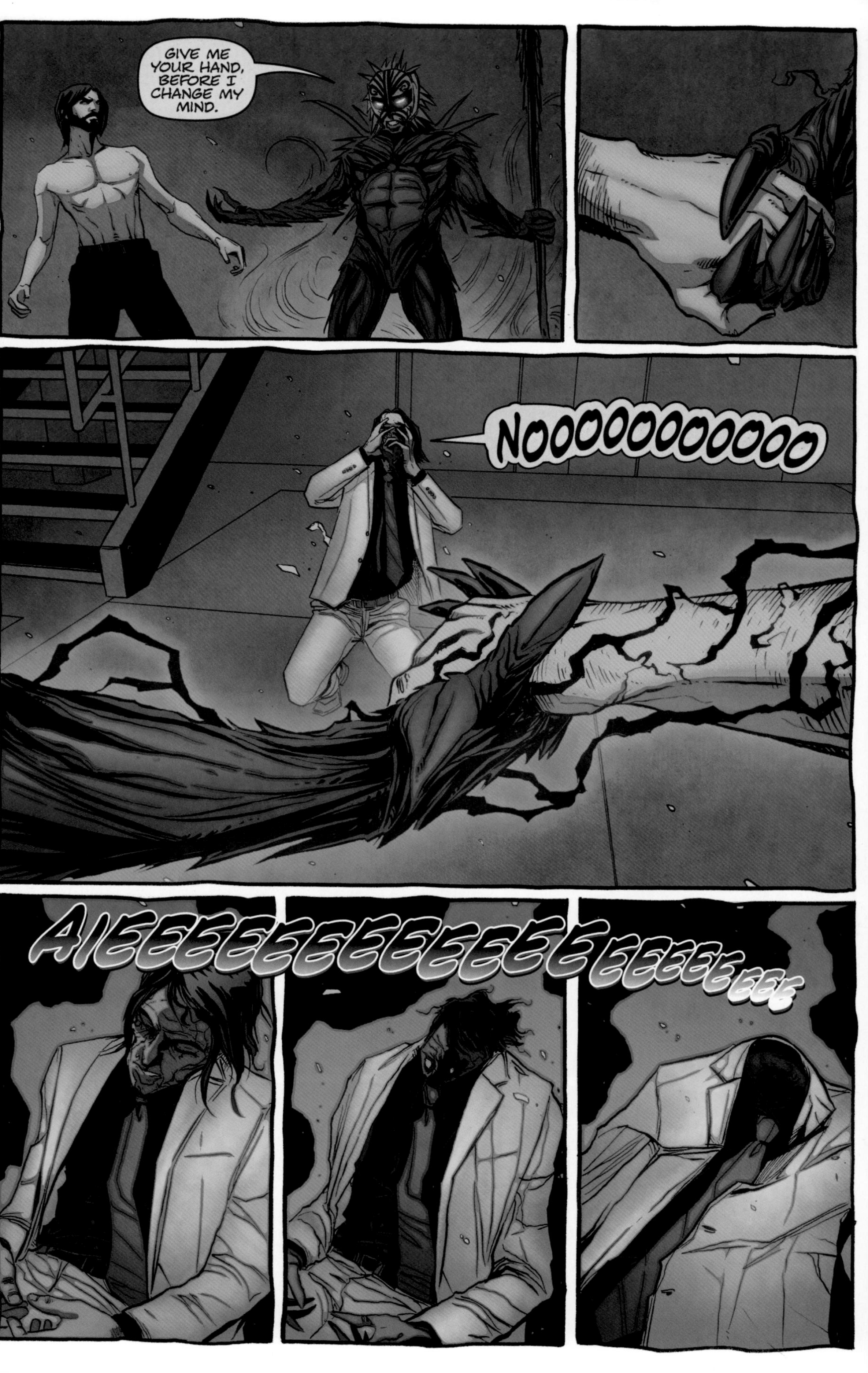
GIVE ME YOUR HAND, BEFORE I CHANGE MY MIND.
NOOOOOOOOOOO
AIEEEEEEEEEEEEEEEEEEEEEE

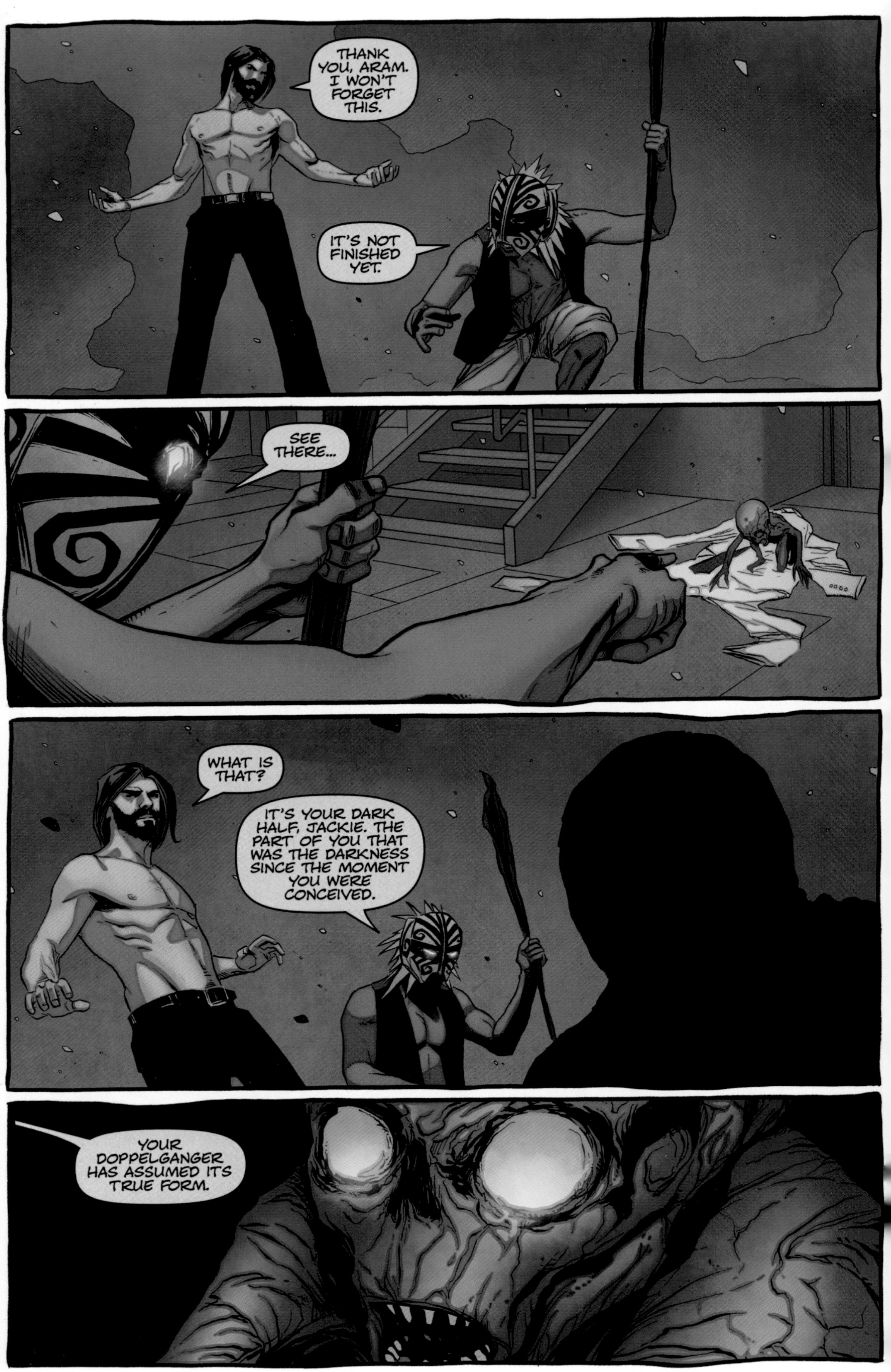
THANK YOU, ARAM. I WON'T FORGET THIS.
IT'S NOT FINISHED YET.
SEE THERE...
WHAT IS THAT?
IT'S YOUR DARK HALF, JACKIE. THE PART OF YOU THAT WAS THE DARKNESS SINCE THE MOMENT YOU WERE CONCEIVED.
YOUR DOPPELGANGER HAS ASSUMED ITS TRUE FORM.

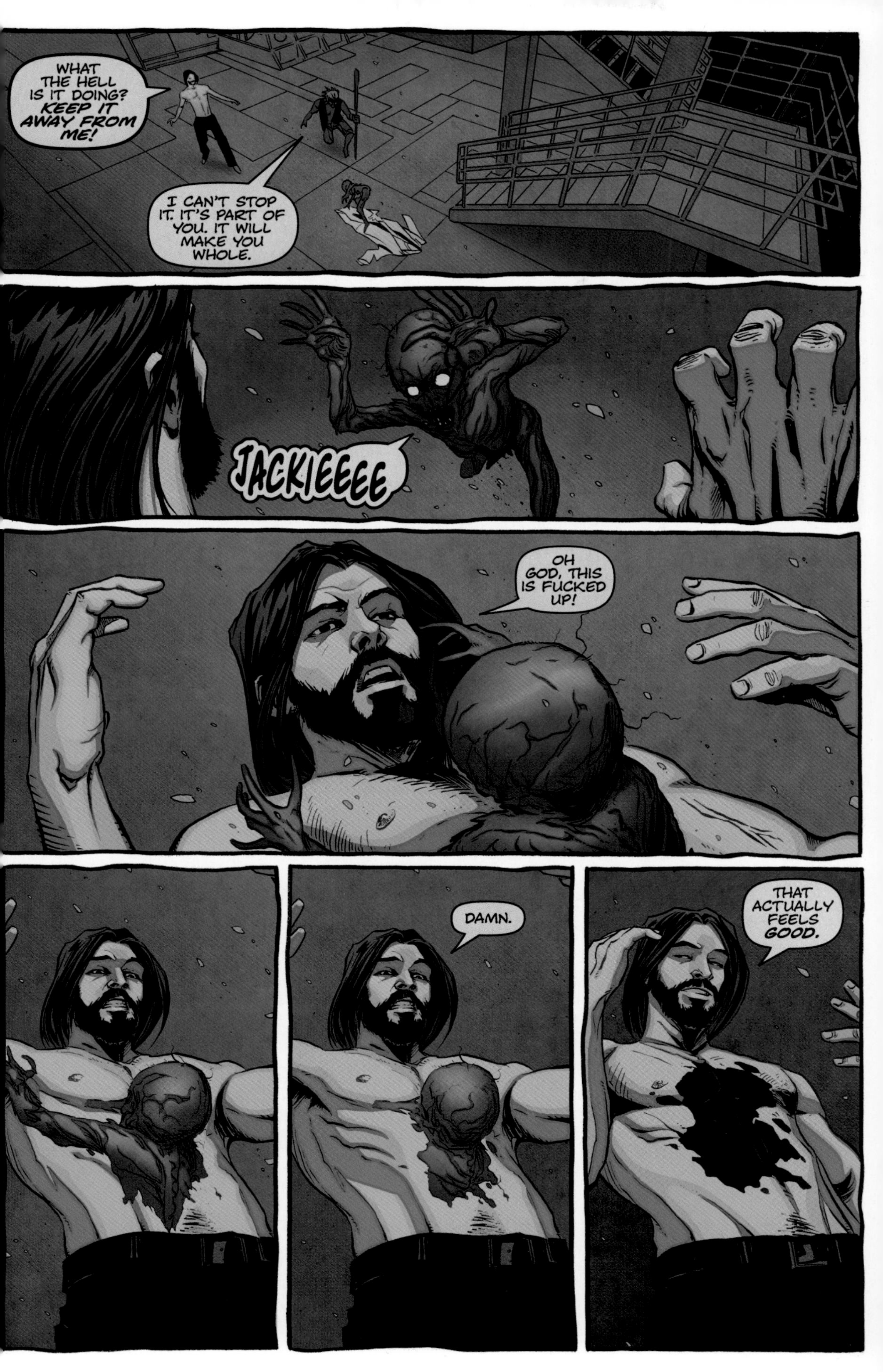
WHAT THE HELL IS IT DOING? KEEP IT AWAY FROM ME!
I CAN'T STOP IT. IT'S PART OF YOU. IT WILL MAKE YOU WHOLE.
JACKIEEEEE
OH GOD, THIS IS FUCKED UP!
DAMN.
THAT ACTUALLY FEELS GOOD.

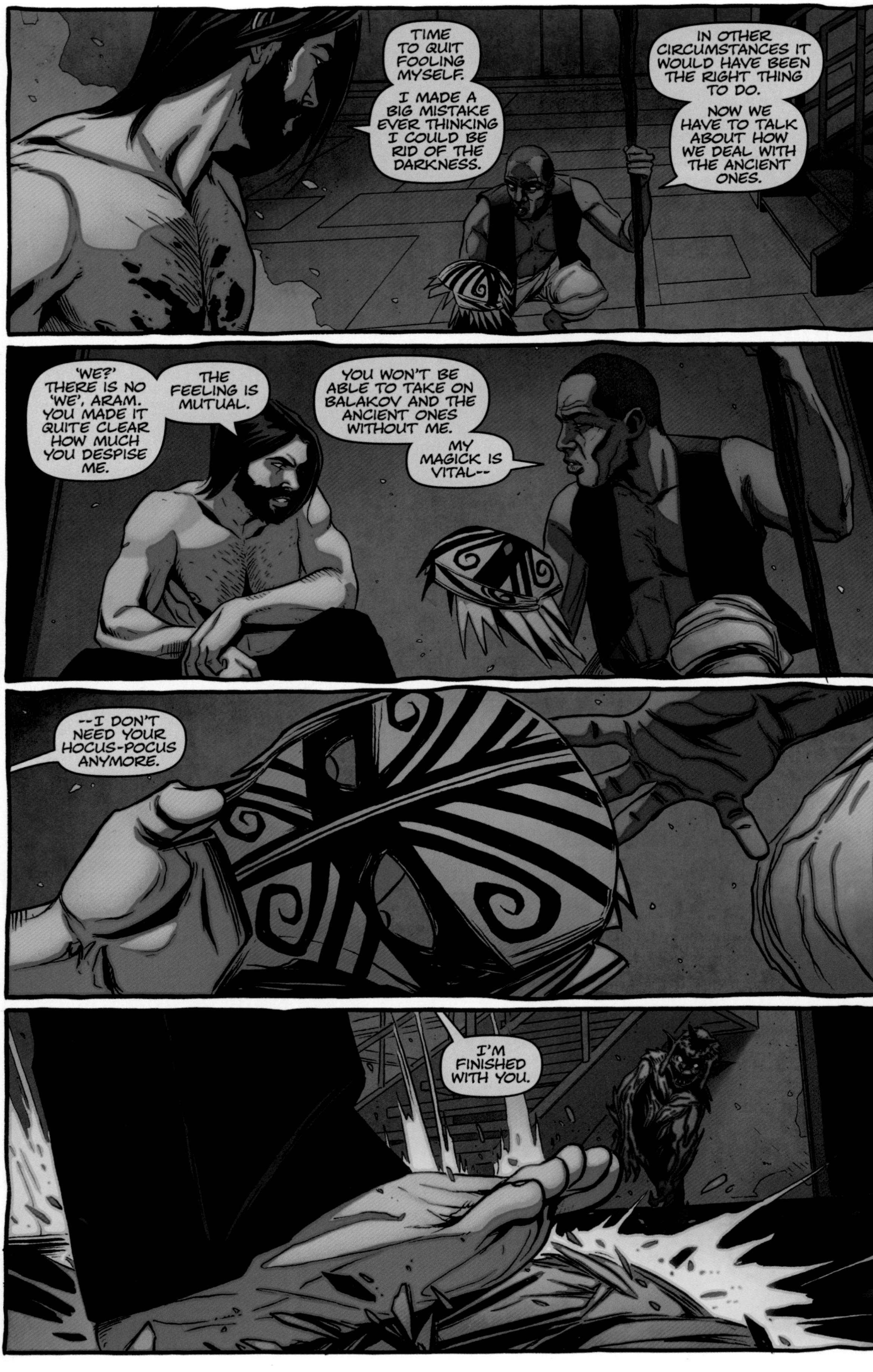
TIME TO QUIT FOOLING MYSELF.
I MADE A BIG MISTAKE EVER THINKING I COULD BE RID OF THE DARKNESS.
IN OTHER CIRCUMSTANCES IT WOULD HAVE BEEN THE RIGHT THING TO DO.
NOW WE HAVE TO TALK ABOUT HOW WE DEAL WITH THE ANCIENT ONES.
'WE?' THERE IS NO 'WE', ARAM. YOU MADE IT QUITE CLEAR HOW MUCH YOU DESPISE ME.
THE FEELING IS MUTUAL.
YOU WON'T BE ABLE TO TAKE ON BALAKOV AND THE ANCIENT ONES WITHOUT ME.
MY MAGICK IS VITAL--
--I DON'T NEED YOUR HOCUS-POCUS ANYMORE.
I'M FINISHED WITH YOU.

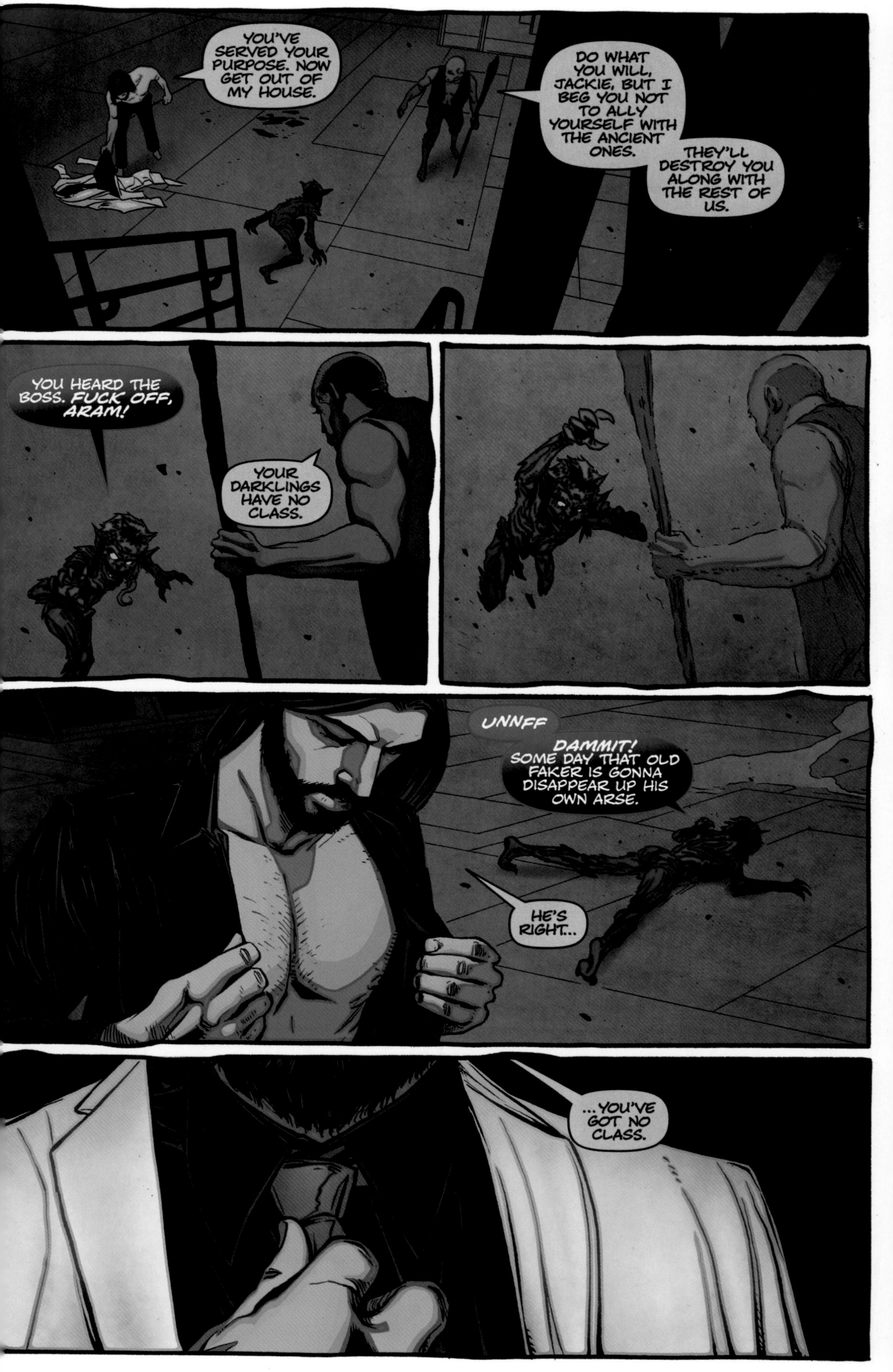
YOU'VE SERVED YOUR PURPOSE. NOW GET OUT OF MY HOUSE.
DO WHAT YOU WILL, JACKIE, BUT I BEG YOU NOT TO ALLY YOURSELF WITH THE ANCIENT ONES.
THEY'LL DESTROY YOU ALONG WITH THE REST OF US.
YOU HEARD THE BOSS. FUCK OFF, ARAM!
YOUR DARKLINGS HAVE NO CLASS.
UNNFF
DAMMIT! SOME DAY THAT OLD FAKER IS GONNA DISAPPEAR UP HIS OWN ARSE.
HE'S RIGHT...
...YOU'VE GOT NO CLASS.

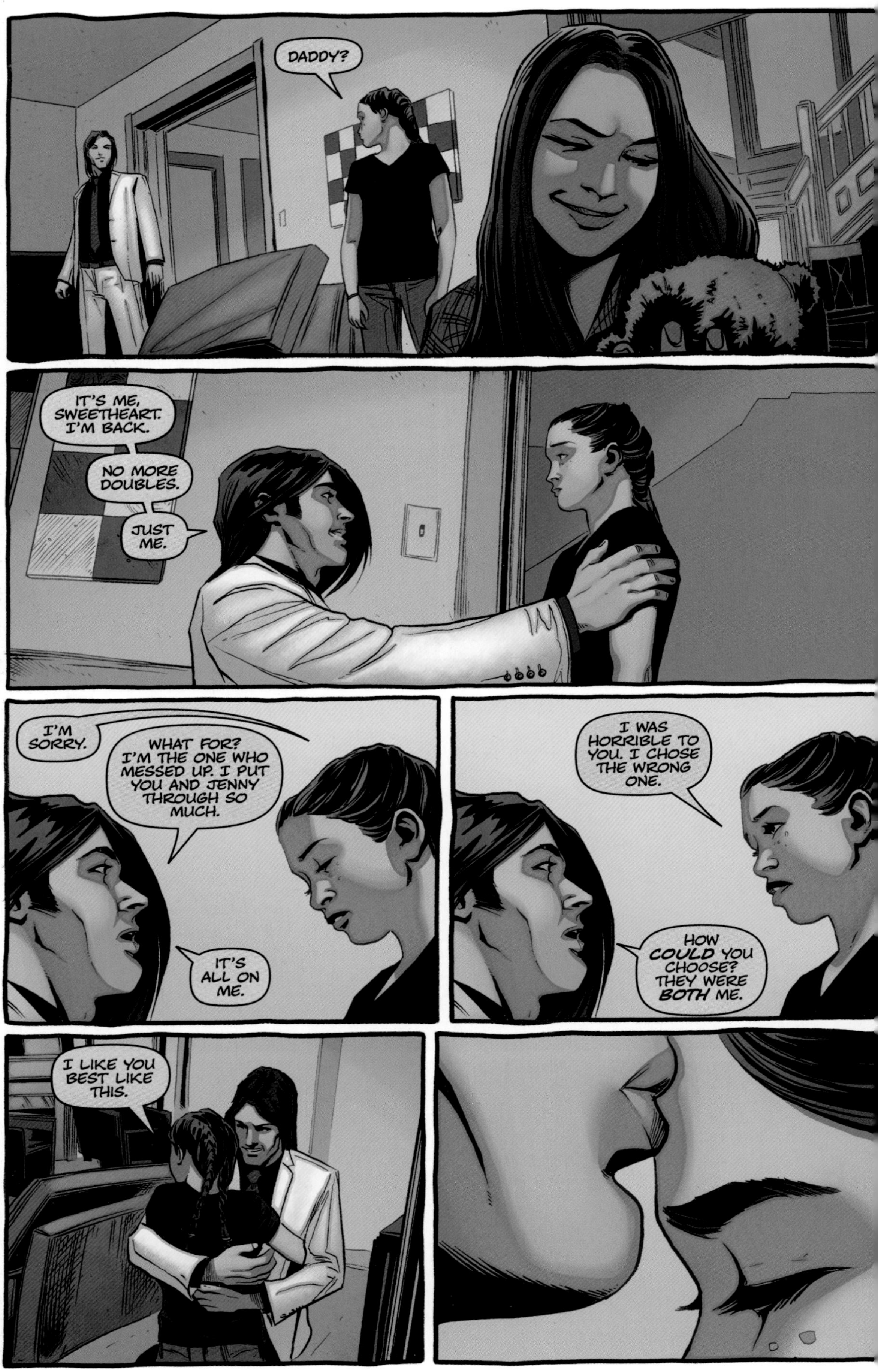
DADDY?
IT'S ME, SWEETHEART. I'M BACK.
NO MORE DOUBLES.
JUST ME.
I'M SORRY.
WHAT FOR? I'M THE ONE WHO MESSED UP. I PUT YOU AND JENNY THROUGH SO MUCH.
IT'S ALL ON ME.
I WAS HORRIBLE TO YOU. I CHOSE THE WRONG ONE.
HOW COULD YOU CHOOSE? THEY WERE BOTH ME.
I LIKE YOU BEST LIKE THIS.

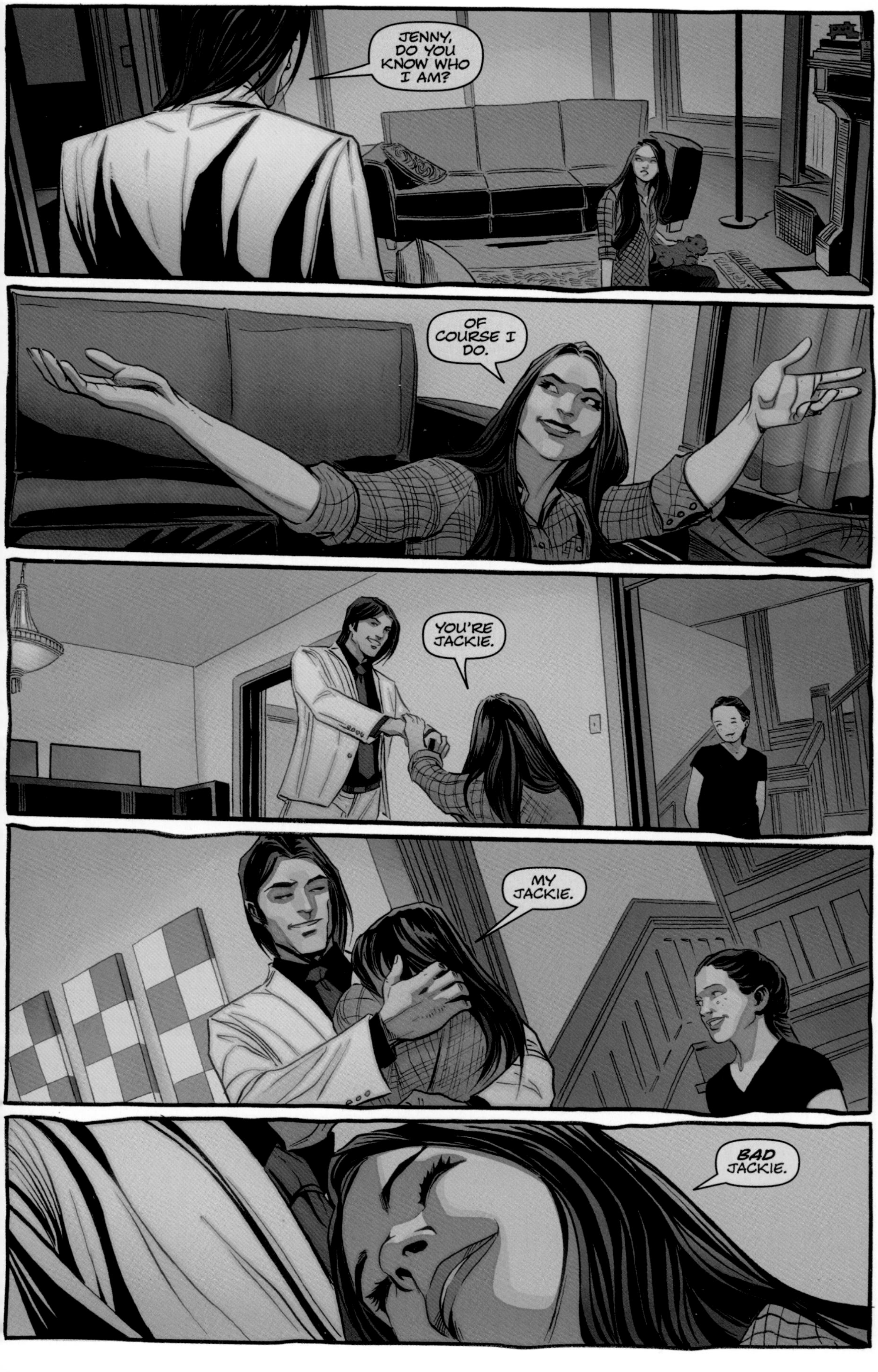
JENNY, DO YOU KNOW WHO I AM?
OF COURSE I DO.
YOU'RE JACKIE.
MY JACKIE.
BAD JACKIE.

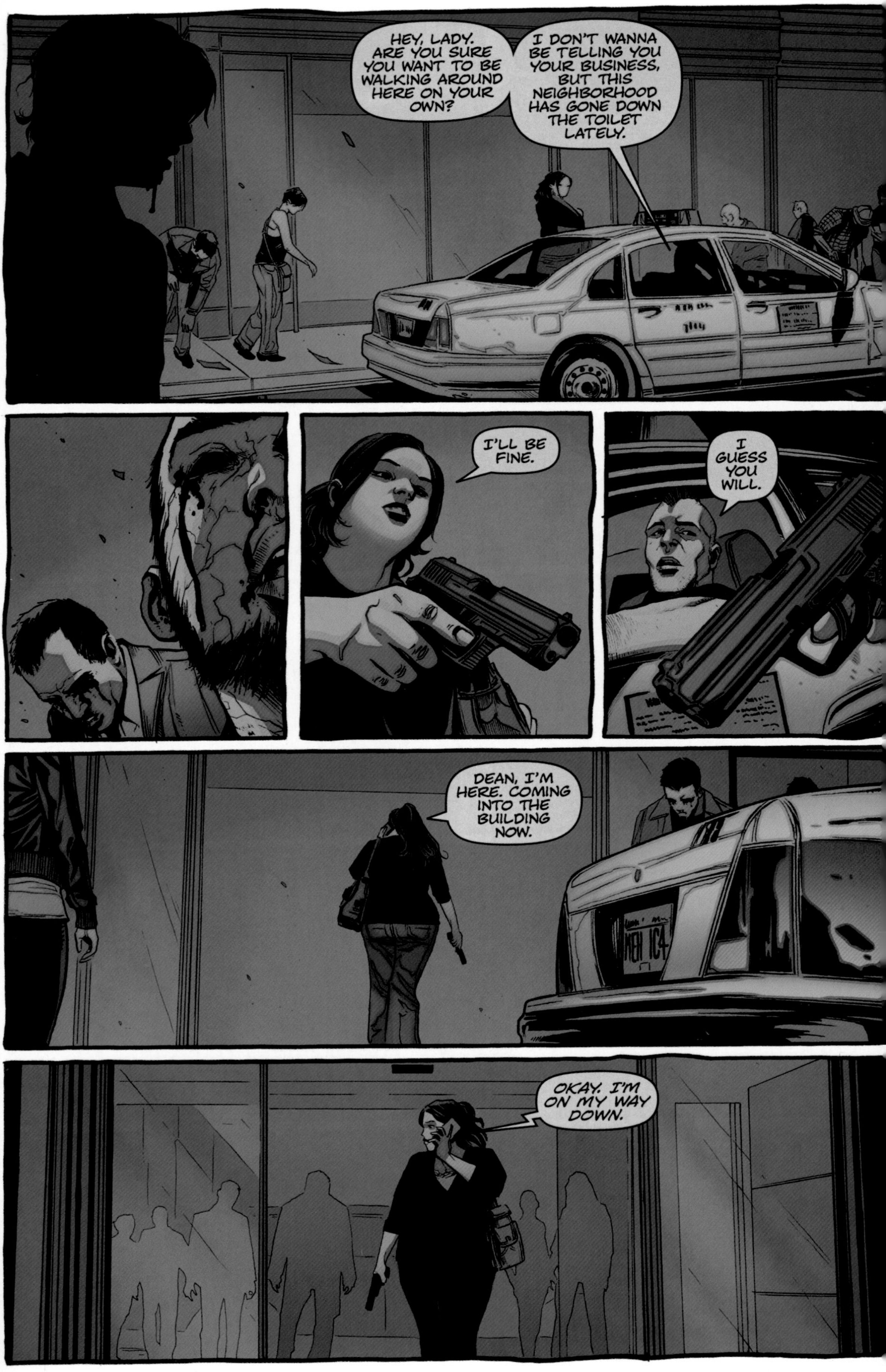
HEY, LADY. ARE YOU SURE YOU WANT TO BE WALKING AROUND HERE ON YOUR OWN?
I DON'T WANNA BE TELLING YOU YOUR BUSINESS, BUT THIS NEIGHBORHOOD HAS GONE DOWN THE TOILET LATELY.
I'LL BE FINE.
I GUESS YOU WILL.
DEAN, I'M HERE. COMING INTO THE BUILDING NOW.
OKAY. I'M ON MY WAY DOWN.

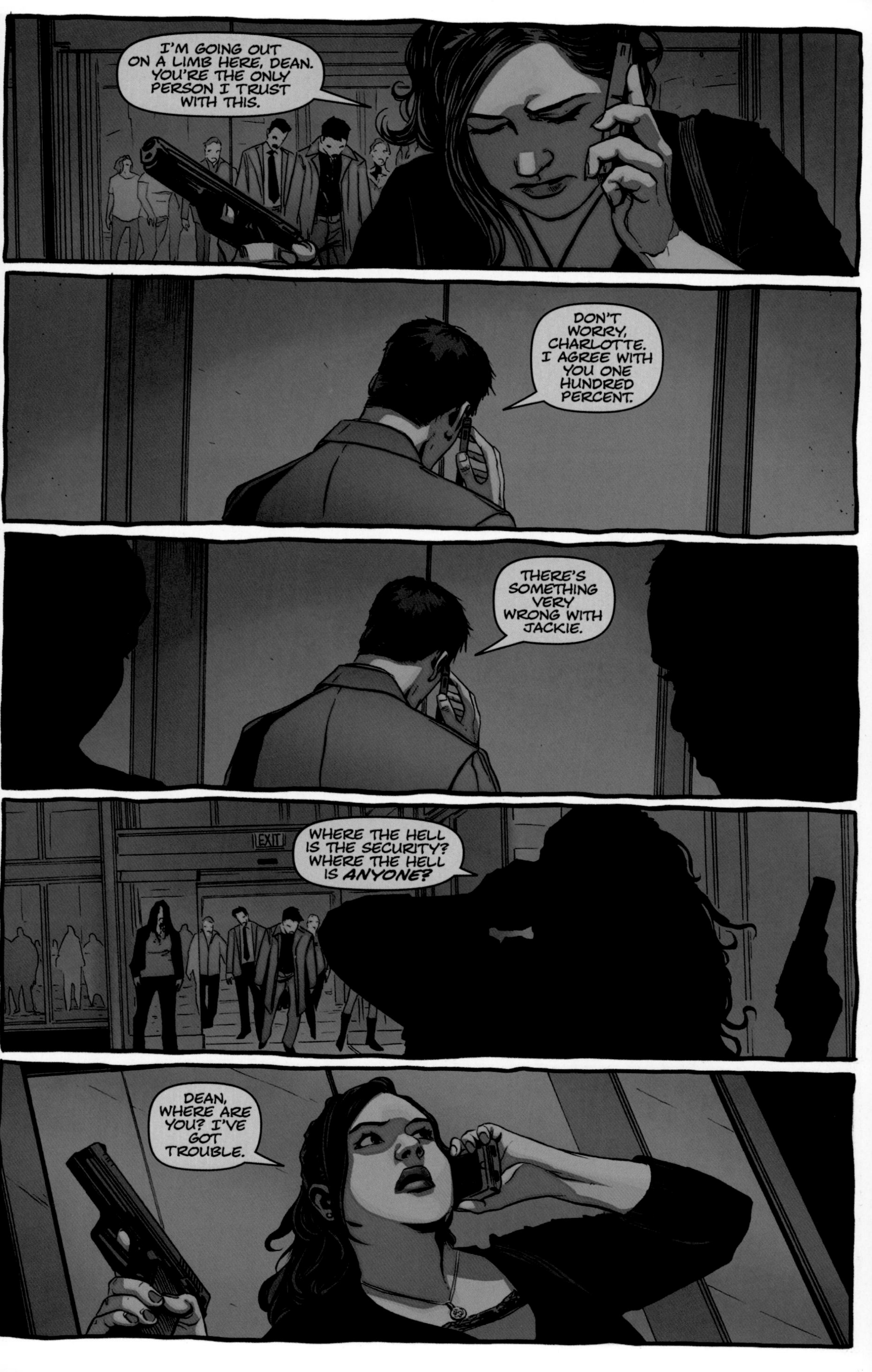

I'M GOING OUT ON A LIMB HERE, DEAN. YOU'RE THE ONLY PERSON I TRUST WITH THIS.
DON'T WORRY, CHARLOTTE. I AGREE WITH YOU ONE HUNDRED PERCENT.
THERE'S SOMETHING VERY WRONG WITH JACKIE.
EXIT
WHERE THE HELL IS THE SECURITY? WHERE THE HELL IS *ANYONE?*
DEAN, WHERE ARE YOU? I'VE GOT TROUBLE.

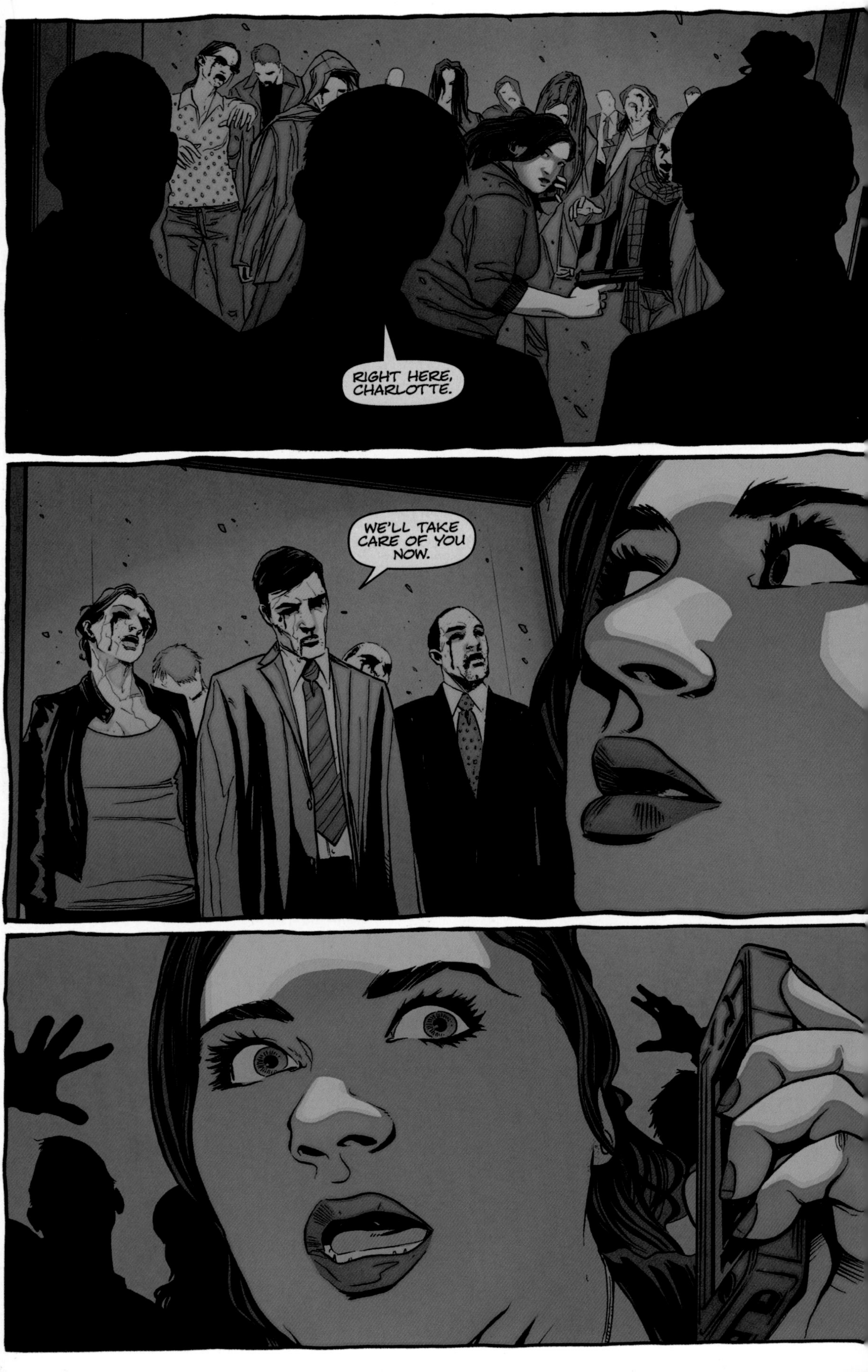
RIGHT HERE, CHARLOTTE.
WE'LL TAKE CARE OF YOU NOW.

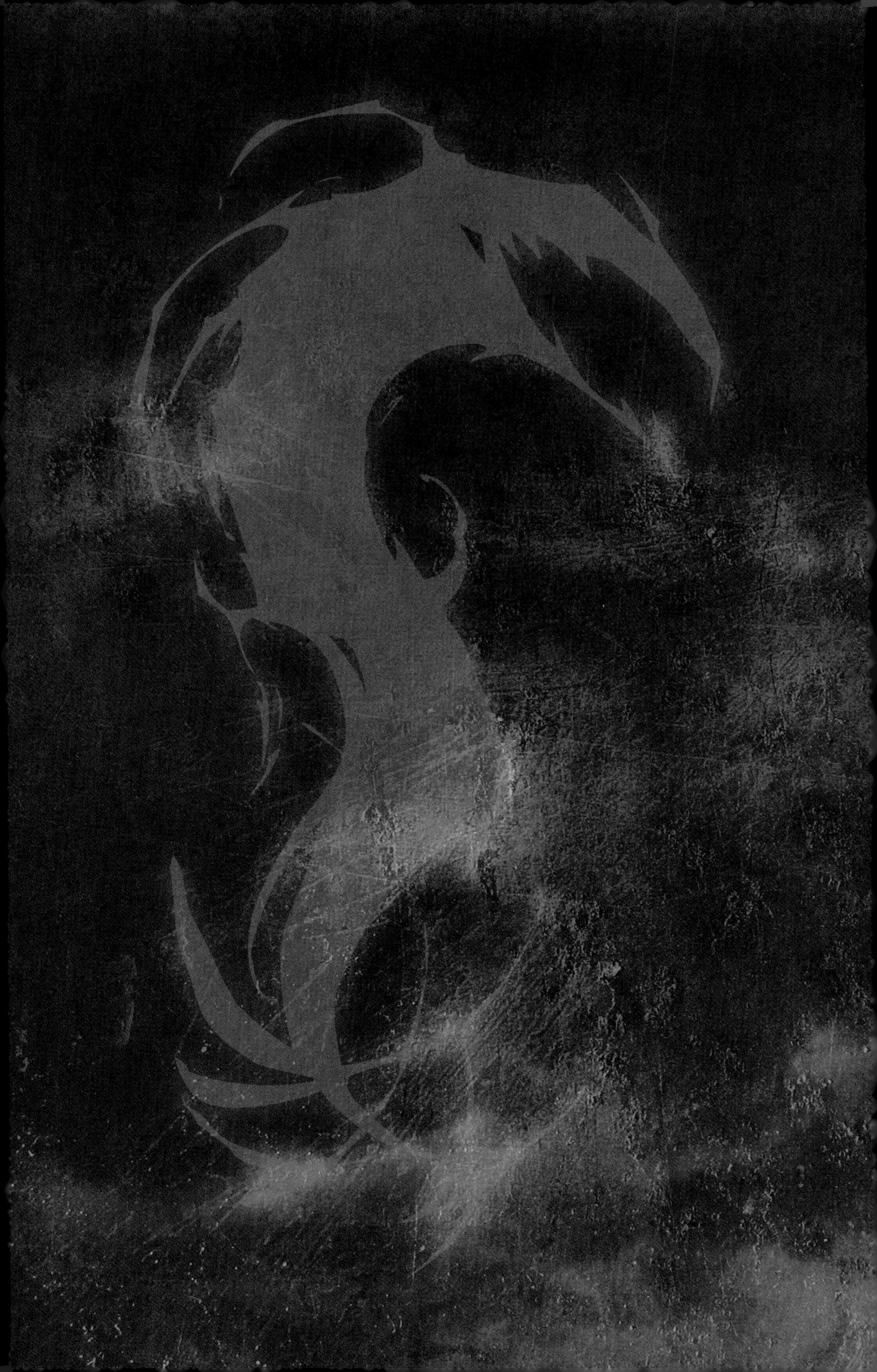

"THE AGE OF REASON"
PART
3

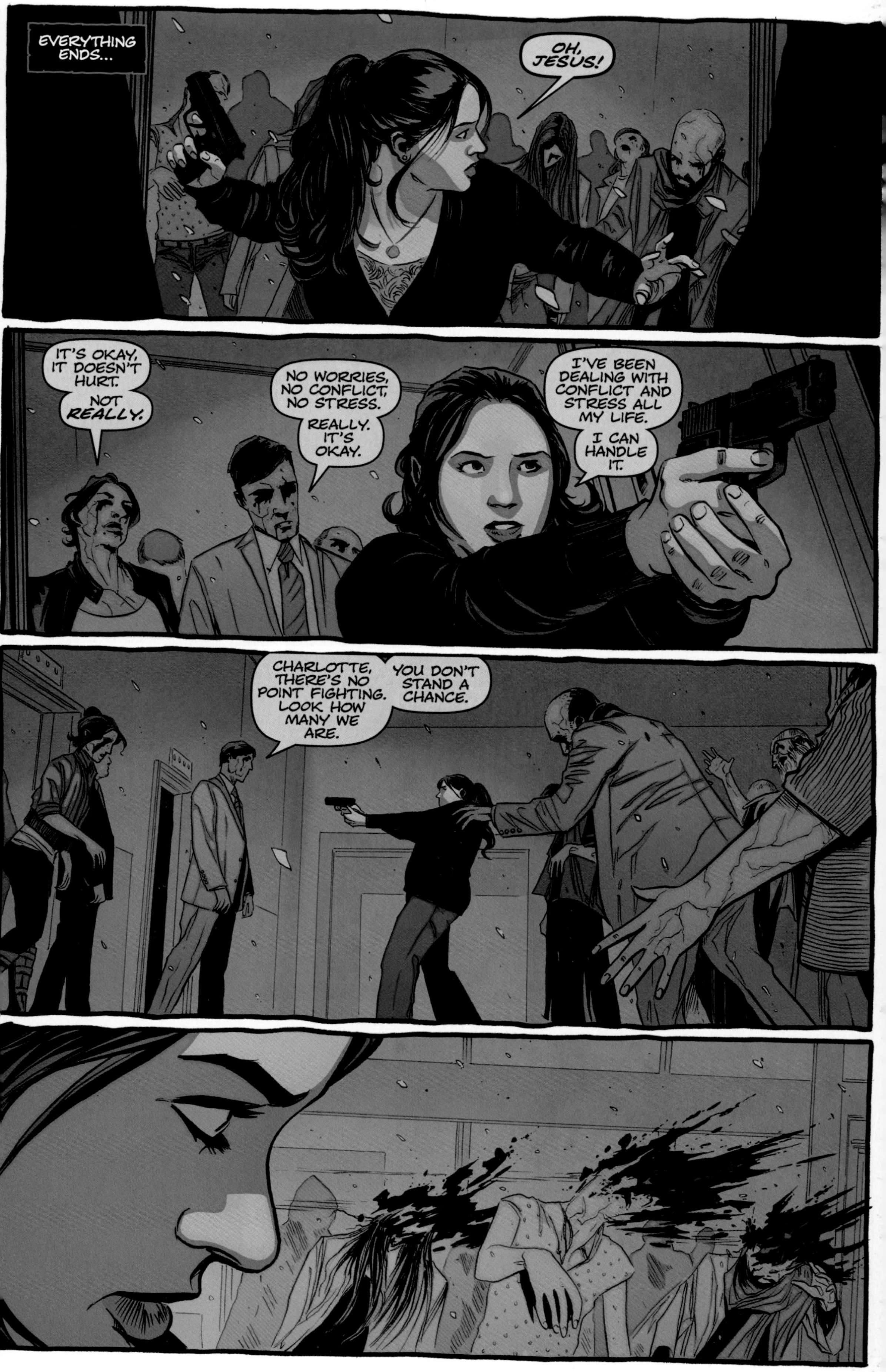
EVERYTHING ENDS...
OH, JESUS!
IT'S OKAY, IT DOESN'T HURT.
NOT REALLY.
NO WORRIES, NO CONFLICT, NO STRESS.
REALLY. IT'S OKAY.
I'VE BEEN DEALING WITH CONFLICT AND STRESS ALL MY LIFE.
I CAN HANDLE IT.
CHARLOTTE, THERE'S NO POINT FIGHTING. LOOK HOW MANY WE ARE.
YOU DON'T STAND A CHANCE.

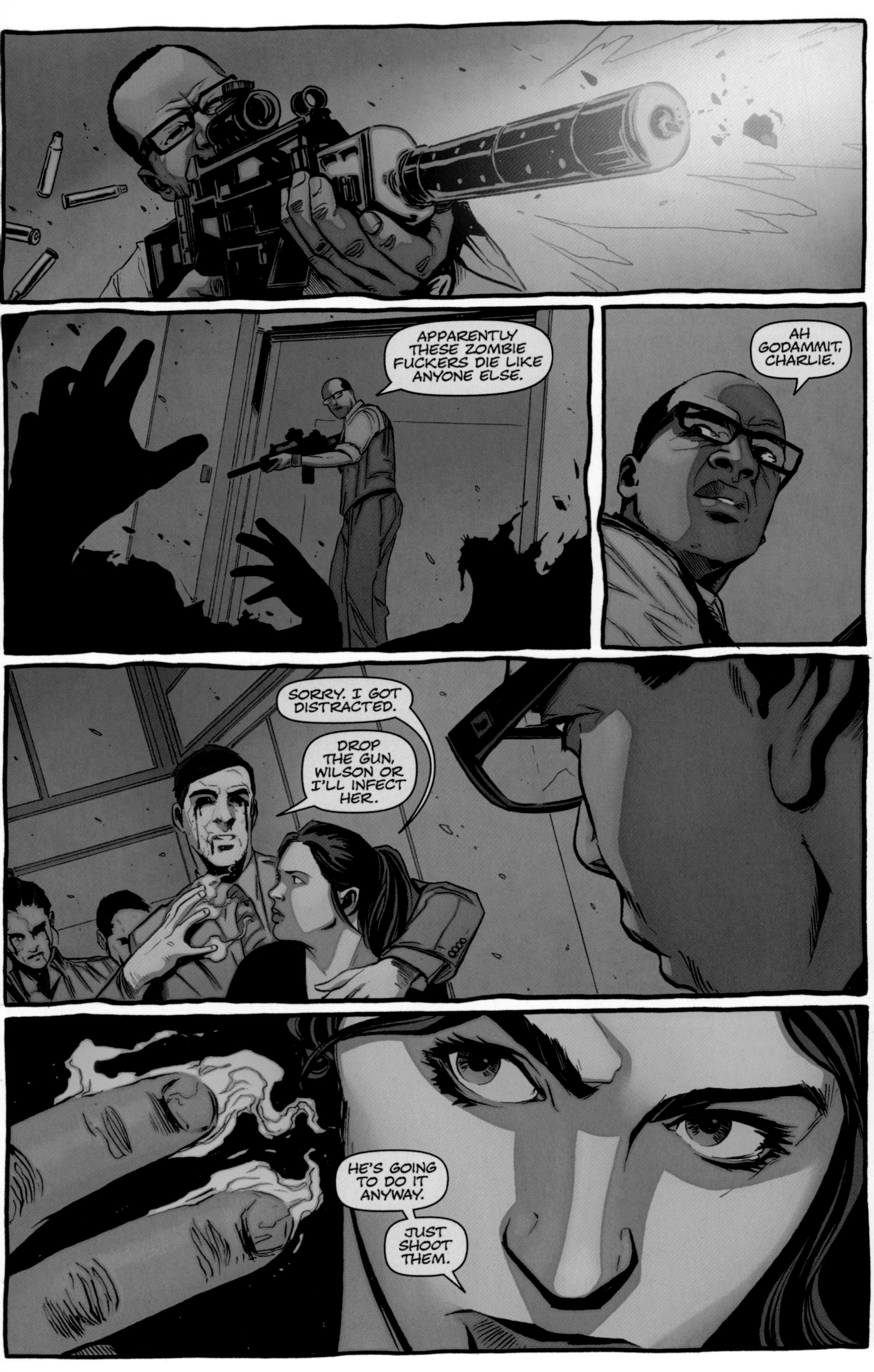
APPARENTLY THESE ZOMBIE FUCKERS DIE LIKE ANYONE ELSE.
AH GODAMMIT, CHARLIE.
SORRY. I GOT DISTRACTED.
DROP THE GUN, WILSON OR I'LL INFECT HER.
HE'S GOING TO DO IT ANYWAY.
JUST SHOOT THEM.

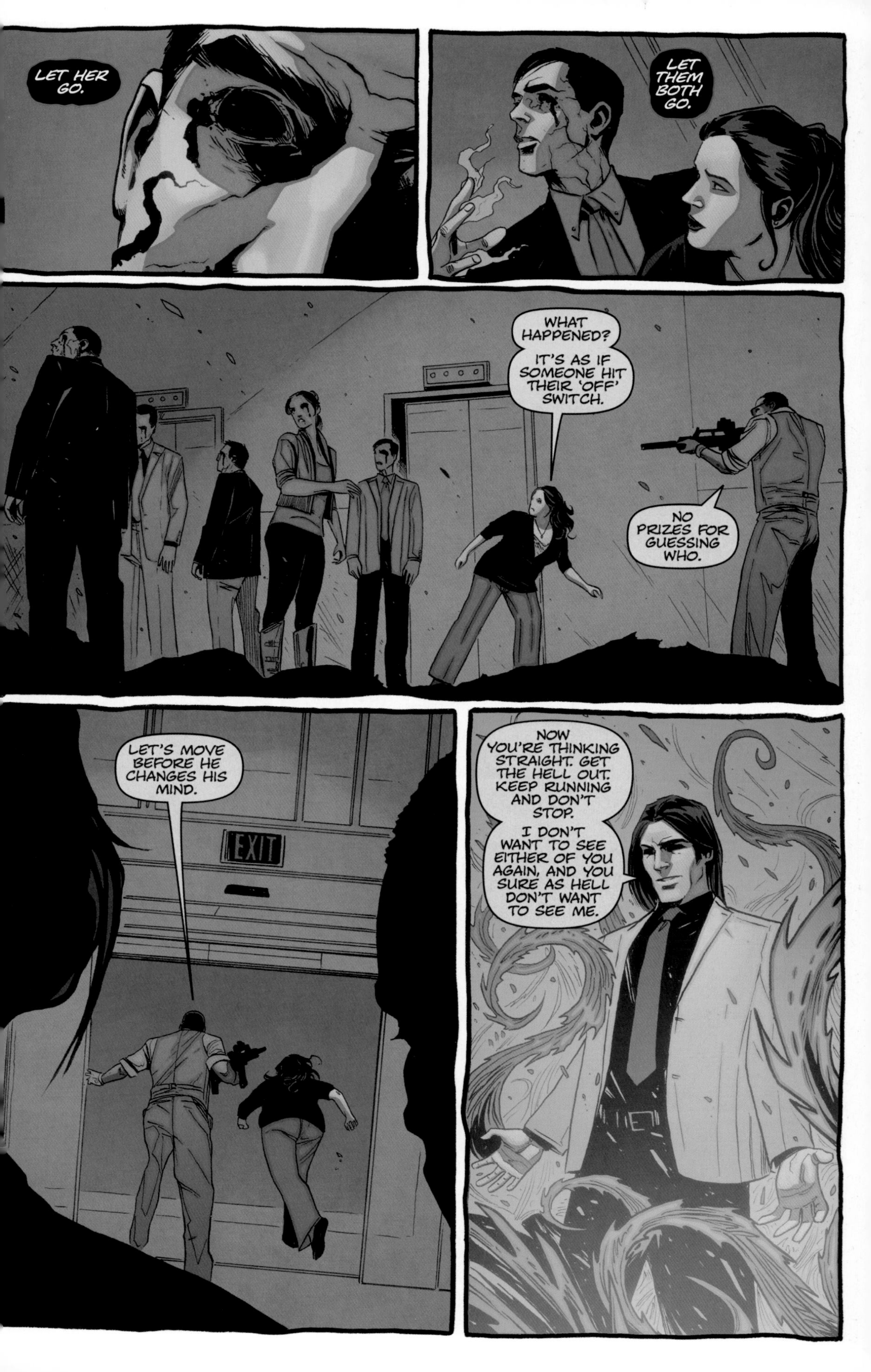
LET HER GO.
LET THEM BOTH GO.
WHAT HAPPENED?
IT'S AS IF SOMEONE HIT THEIR 'OFF' SWITCH.
NO PRIZES FOR GUESSING WHO.
LET'S MOVE BEFORE HE CHANGES HIS MIND.
NOW YOU'RE THINKING STRAIGHT. GET THE HELL OUT. KEEP RUNNING AND DON'T STOP.
I DON'T WANT TO SEE EITHER OF YOU AGAIN, AND YOU SURE AS HELL DON'T WANT TO SEE ME.
EXIT

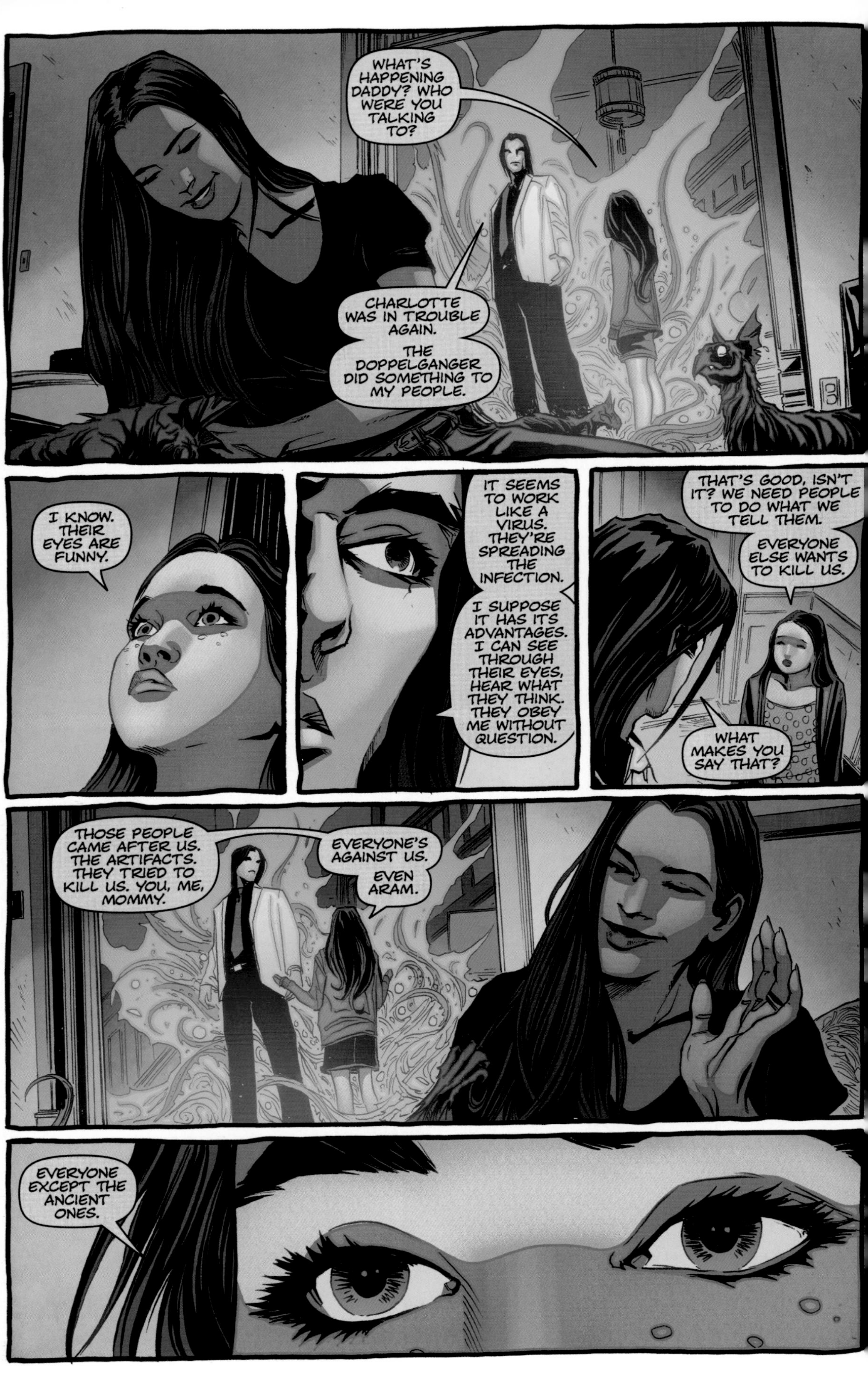
WHAT'S HAPPENING DADDY? WHO WERE YOU TALKING TO?
CHARLOTTE WAS IN TROUBLE AGAIN.
THE DOPPELGANGER DID SOMETHING TO MY PEOPLE.
I KNOW. THEIR EYES ARE FUNNY.
IT SEEMS TO WORK LIKE A VIRUS. THEY'RE SPREADING THE INFECTION.
I SUPPOSE IT HAS ITS ADVANTAGES. I CAN SEE THROUGH THEIR EYES, HEAR WHAT THEY THINK. THEY OBEY ME WITHOUT QUESTION.
THAT'S GOOD, ISN'T IT? WE NEED PEOPLE TO DO WHAT WE TELL THEM.
EVERYONE ELSE WANTS TO KILL US.
WHAT MAKES YOU SAY THAT?
THOSE PEOPLE CAME AFTER US. THE ARTIFACTS. THEY TRIED TO KILL US. YOU, ME, MOMMY.
EVERYONE'S AGAINST US.
EVEN ARAM.
EVERYONE EXCEPT THE ANCIENT ONES.

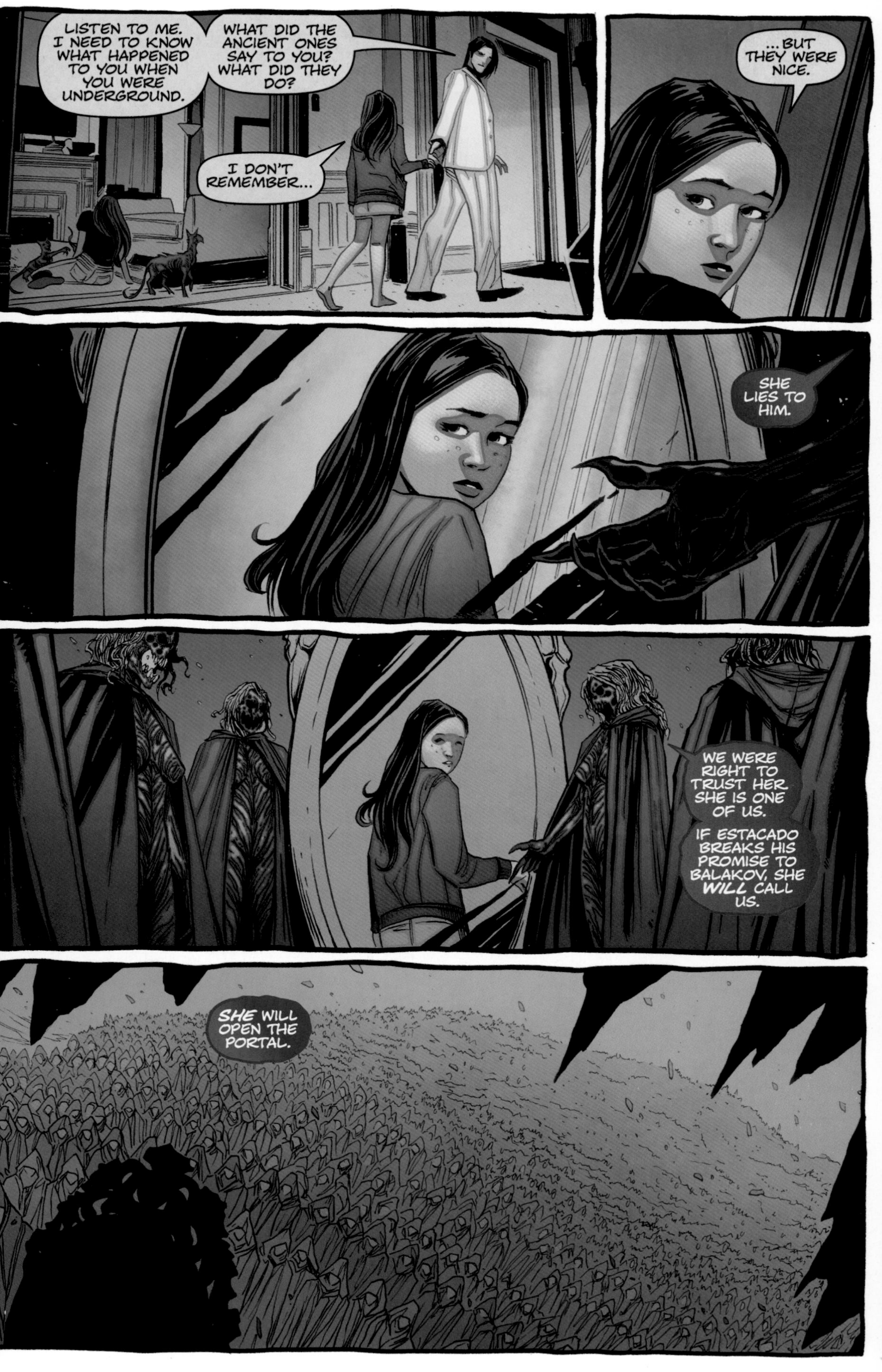
LISTEN TO ME. I NEED TO KNOW WHAT HAPPENED TO YOU WHEN YOU WERE UNDERGROUND.
WHAT DID THE ANCIENT ONES SAY TO YOU? WHAT DID THEY DO?
I DON'T REMEMBER...
...BUT THEY WERE NICE.
SHE LIES TO HIM.
WE WERE RIGHT TO TRUST HER SHE IS ONE OF US.
IF ESTACADO BREAKS HIS PROMISE TO BALAKOV, SHE WILL CALL US.
SHE WILL OPEN THE PORTAL.

YOU WANT TO TELL ME WHY YOU WERE THERE? I HEARD JACKIE FIRED YOU. IF YOU HAD ANY SENSE YOU'D BE A THOUSAND MILES FROM HERE.

SO WOULD YOU. WE BOTH KNOW SOMETHING HAS HAPPENED TO JACKIE THESE PAST FEW WEEKS. YOU SAW DEAN AND THE OTHERS.

I'M GUESSING WE BOTH HAVE THE SAME REASON FOR STICKING AROUND.

MISPLACED LOYALTY?

NOT ANY MORE. WHAT JACKIE IS DOING HAS NOTHING TO DO WITH TURF WARS. AT LEAST, NOT THE KIND WE'RE USED TO.

IT'S NOT ABOUT RIVAL MOBS. I HAVE A FEELING THIS IS...

BIGGER?

A LOT BIGGER.

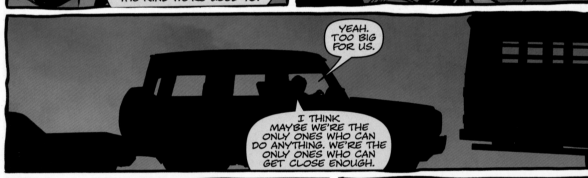

YEAH. TOO BIG FOR US.

I THINK MAYBE WE'RE THE ONLY ONES WHO CAN DO ANYTHING. WE'RE THE ONLY ONES WHO CAN GET CLOSE ENOUGH.

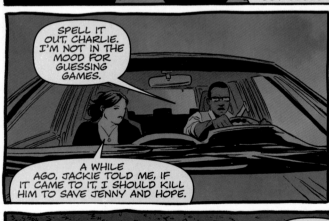

SPELL IT OUT, CHARLIE. I'M NOT IN THE MOOD FOR GUESSING GAMES.

A WHILE AGO, JACKIE TOLD ME, IF IT CAME TO IT, I SHOULD KILL HIM TO SAVE JENNY AND HOPE.

KILL HIM? HE SAID THAT?

YES.

THEN WE'RE ALL AGREED.

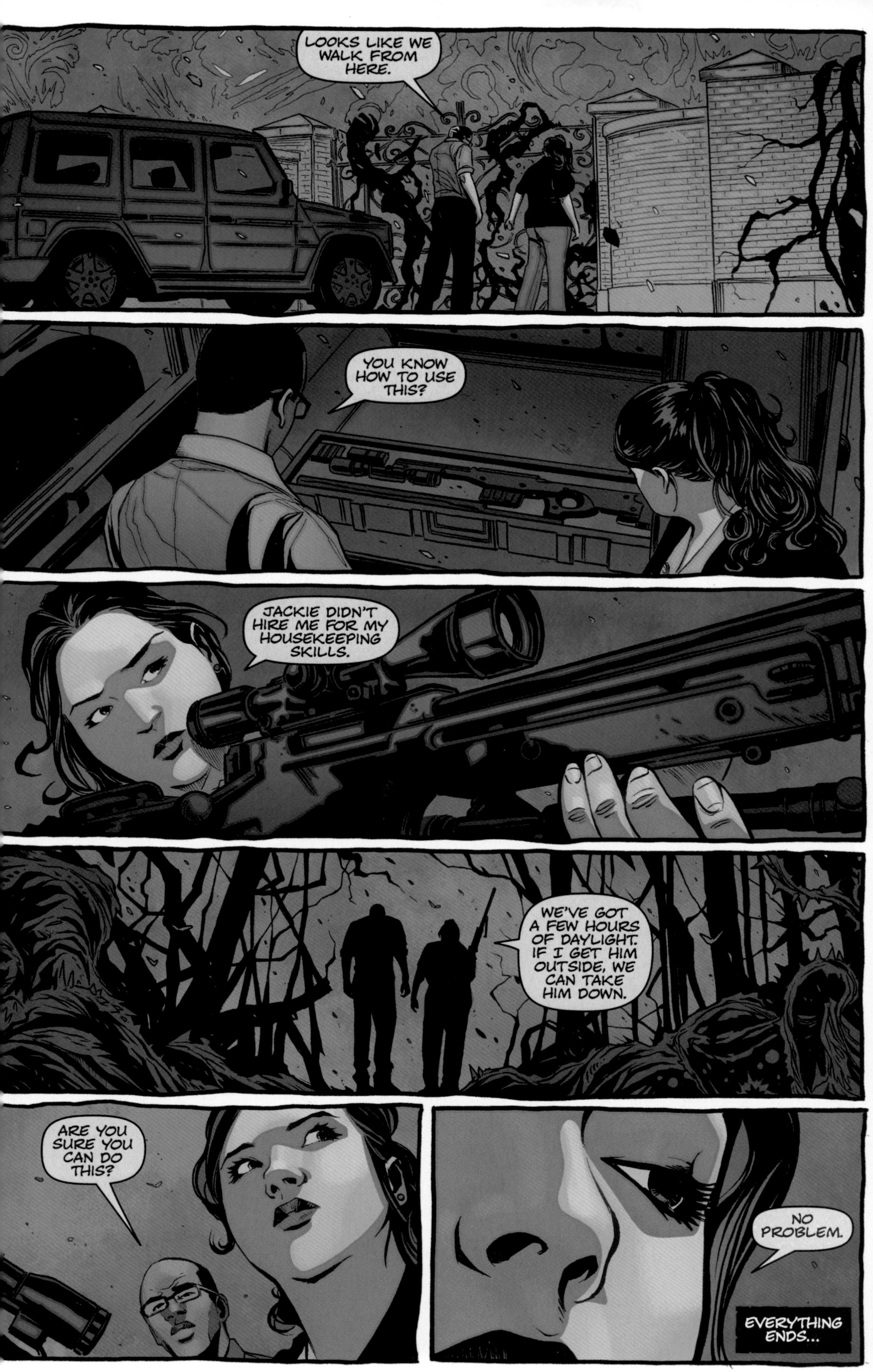
LOOKS LIKE WE WALK FROM HERE.
YOU KNOW HOW TO USE THIS?
JACKIE DIDN'T HIRE ME FOR MY HOUSEKEEPING SKILLS.
WE'VE GOT A FEW HOURS OF DAYLIGHT. IF I GET HIM OUTSIDE, WE CAN TAKE HIM DOWN.
ARE YOU SURE YOU CAN DO THIS?
NO PROBLEM.
EVERYTHING ENDS...

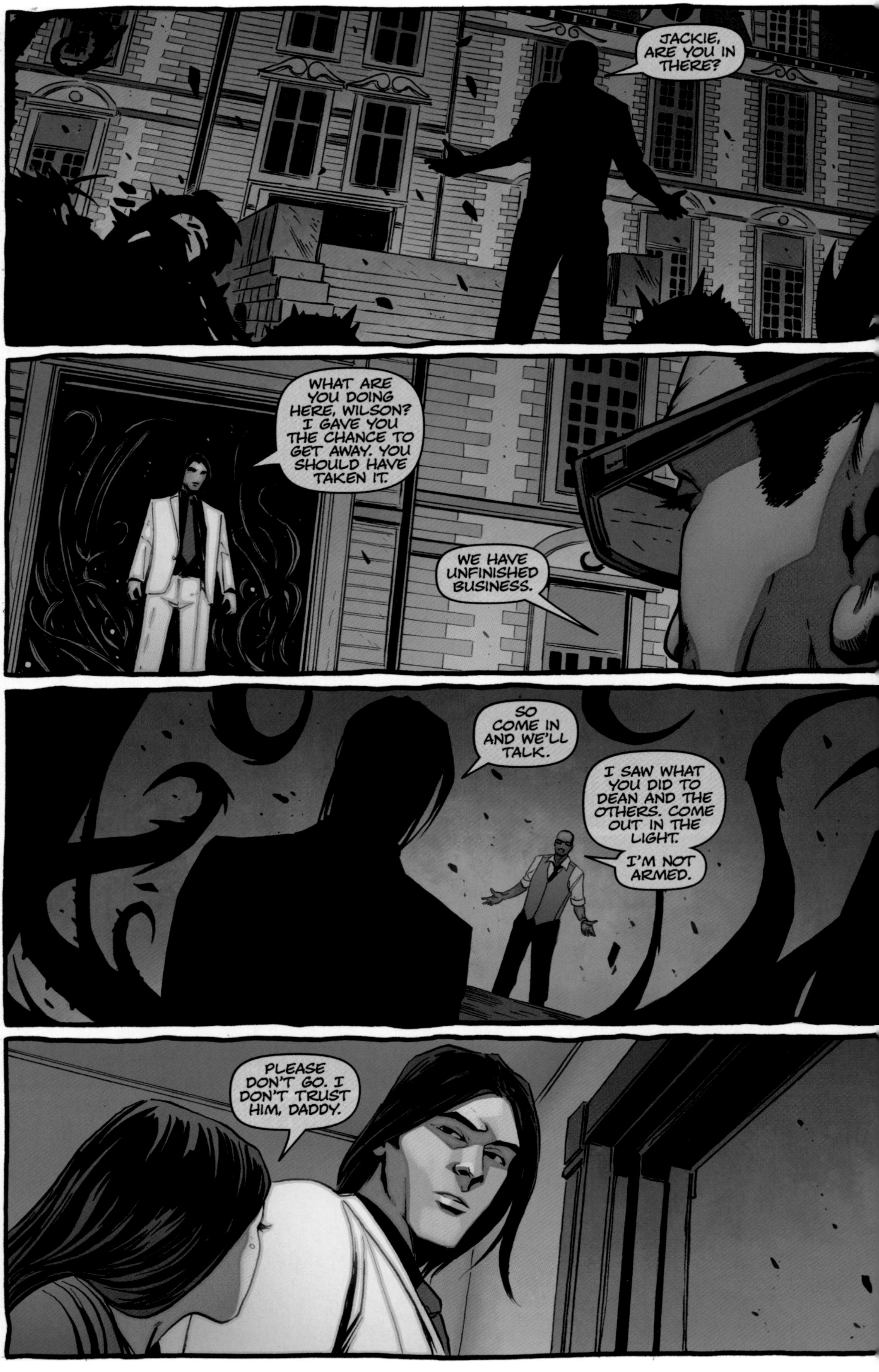
JACKIE, ARE YOU IN THERE?
WHAT ARE YOU DOING HERE, WILSON? I GAVE YOU THE CHANCE TO GET AWAY. YOU SHOULD HAVE TAKEN IT.
WE HAVE UNFINISHED BUSINESS.
SO COME IN AND WE'LL TALK.
I SAW WHAT YOU DID TO DEAN AND THE OTHERS. COME OUT IN THE LIGHT.
I'M NOT ARMED.
PLEASE DON'T GO. I DON'T TRUST HIM, DADDY.

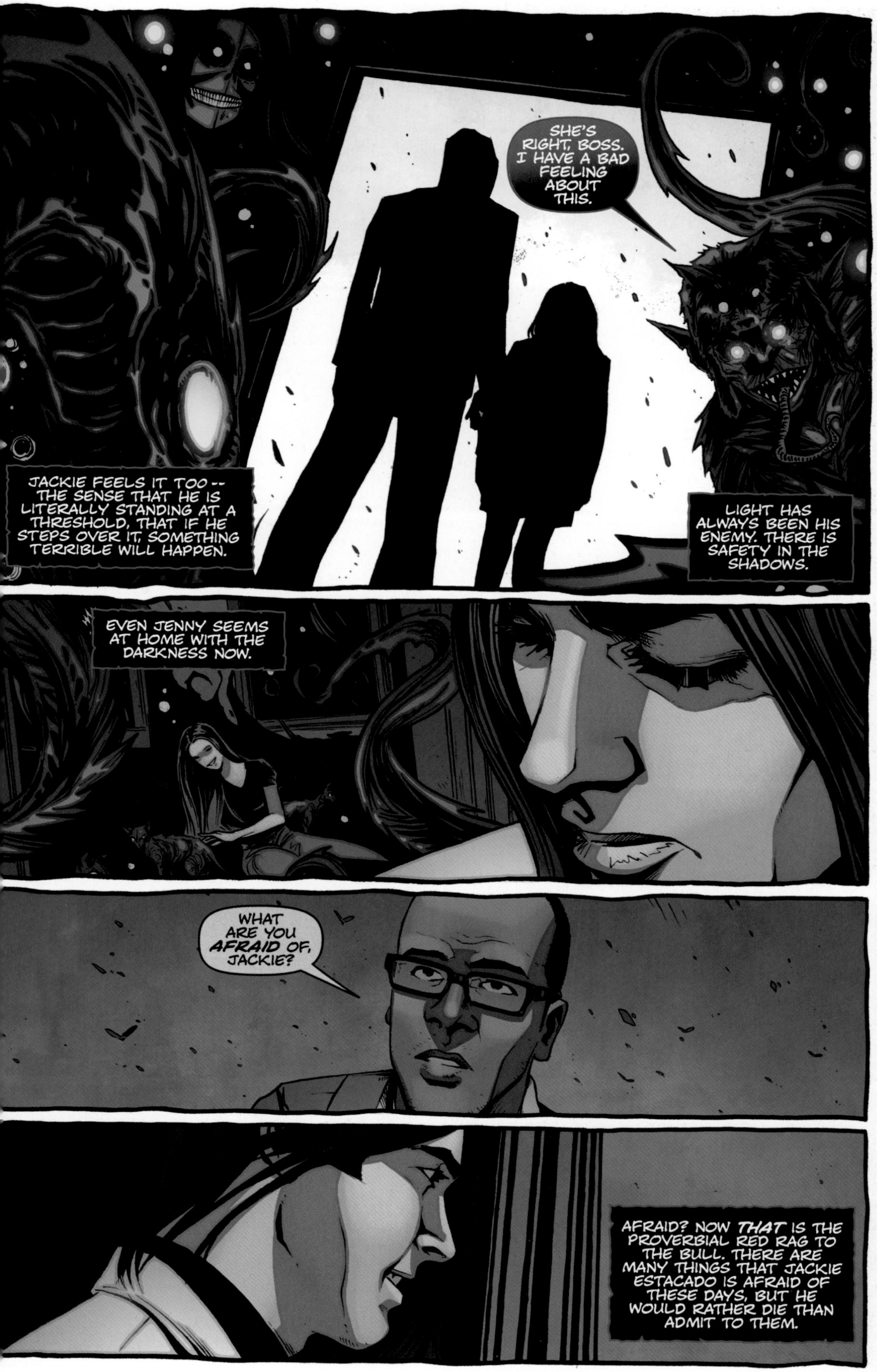
SHE'S RIGHT, BOSS. I HAVE A BAD FEELING ABOUT THIS.
JACKIE FEELS IT TOO -- THE SENSE THAT HE IS LITERALLY STANDING AT A THRESHOLD, THAT IF HE STEPS OVER IT, SOMETHING TERRIBLE WILL HAPPEN.
LIGHT HAS ALWAYS BEEN HIS ENEMY. THERE IS SAFETY IN THE SHADOWS.
EVEN JENNY SEEMS AT HOME WITH THE DARKNESS NOW.
WHAT ARE YOU AFRAID OF, JACKIE?
AFRAID? NOW THAT IS THE PROVERBIAL RED RAG TO THE BULL. THERE ARE MANY THINGS THAT JACKIE ESTACADO IS AFRAID OF THESE DAYS, BUT HE WOULD RATHER DIE THAN ADMIT TO THEM.

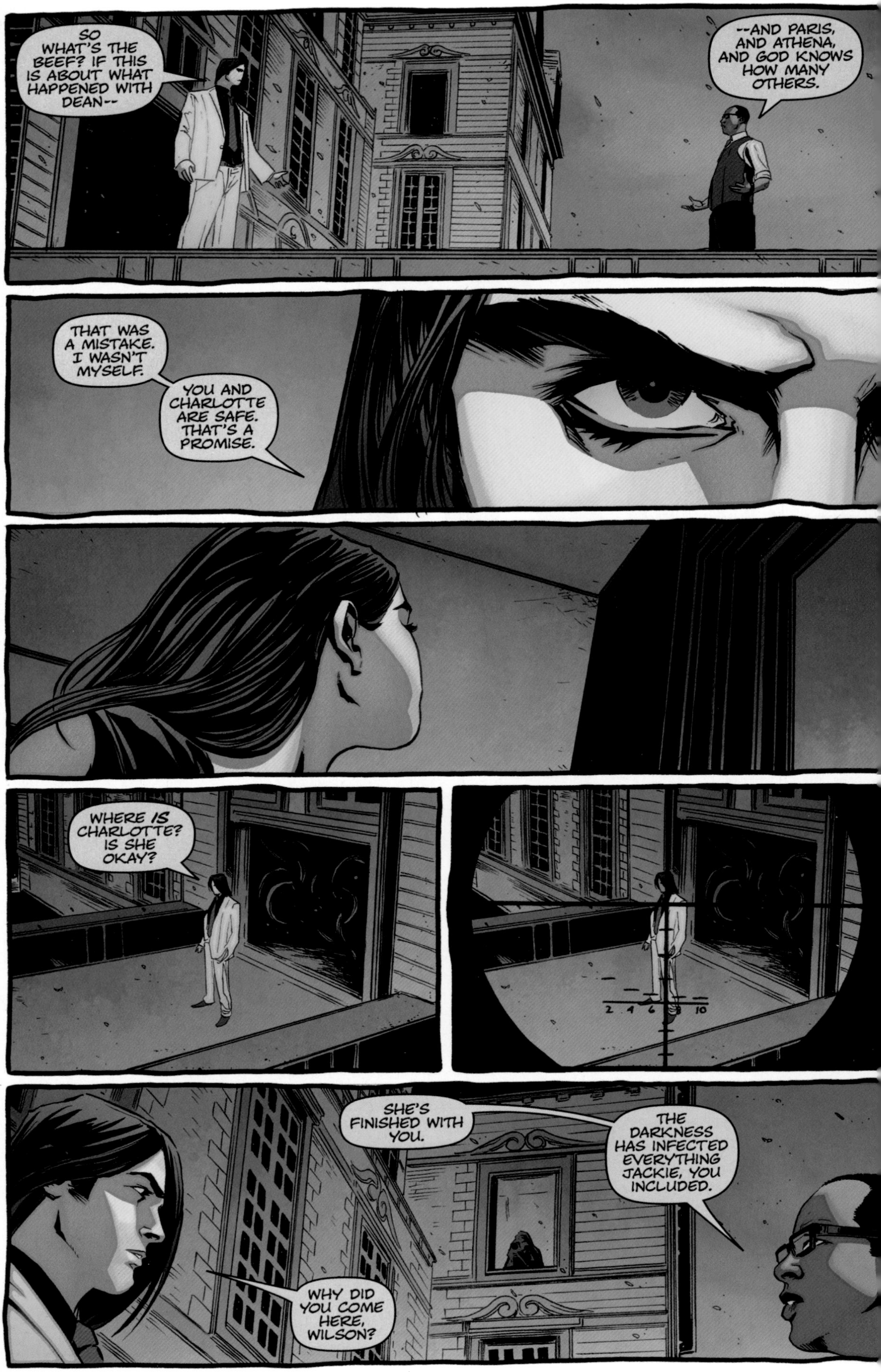
SO WHAT'S THE BEEF? IF THIS IS ABOUT WHAT HAPPENED WITH DEAN--
--AND PARIS, AND ATHENA, AND GOD KNOWS HOW MANY OTHERS.
THAT WAS A MISTAKE. I WASN'T MYSELF.
YOU AND CHARLOTTE ARE SAFE. THAT'S A PROMISE.
WHERE IS CHARLOTTE? IS SHE OKAY?
2 4 6 8 10
SHE'S FINISHED WITH YOU.
THE DARKNESS HAS INFECTED EVERYTHING JACKIE, YOU INCLUDED.
WHY DID YOU COME HERE, WILSON?

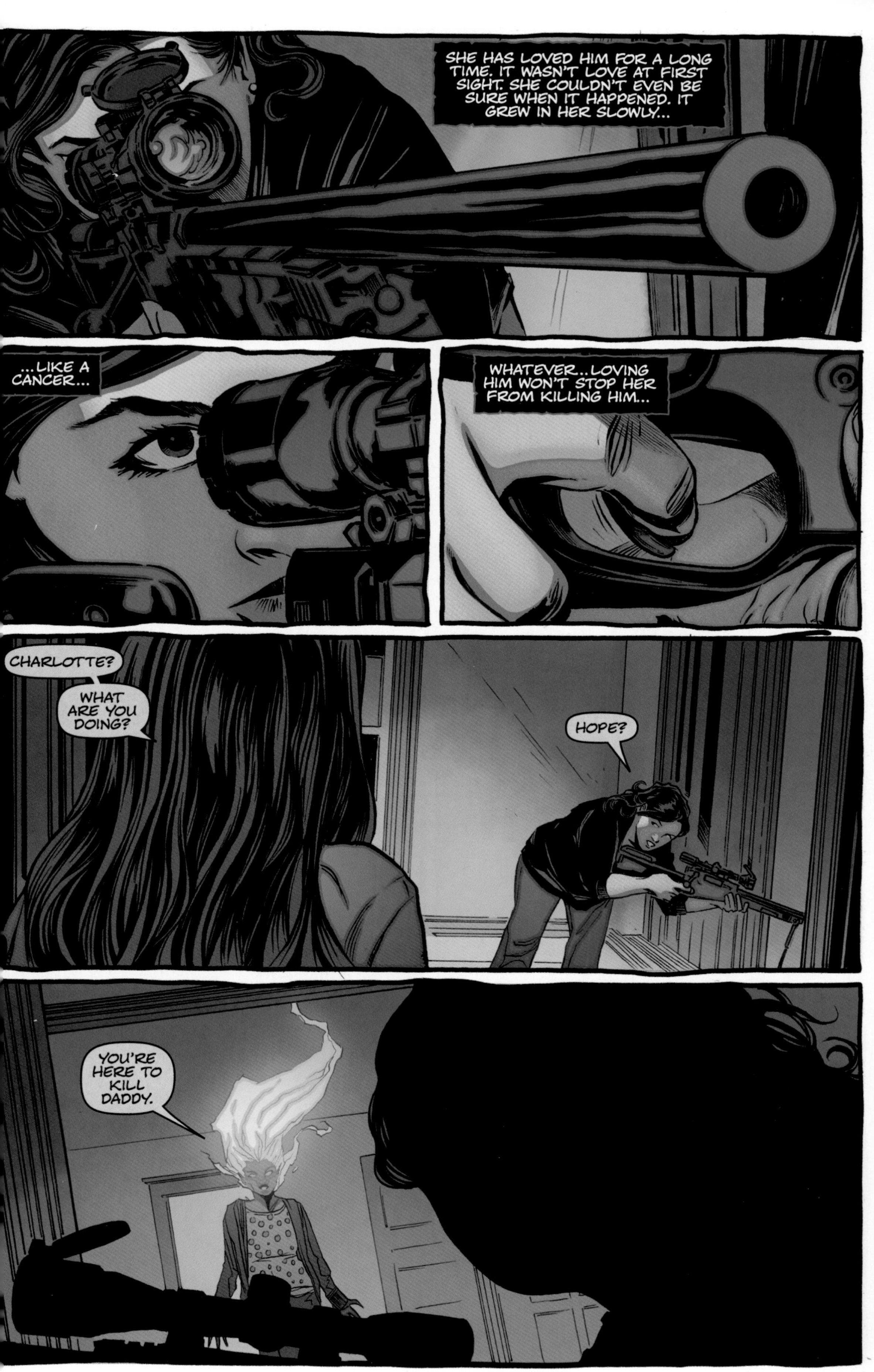
SHE HAS LOVED HIM FOR A LONG TIME. IT WASN'T LOVE AT FIRST SIGHT. SHE COULDN'T EVEN BE SURE WHEN IT HAPPENED. IT GREW IN HER SLOWLY...
...LIKE A CANCER...
WHATEVER...LOVING HIM WON'T STOP HER FROM KILLING HIM...
CHARLOTTE?
WHAT ARE YOU DOING?
HOPE?
YOU'RE HERE TO KILL DADDY.

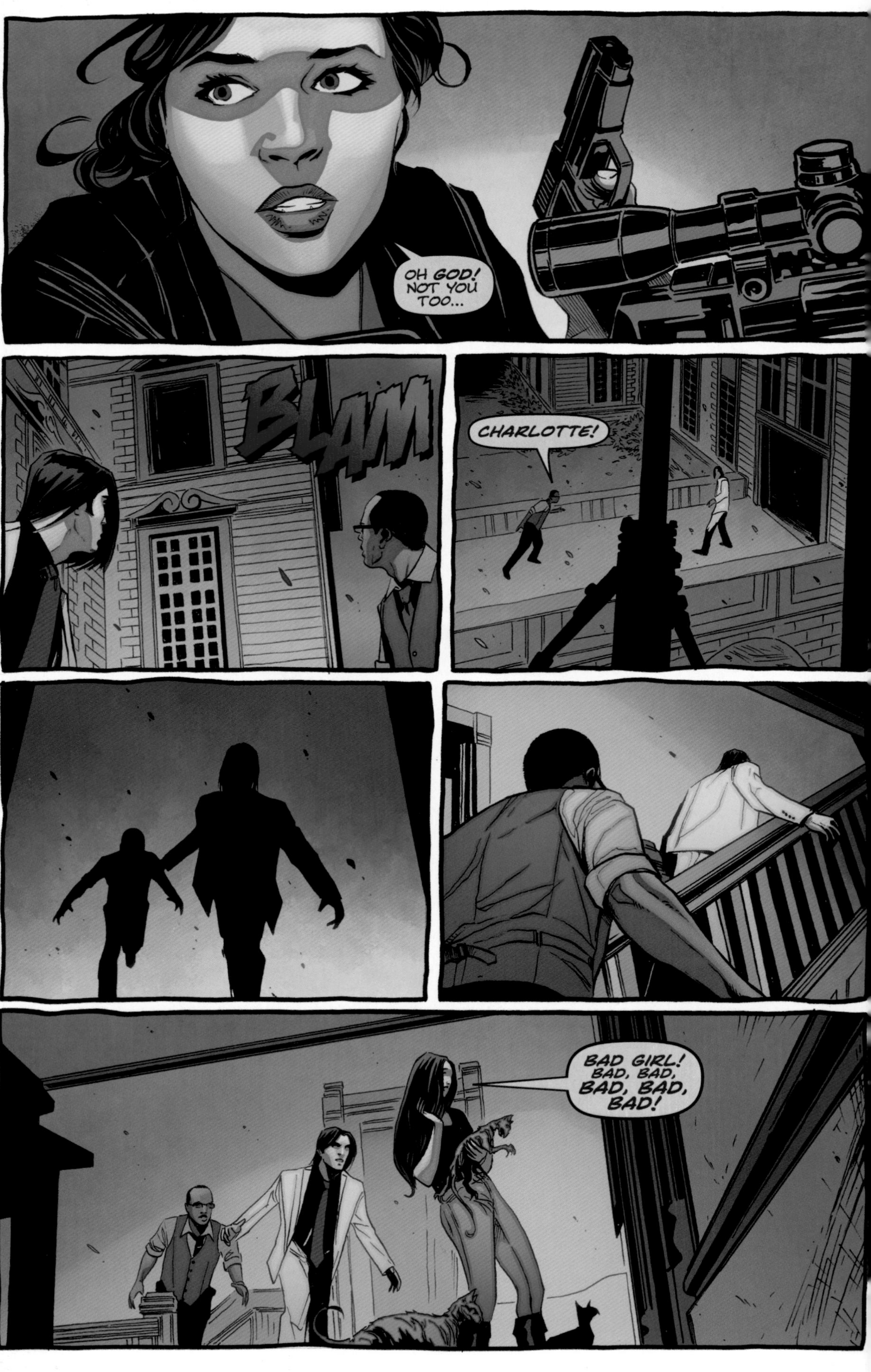

OH GOD! NOT YOU TOO...
BLAM
CHARLOTTE!
BAD GIRL! BAD, BAD, BAD, BAD, BAD!

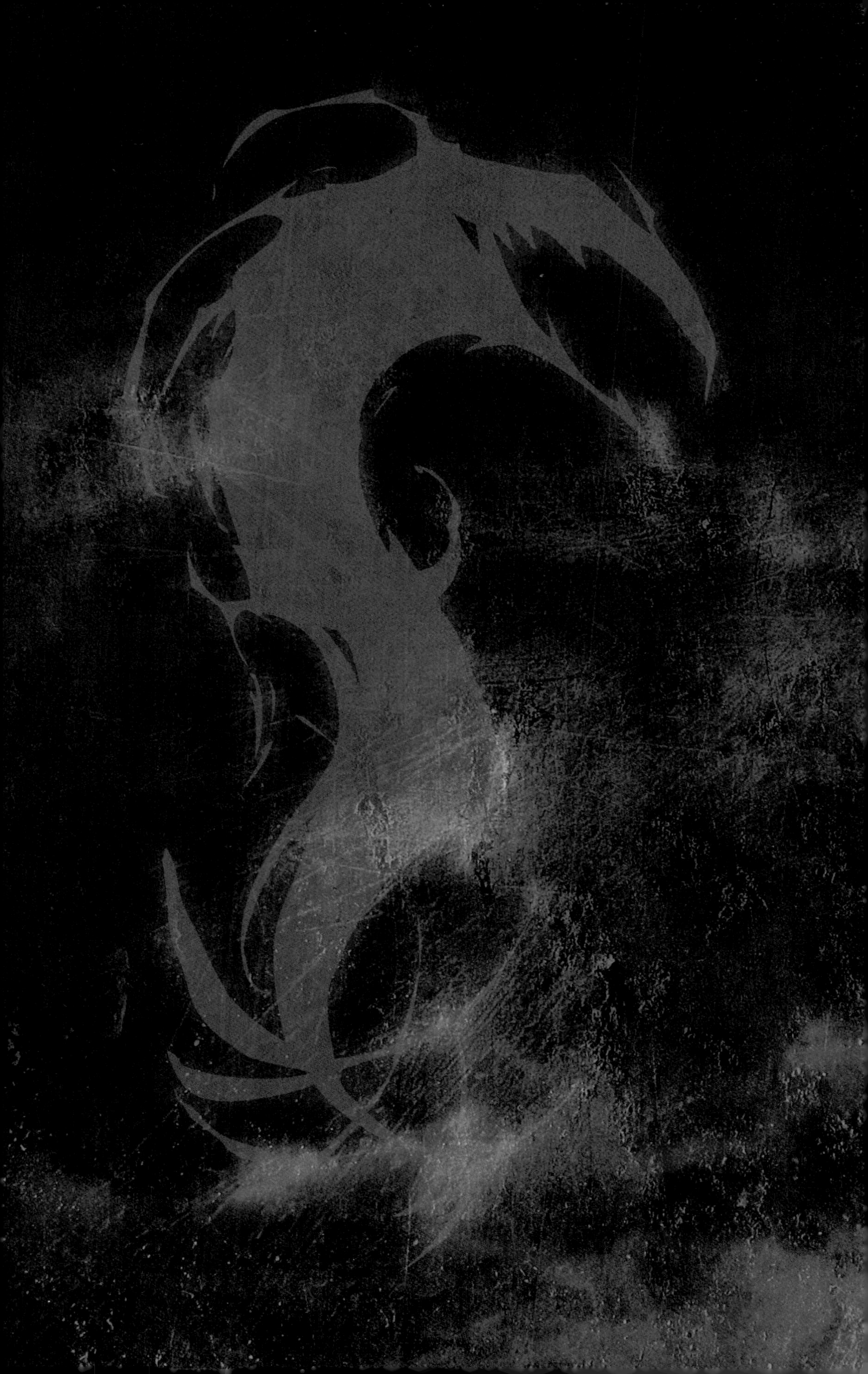

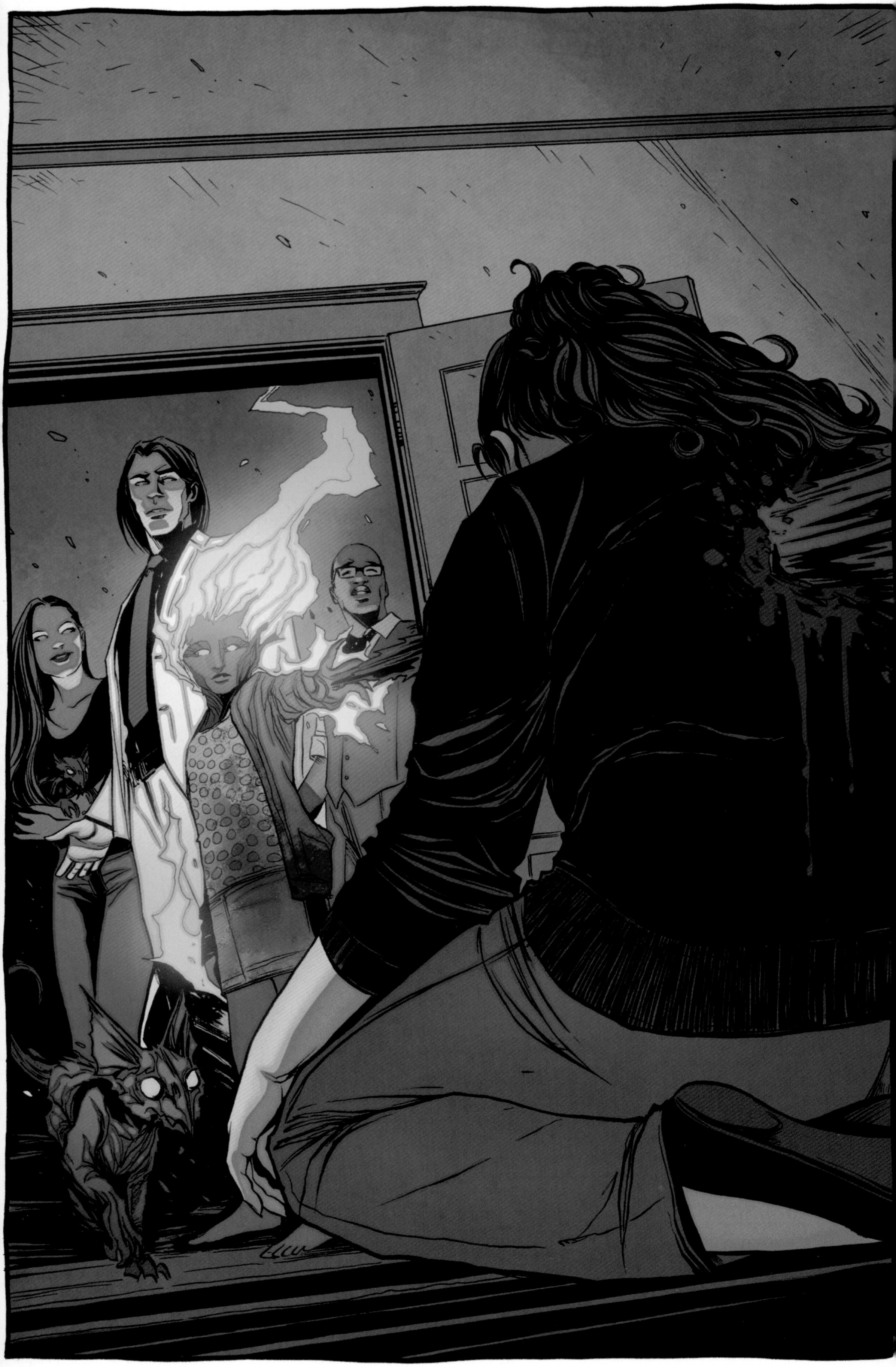

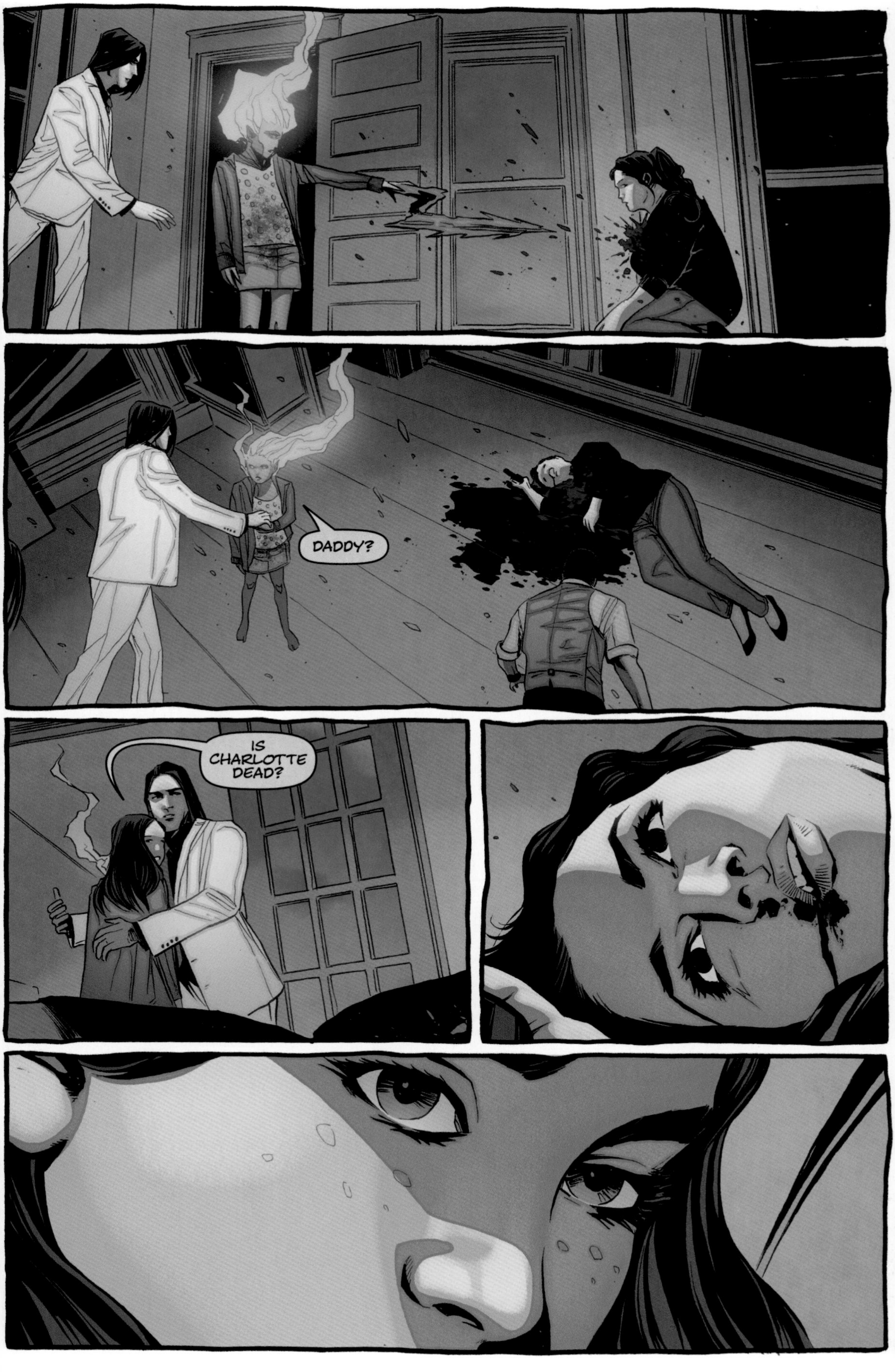
DADDY?
IS CHARLOTTE DEAD?

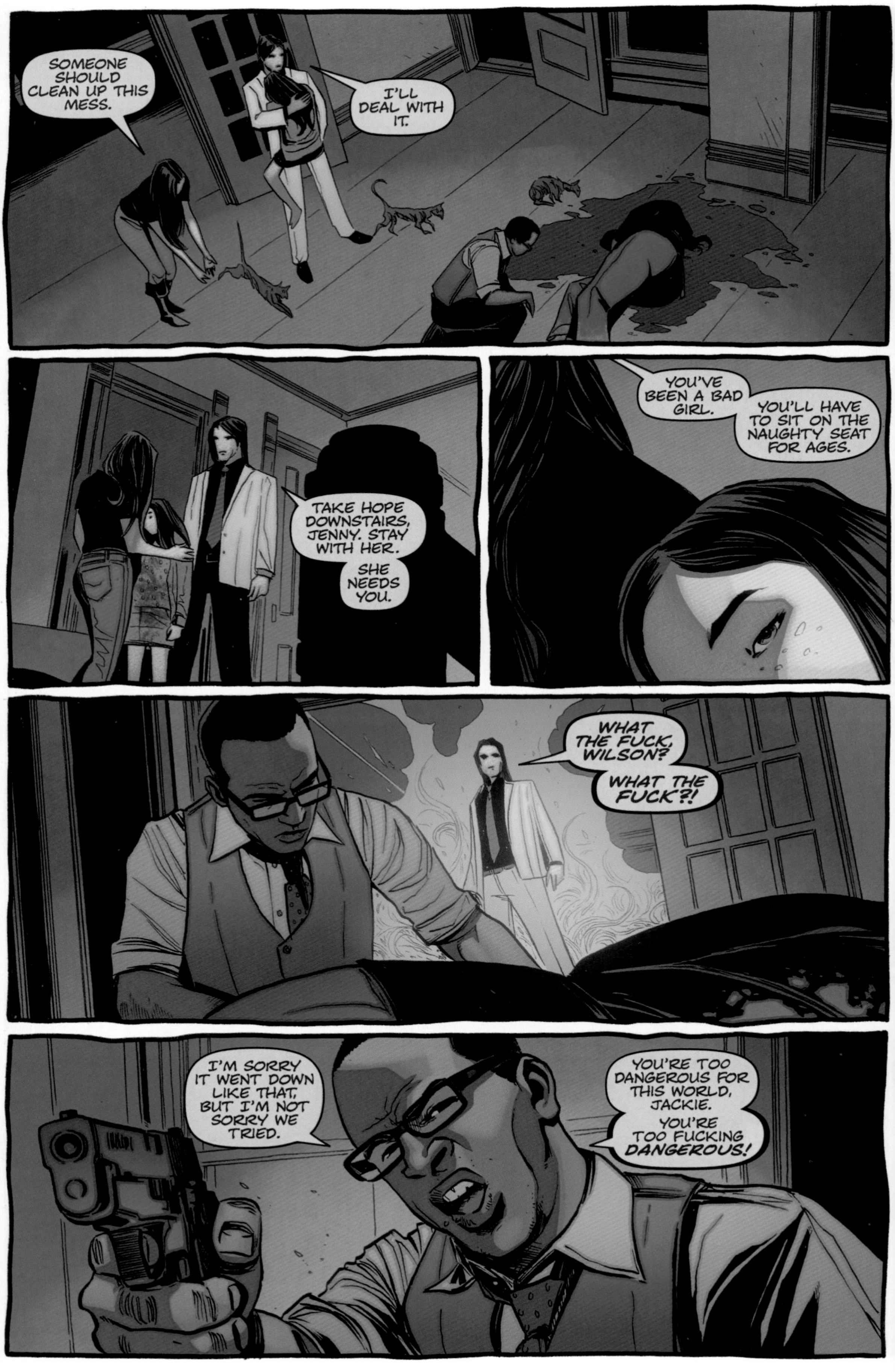
SOMEONE SHOULD CLEAN UP THIS MESS.
I'LL DEAL WITH IT.
TAKE HOPE DOWNSTAIRS, JENNY. STAY WITH HER.
SHE NEEDS YOU.
YOU'VE BEEN A BAD GIRL.
YOU'LL HAVE TO SIT ON THE NAUGHTY SEAT FOR AGES.
WHAT THE FUCK, WILSON?
WHAT THE FUCK?!
I'M SORRY IT WENT DOWN LIKE THAT, BUT I'M NOT SORRY WE TRIED.
YOU'RE TOO DANGEROUS FOR THIS WORLD, JACKIE.
YOU'RE TOO FUCKING DANGEROUS!

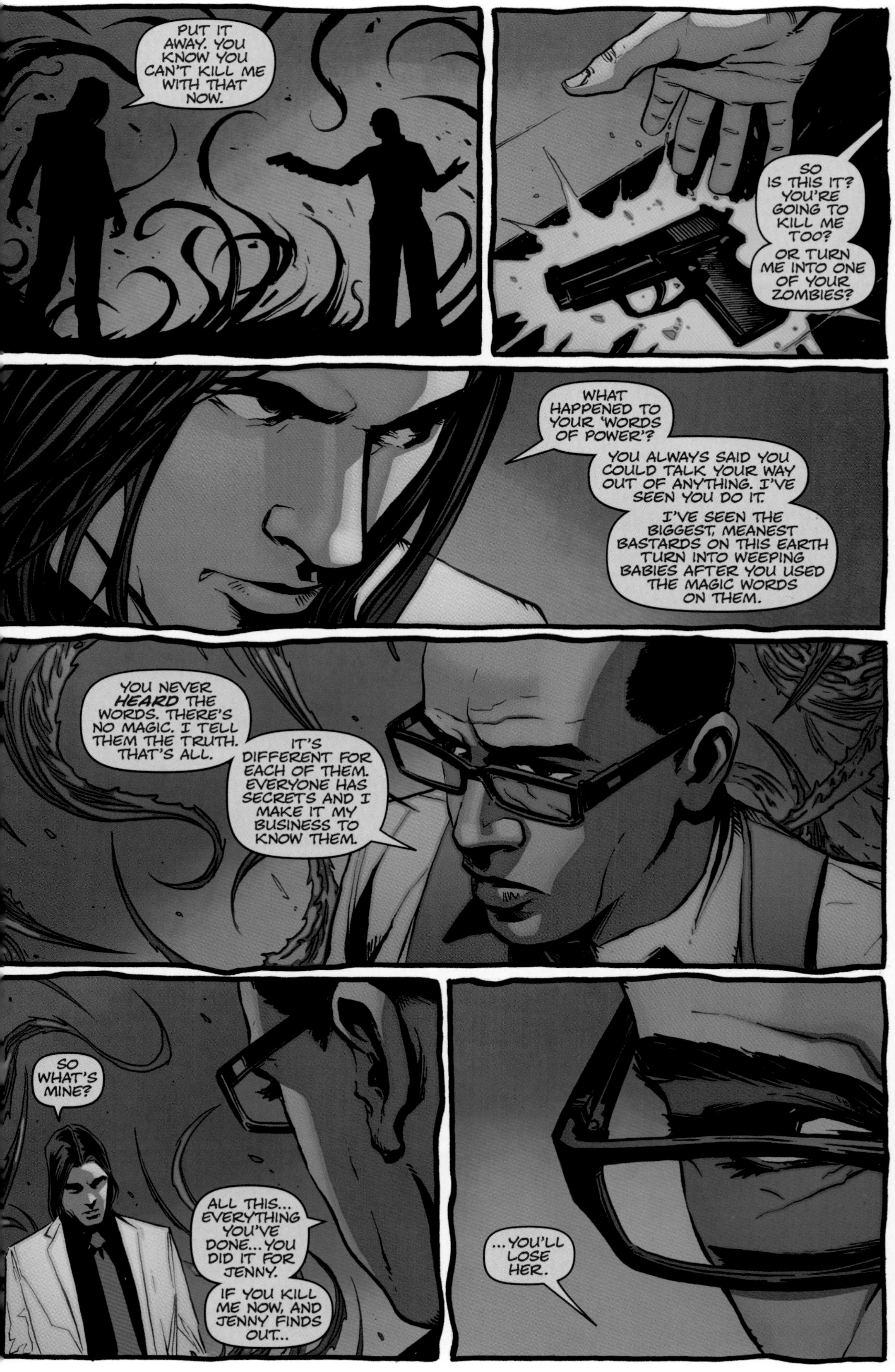
PUT IT AWAY. YOU KNOW YOU CAN'T KILL ME WITH THAT NOW.
SO IS THIS IT? YOU'RE GOING TO KILL ME TOO?
OR TURN ME INTO ONE OF YOUR ZOMBIES?
WHAT HAPPENED TO YOUR 'WORDS OF POWER'?
YOU ALWAYS SAID YOU COULD TALK YOUR WAY OUT OF ANYTHING. I'VE SEEN YOU DO IT.
I'VE SEEN THE BIGGEST, MEANEST BASTARDS ON THIS EARTH TURN INTO WEEPING BABIES AFTER YOU USED THE MAGIC WORDS ON THEM.
YOU NEVER HEARD THE WORDS. THERE'S NO MAGIC. I TELL THEM THE TRUTH. THAT'S ALL.
IT'S DIFFERENT FOR EACH OF THEM. EVERYONE HAS SECRETS AND I MAKE IT MY BUSINESS TO KNOW THEM.
SO WHAT'S MINE?
ALL THIS... EVERYTHING YOU'VE DONE... YOU DID IT FOR JENNY.
IF YOU KILL ME NOW, AND JENNY FINDS OUT...
...YOU'LL LOSE HER.

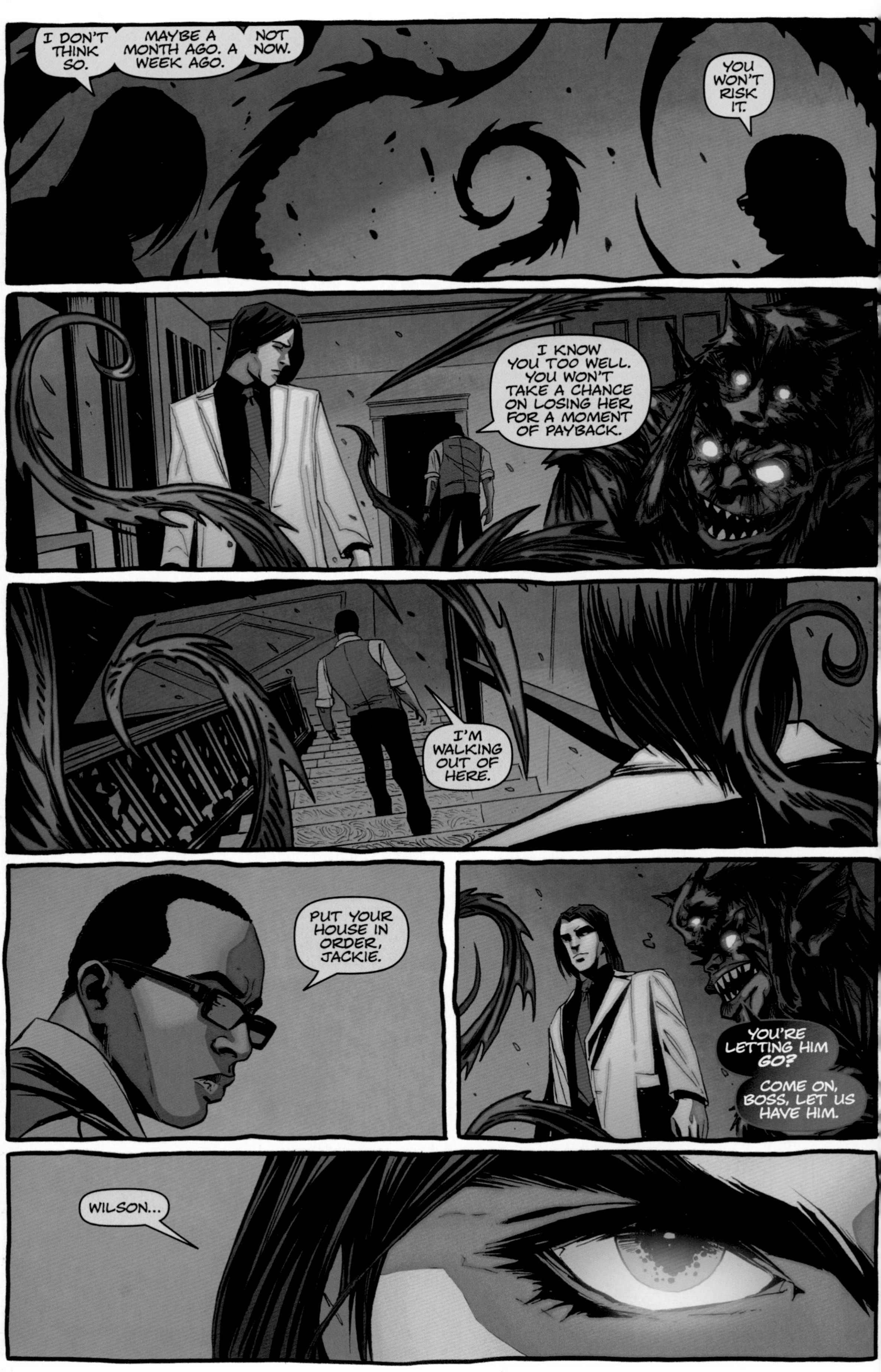
I DON'T THINK SO.
MAYBE A MONTH AGO. A WEEK AGO.
NOT NOW.
YOU WON'T RISK IT.
I KNOW YOU TOO WELL. YOU WON'T TAKE A CHANCE ON LOSING HER FOR A MOMENT OF PAYBACK.
I'M WALKING OUT OF HERE.
PUT YOUR HOUSE IN ORDER, JACKIE.
YOU'RE LETTING HIM GO?
COME ON, BOSS, LET US HAVE HIM.
WILSON...

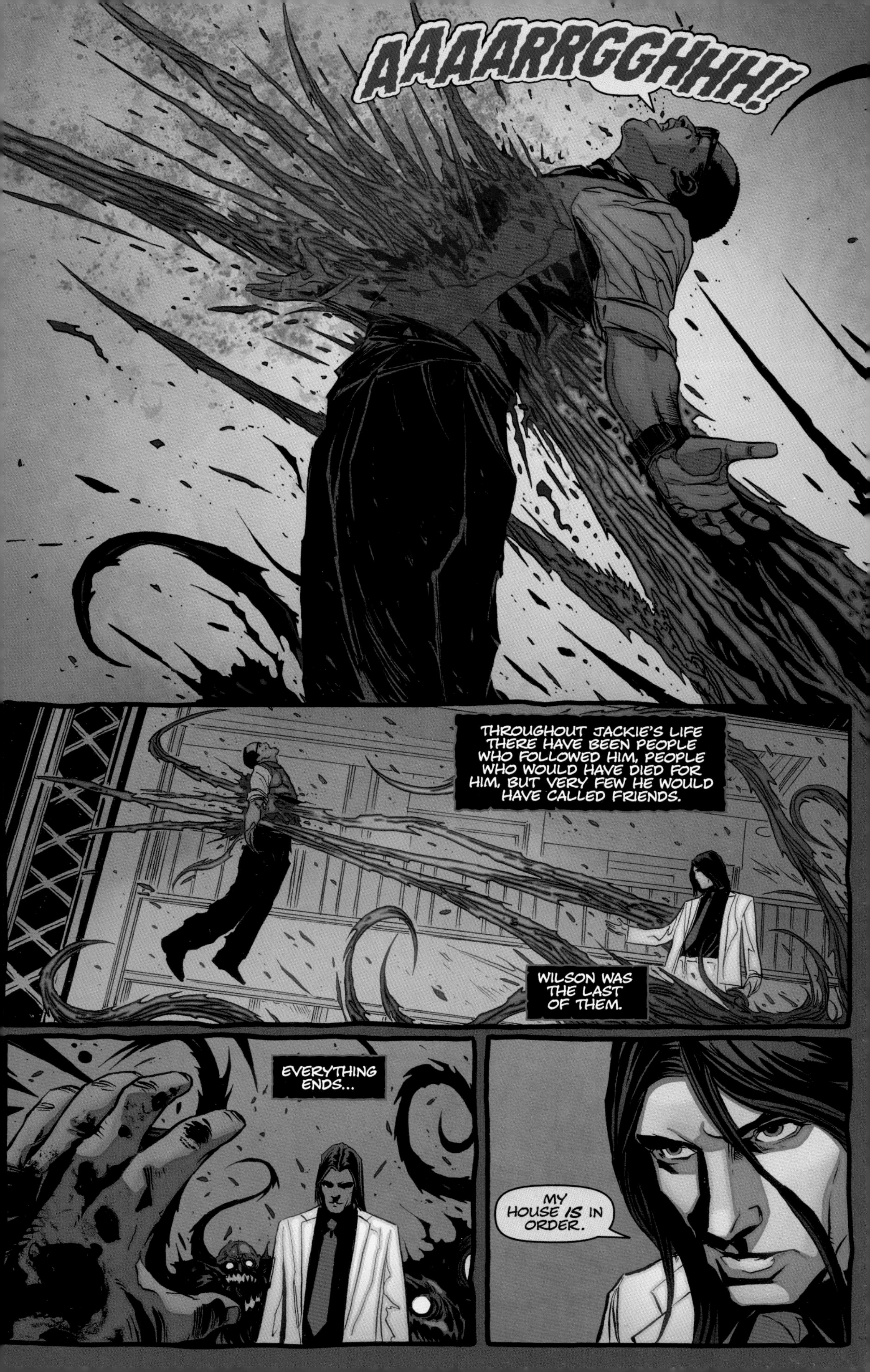
AAAARRGGHHH!
THROUGHOUT JACKIE'S LIFE THERE HAVE BEEN PEOPLE WHO FOLLOWED HIM, PEOPLE WHO WOULD HAVE DIED FOR HIM, BUT VERY FEW HE WOULD HAVE CALLED FRIENDS.
WILSON WAS THE LAST OF THEM.
EVERYTHING ENDS...
MY HOUSE *IS* IN ORDER.

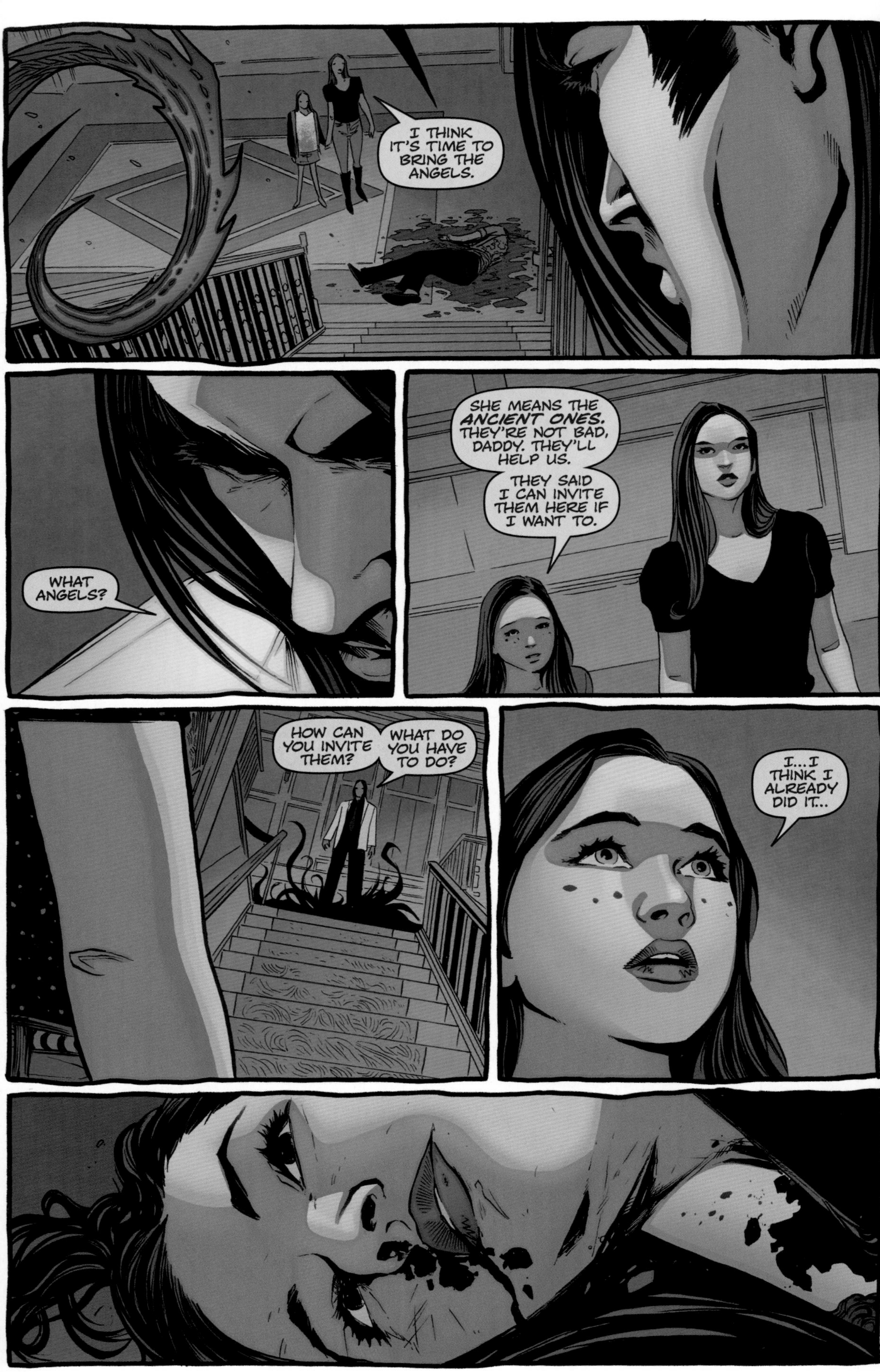
I THINK IT'S TIME TO BRING THE ANGELS.
WHAT ANGELS?
SHE MEANS THE ANCIENT ONES. THEY'RE NOT BAD, DADDY. THEY'LL HELP US.
THEY SAID I CAN INVITE THEM HERE IF I WANT TO.
HOW CAN YOU INVITE THEM?
WHAT DO YOU HAVE TO DO?
I...I THINK I ALREADY DID IT...

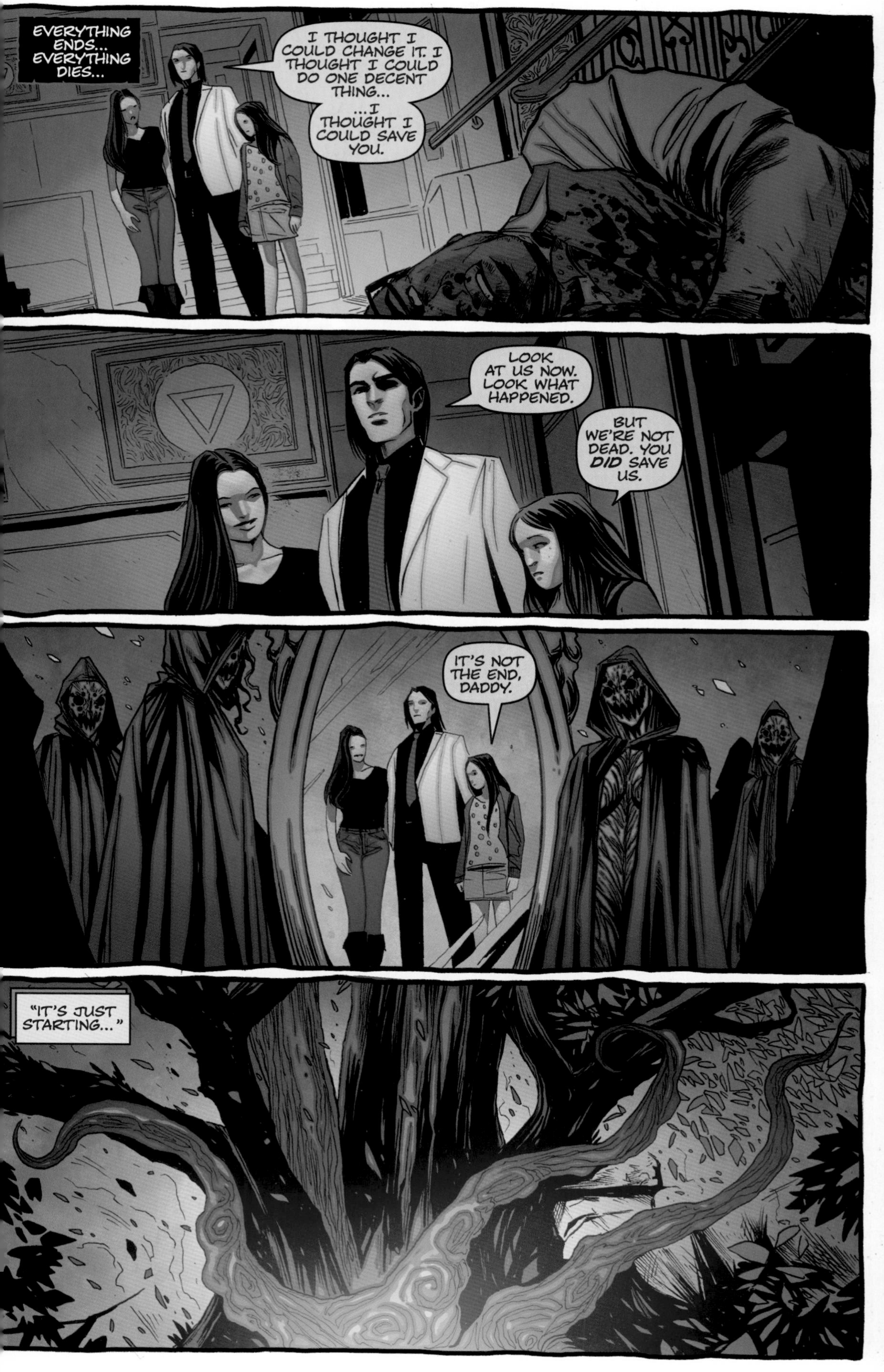
EVERYTHING ENDS... EVERYTHING DIES...
I THOUGHT I COULD CHANGE IT. I THOUGHT I COULD DO ONE DECENT THING...
...I THOUGHT I COULD SAVE YOU.
LOOK AT US NOW. LOOK WHAT HAPPENED.
BUT WE'RE NOT DEAD. YOU *DID* SAVE US.
IT'S NOT THE END, DADDY.
"IT'S JUST STARTING..."

COVER GALLERY

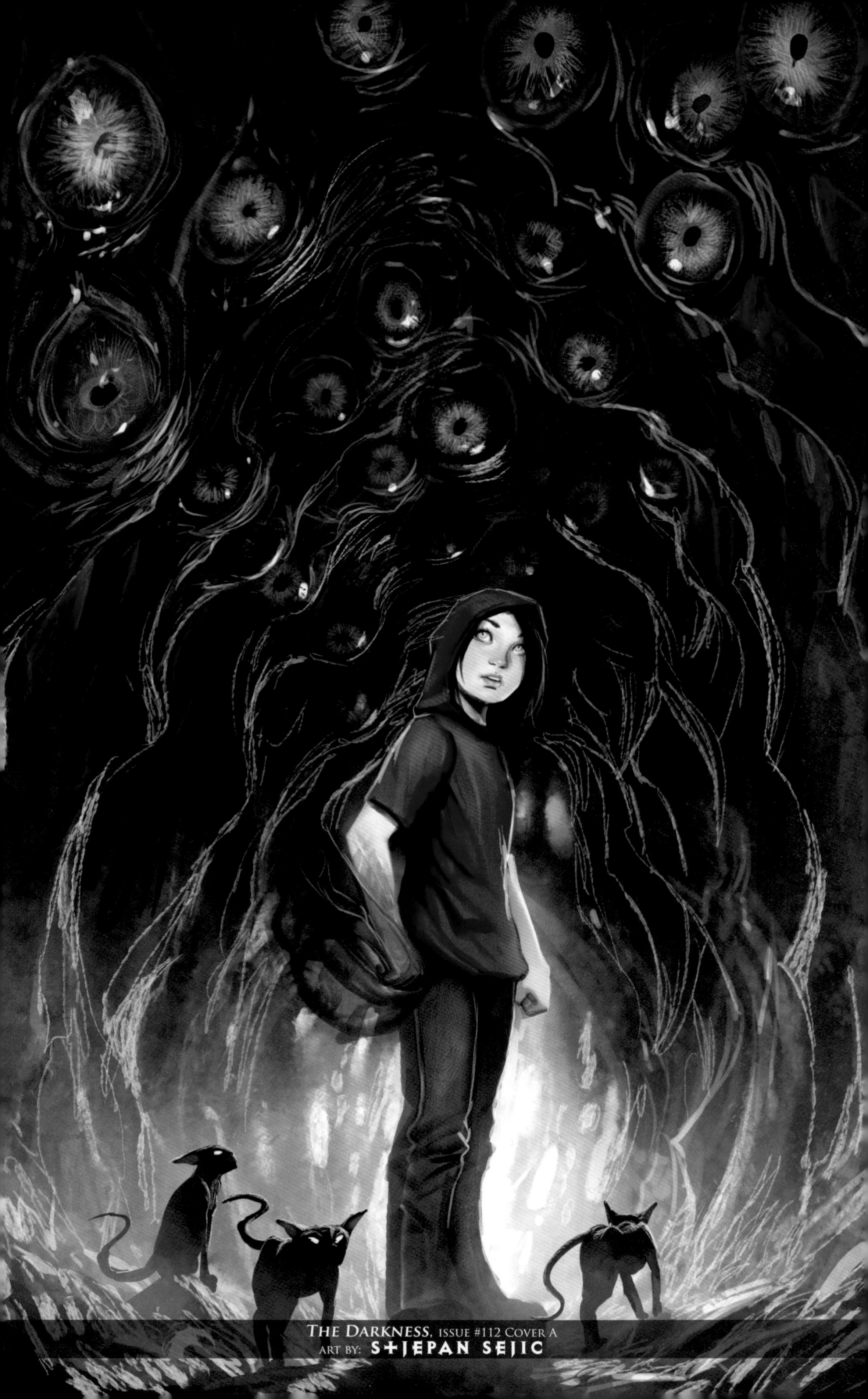

THE DARKNESS, ISSUE #112 COVER A
ART BY: STJEPAN SEJIC

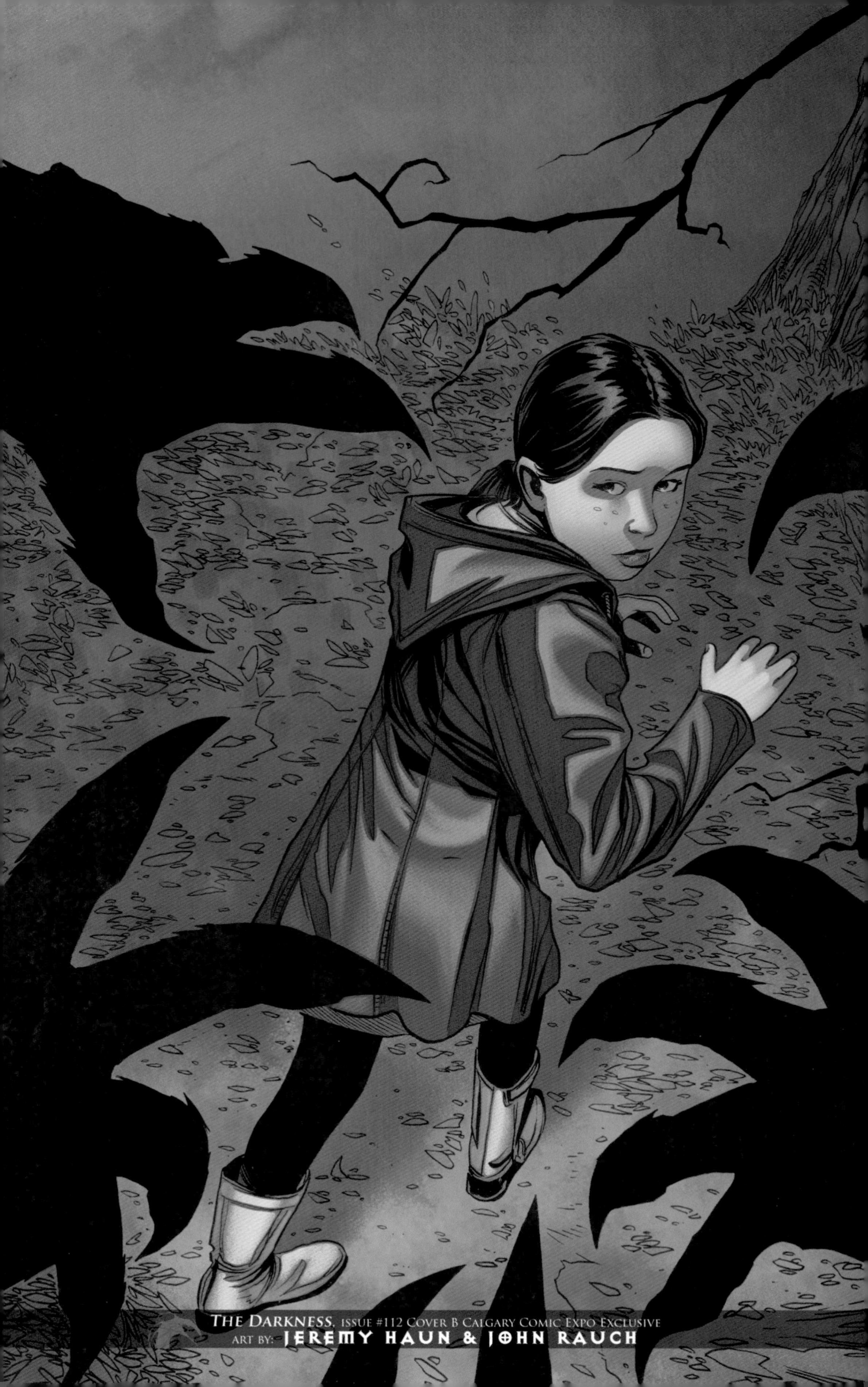

The Darkness, issue #112 Cover B Calgary Comic Expo Exclusive
Art by: **JEREMY HAUN & JOHN RAUCH**

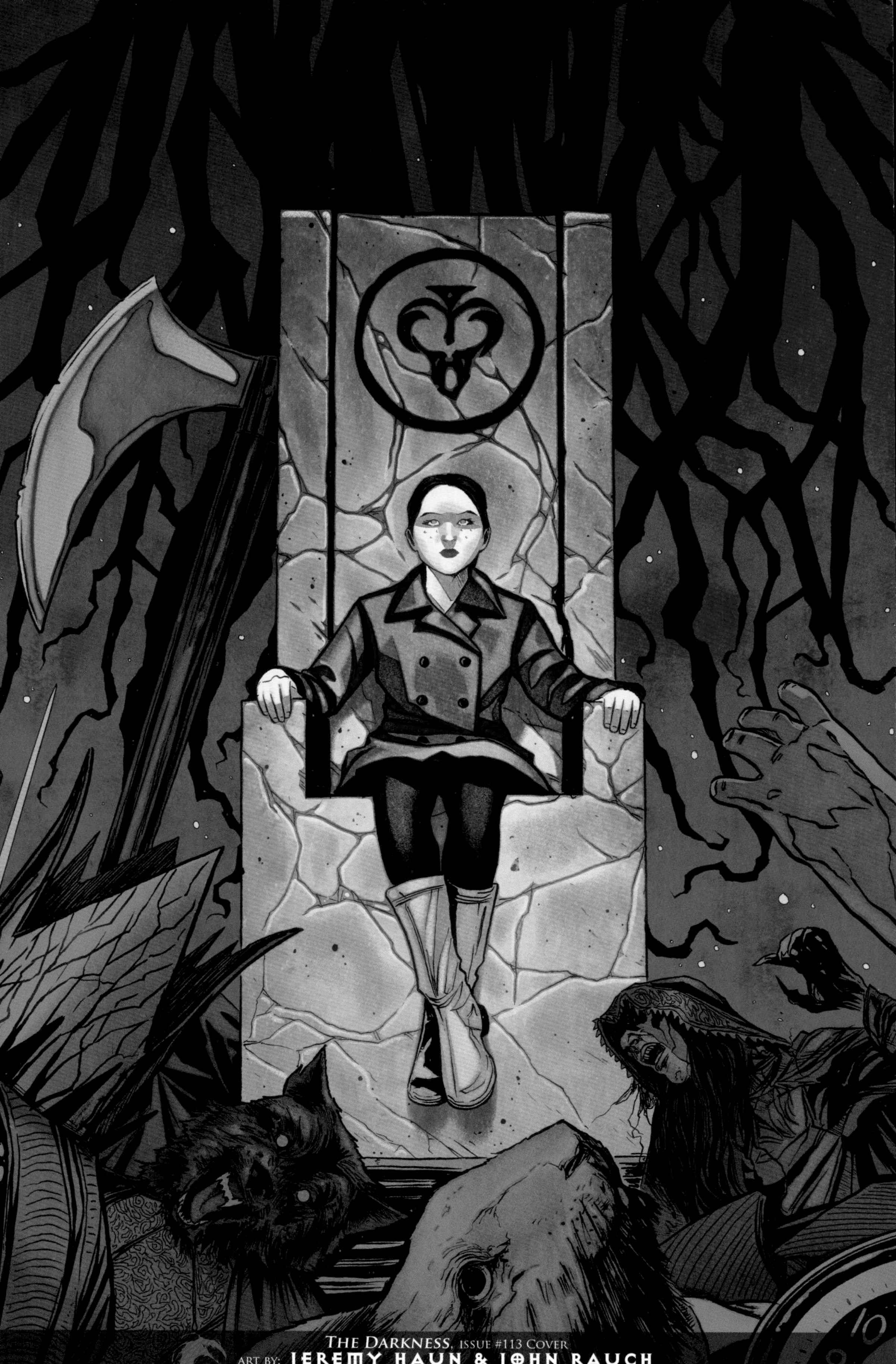

The Darkness, issue #113 Cover
Art by: **Jeremy Haun & John Rauch**

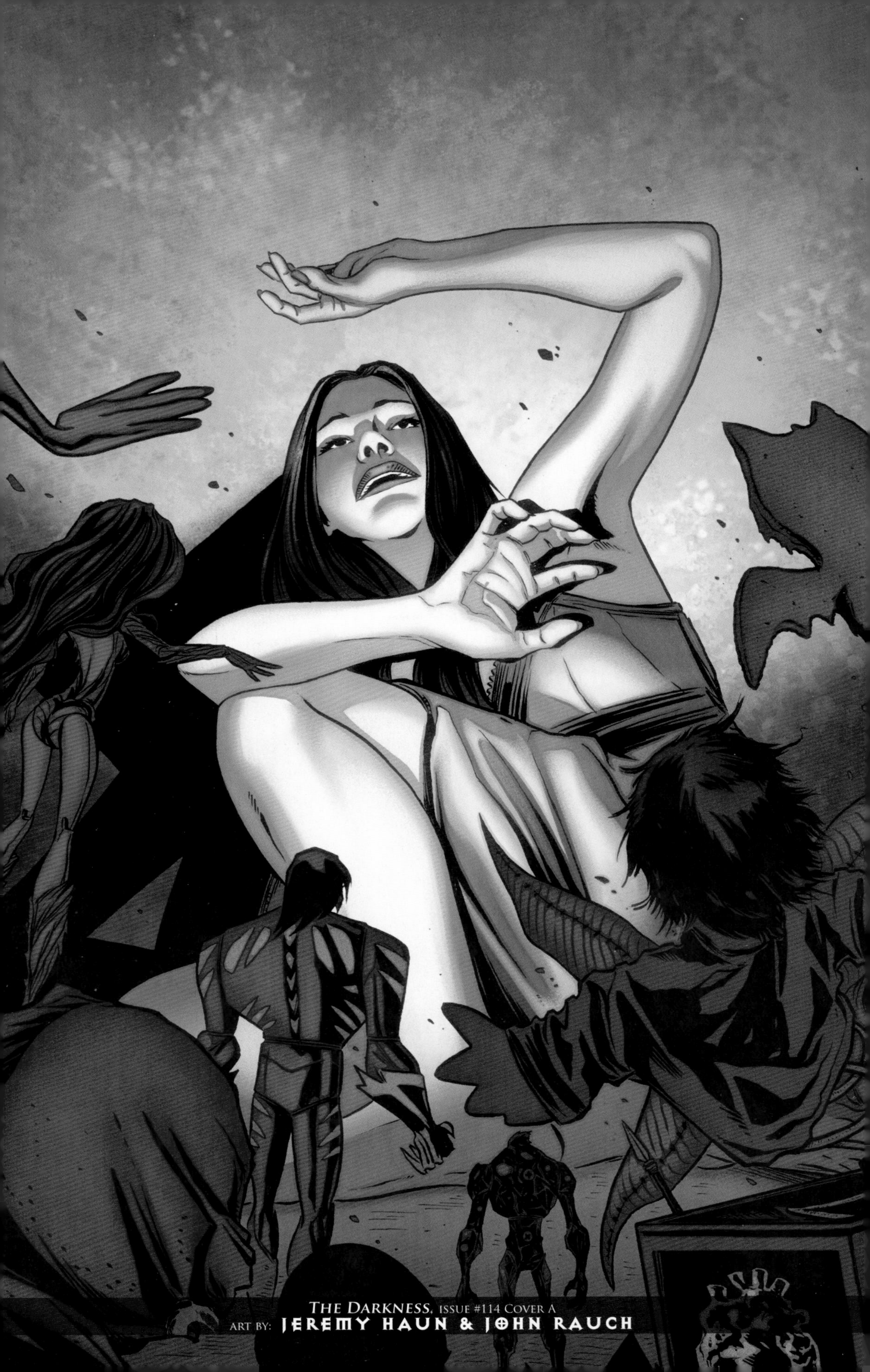

The Darkness, issue #114 Cover A
art by: Jeremy Haun & John Rauch

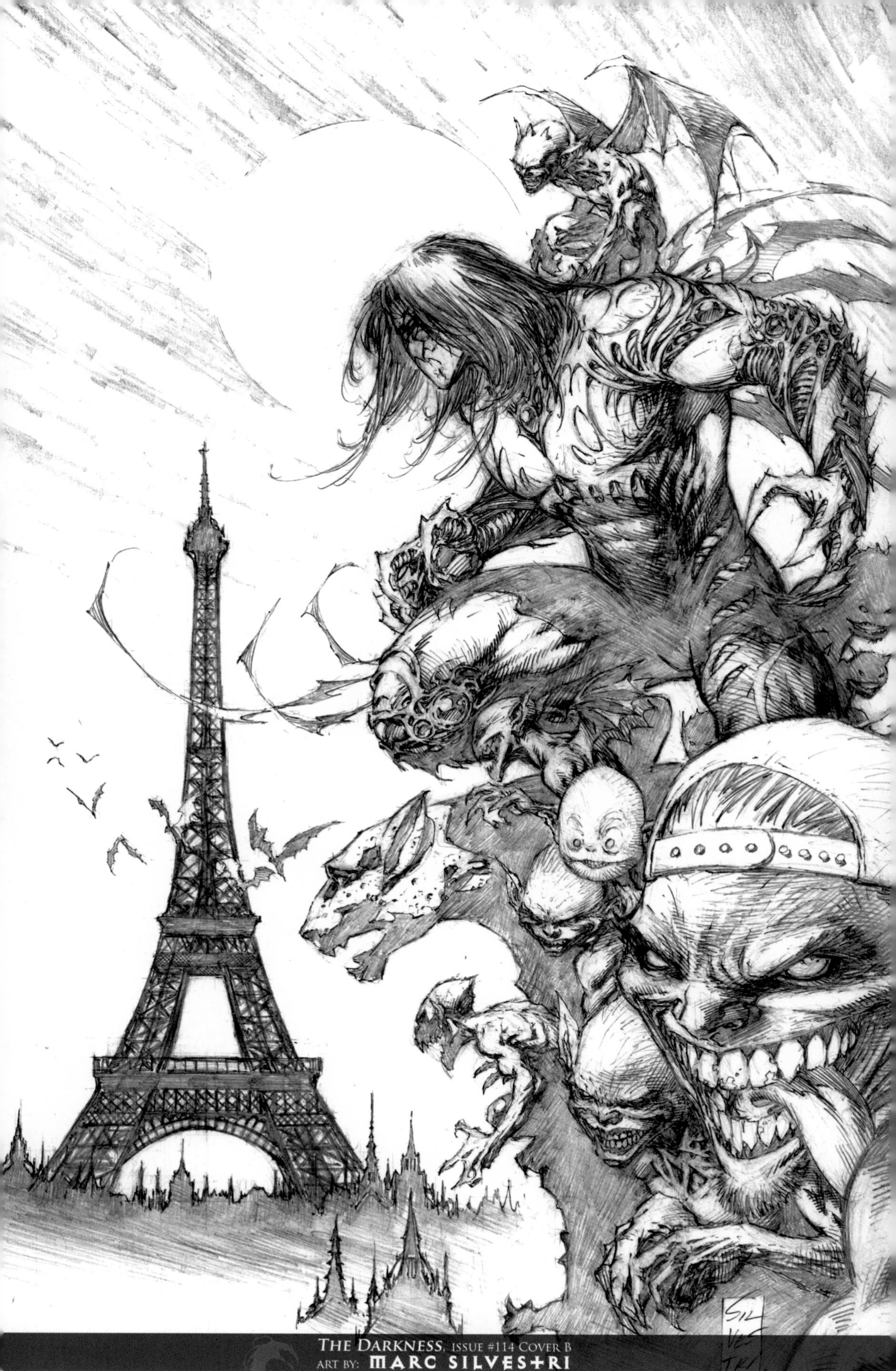
SIL
VES
TRI

THE DARKNESS, ISSUE #114 COVER B
ART BY: MARC SILVESTRI

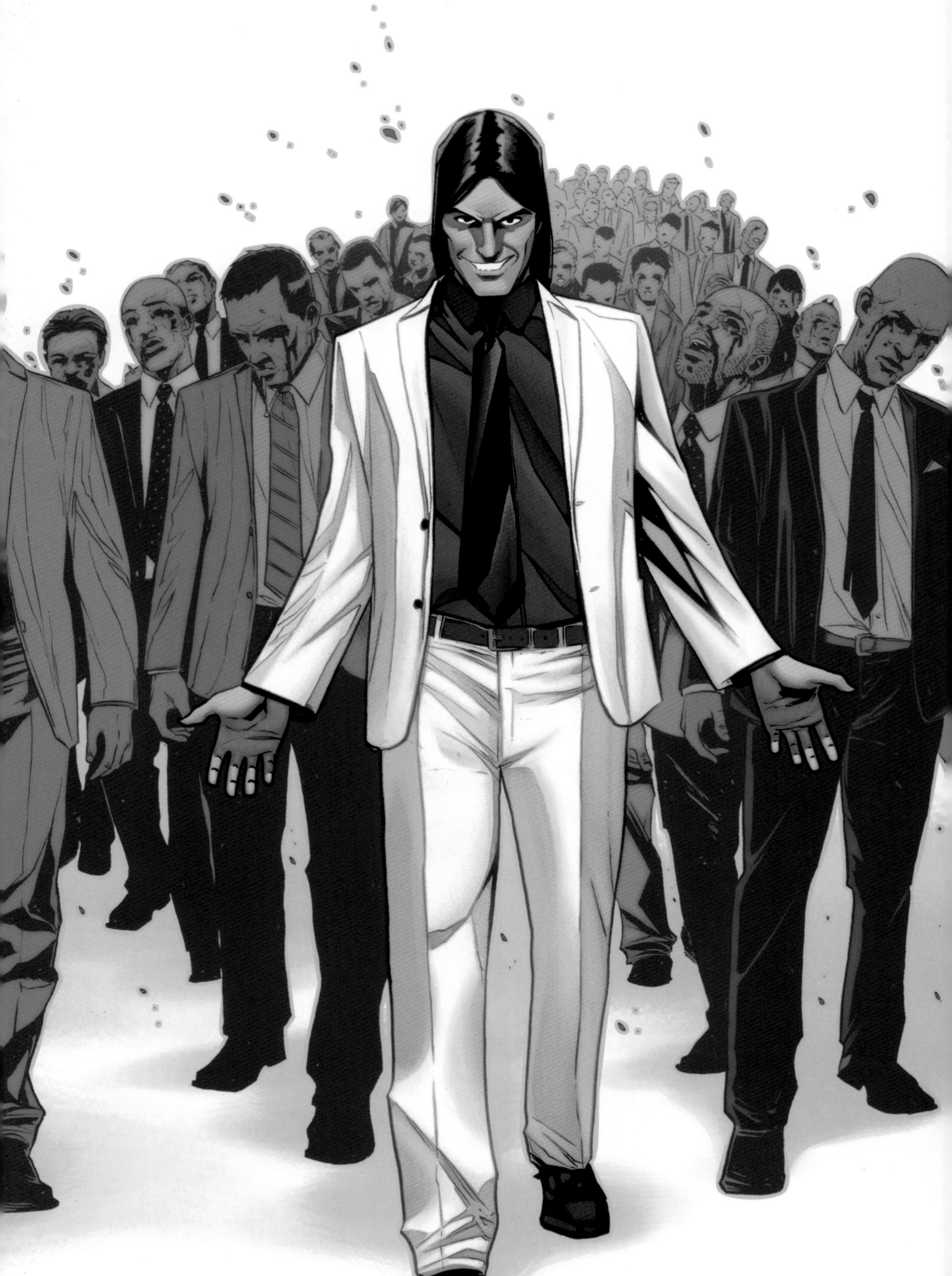

THE DARKNESS, ISSUE #115 COVER
ART BY: JEREMY HAUN & JOHN RAUCH

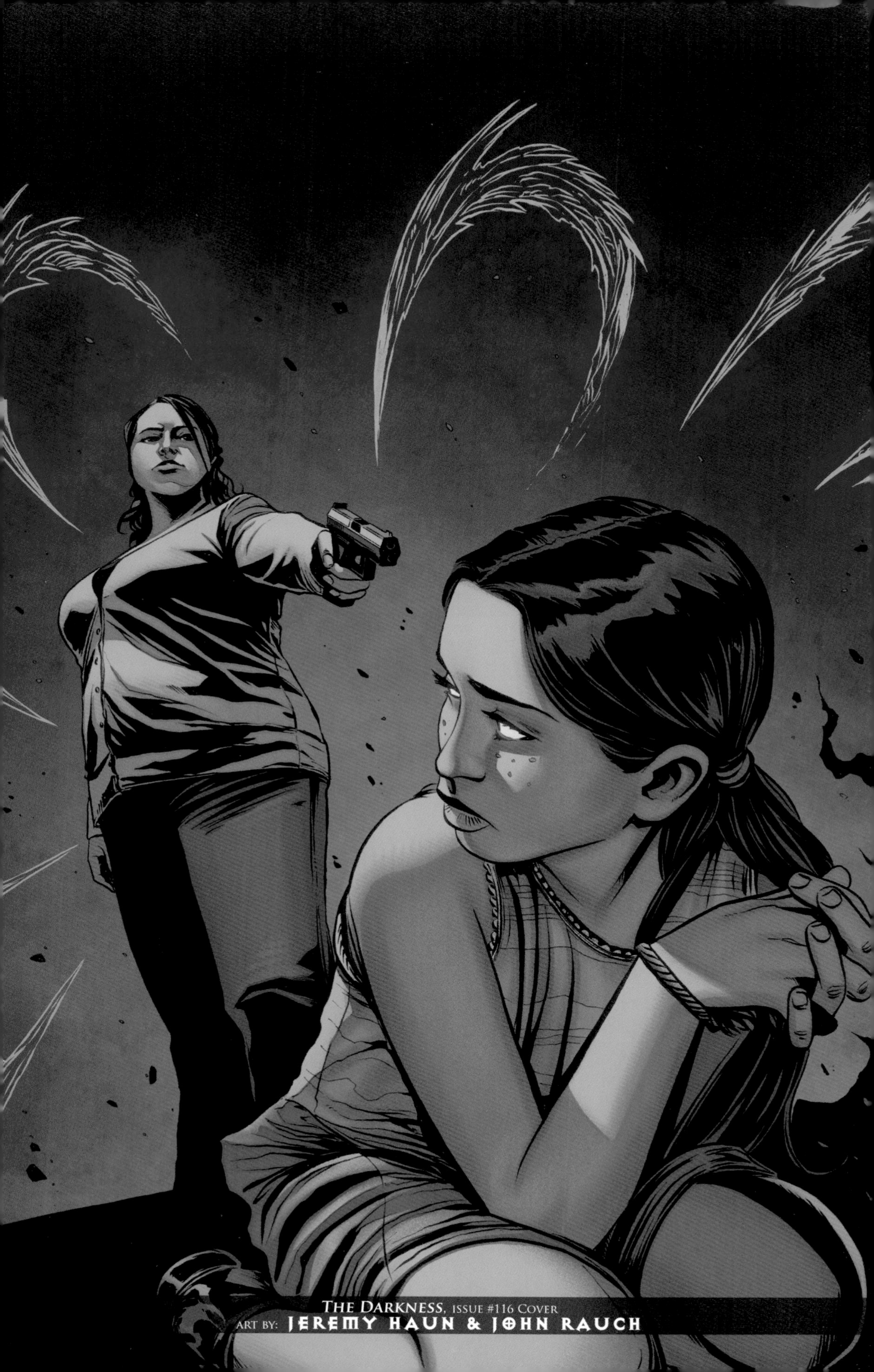

THE DARKNESS, ISSUE #116 COVER
ART BY: JEREMY HAUN & JOHN RAUCH

TOP COW UNIVERSE

ACCURSED

- The Darkness: Accursed Vol. 1-7

BROKEN TRINITY

- Broken Trinity Vol. 1-2
- The Magdalena Vol. 1-2

REDEMPTION

- Witchblade: Redemption Vol. 1-4

ARTIFACTS

- Angelus Vol. 1
- Artifacts Vol. 1-3

REBIRTH

READ MORE TOP COW

Ron Marz • Michael Broussard
ARTIFACTS
volume 1
FEATURING AN INTRODUCTION BY
MARC SILVESTRI

ISBN# 978-1-60706-201-1

CATCH UP ON ARTIFACTS FROM VOLUME 1!

Writer: Ron Marz
Artists: Michael Broussard, Stjepan Sejic

Separately, thirteen mystical Artifacts will guide the fate of the Universe. Together, thirteen Artifacts will end the Universe. When a mysterious antagonist kidnaps Hope, the daughter of Sara Pezzini and Jackie Estacado, Armageddon is put into motion. Starring virtually every character in the Top Cow Universe, this is a series for diehard fans and new readers alike. Pick up Volumes 1-5 today!

Ron Marz • Whilce Portacio
ARTIFACTS
volume 2

ISBN# 978-1-60706-672-9

Ron Marz • Jeremy Haun • Dale Keown
ARTIFACTS
volume 3

ISBN# 978-1-60706-425-1

ARTIFACTS
volume 4
REBIRTH
Ron Marz • Stjepan Sejic

ISBN# 978-1-60706-562-3

ARTIFACTS
volume 5
Ron Marz • Stjepan Sejic

ISBN# 978-1-60706-664-4

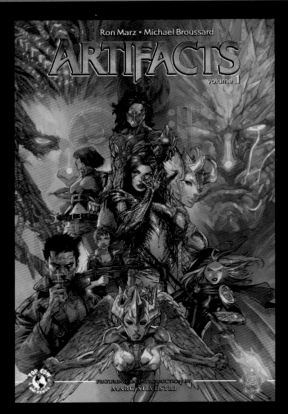

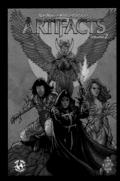

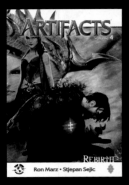

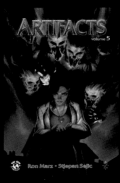

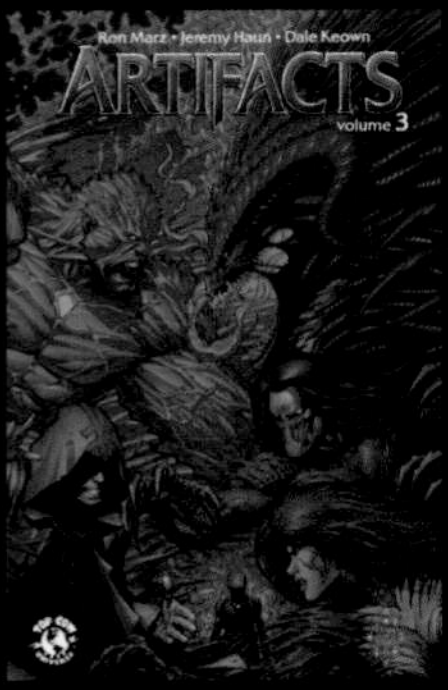

READ MORE TOP COW

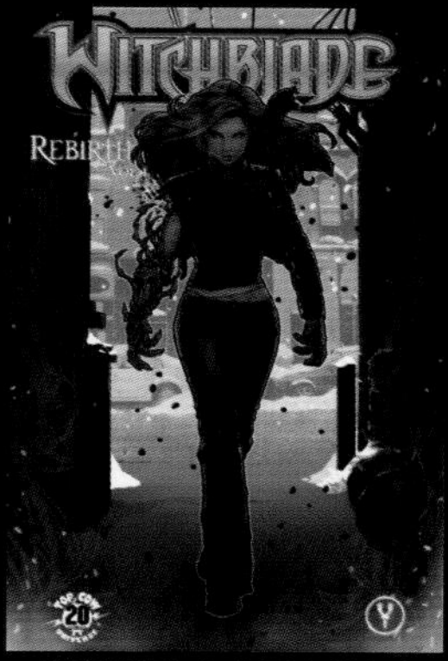
WITCHBLADE
REBIRTH

ISBN# 978-1-60706-532-6

WITCHBLADE REBIRTH VOLUME 1

Writer: Tim Seeley
Artists: Diego Bernard, Fred Benes, Arif Prianto

In the wake of Top Cow's REBIRTH, Sara Pezzini has relocated from New York to Chicago and struggles to adapt to being a private detective.

WITCHBLADE REBIRTH VOLUME 2

Writer: Tim Seeley
Artists: Diego Bernard, Fred Benes, Arif Prianto

This volume sees Sara Pezzini dealing with mercenary mana-hunters, spirit realms, fantastical steampunk warriors, and the most distilled embodiment of evil she's ever encountered.

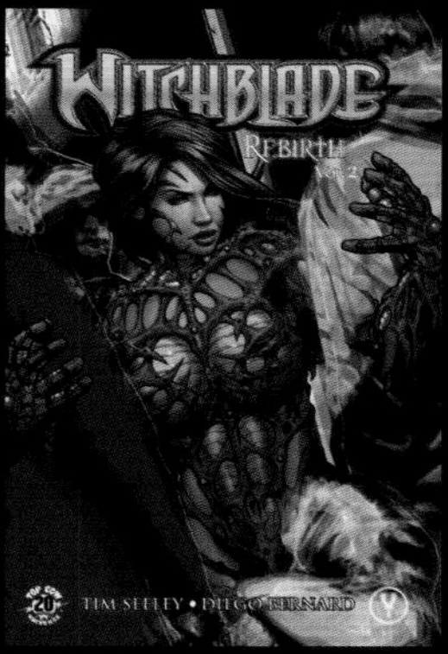
WITCHBLADE
REBIRTH
TIM SEELEY • DIEGO BERNARD

ISBN# 978-1-60706-637-8

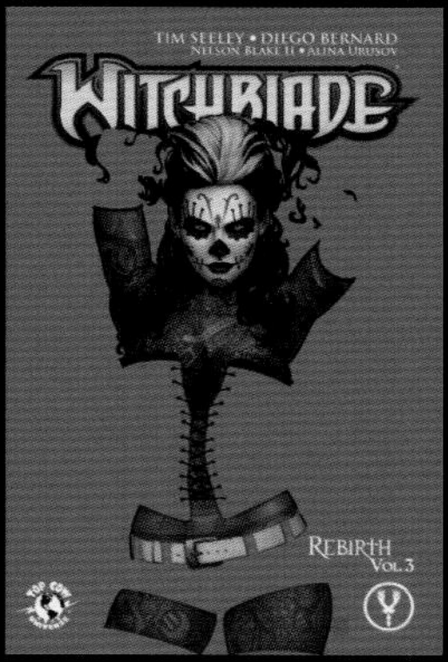
TIM SEELEY • DIEGO BERNARD
WITCHBLADE
REBIRTH
VOL. 3

ISBN# 978-1-60706-681-1

WITCHBLADE REBIRTH VOLUME 3

Writer: Tim Seeley
Artists: Diego Bernard, Fred Benes, Arif Prianto

Attempting to abandon her past and settle into a new life in Chicago, Sara Pezzini will have to contend against mercenaries, gangsters, and power hungry leprechauns, all while suffering the drudgeries of trying to stay profitable.

WITCHBLADE REBIRTH VOLUME 4

Writer: Tim Seeley
Artists: Diego Bernard, Fred Benes, Arif Prianto

It's all in a day's work for Sara Pezzini when Chicago is overrun with supernatural corruption and dark recreations of the Artifacts - including the devious "Anti-Magdalena" herself!

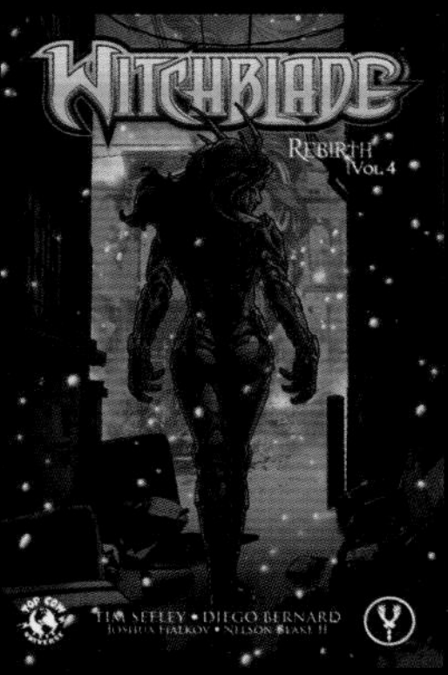
WITCHBLADE
REBIRTH
VOL. 4
TIM SEELEY • DIEGO BERNARD

ISBN# 978-1-60706-800-6

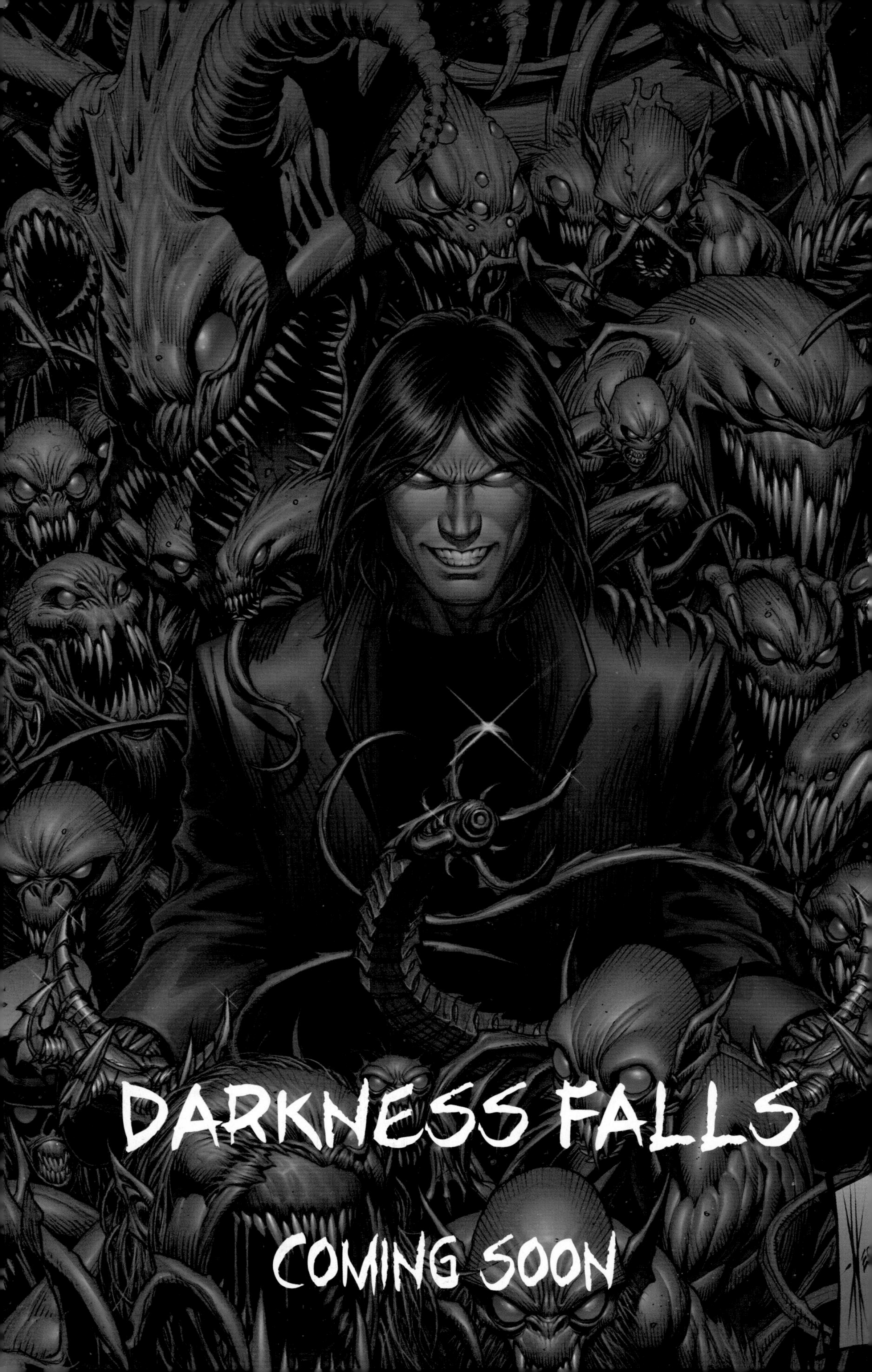
DARKNESS FALLS
COMING SOON